THE DEATH COLLECTORS

Also by Jack Kerley

The Hundredth Man

THE
DEATH COLLECTORS
JACK KERLEY

HarperCollins*Publishers*

HarperCollins*Publishers*
77–85 Fulham Palace Road, London W6 8JB

www.harpercollins.co.uk

First published in Great Britain by
HarperCollins*Publishers* 2005

1

A catalogue record for this book
is available from the British Library

ISBN 0 00 718060 8 (HB)
0 00 720120 6 (TPB)

Typeset in Minion by Palimpsest Book Production Limited,
Polmont, Stirlingshire
Printed in Great Britain by
Clays Limited, St Ives plc

For Elaine,
Who always believed

AUTHOR'S NOTE

I exercised broad license in bending settings, geography and various institutions and law-enforcement agencies to the will and whims of the story. Everything should be regarded as fiction save for the natural beauty of Mobile and its environs. Mention is made of a rare stamp, the "Scarlet Angelus". It is fictional as well. Any similarities between characters in this work and real persons, living or elsewise, is purely coincidental.

ACKNOWLEDGEMENTS

Without readers, I'm just that tree toppling soundlessly in the forest. Thanks to all my readers, especially those who wrote. Your letters are appreciated, I assure you. In a similar vein, thanks to all the booksellers who put my work in the hands of readers, sometimes by grabbing collars and saying, "Read this".

Thanks to friend and writing colleague Dr Dan Handel for suggestions regarding medical procedures and terminology. If you're ever shot, see Dan and tell him I sent you.

Thanks to FBI Special Agent (ret.) Mike McDaniel for input regarding law-enforcement procedures. As with Dr Handel, deviations from expert advice regarding investigative/legal/medical/procedures are mine alone.

Thanks to Duane and Janine Eby, Dave Hansen, and John and Cindy Sabo, just for being who they are.

Thanks to the great folks at HarperCollins UK: Julia Wisdom and editor Anne O'Brien (who set my days straight, among other assists).

And always, a pyrotechnic display of thanks to Aaron and the exceptional folks at the Aaron Priest Literary Agency.

PROLOGUE

Mobile County Courthouse,
Mobile, Alabama, May 15, 1972

Detective Jacob Willow dodged a sign proclaiming, DIE YOU DAM MURDRER, ducked another saying, REPENT SINNER! He shouldered past a pinched-faced preacher waving a bible, and squirmed between two agitated fat ladies in sweaty dresses. Breaking free of the mob surging in front of the courthouse, Willow bounded up the steps two at a time, tried three, tripped, went back to two. He flicked his cigarette into an urn at the door and stepped inside. The trial was upstairs and he ran those steps as well, dizzied when he reached the top. He peered around the corner into the hall leading to the courtroom, hoping he wouldn't see the Crying Woman.

1

Sure as sunrise, there she sat, twenty steps away on an oaken bench the size of a church pew, black dress, veil, elbows on her knees, face in her hands. Willow felt guilt curdle through his stomach. He turned his eyes from the Crying Woman.

Courthouse guard Windell Latham sat behind a folding table at the top of the stairs, a checkpoint for major trials. Latham was tipped back in a chair and trimming his nails with a deer knife, white crescents dappling his outsized belly.

"See you're on your late-as-usual schedule, 'tective Willow," Latham said, barely looking up. "You gonna miss the sentencing you don't get inside that courtroom 'bout now."

Willow nodded toward the Crying Woman. "Doesn't she ever leave?"

Another crescent tumbled. "Should be gone after today, Willow. Won't be nothing to see no more."

Willow walked toward the courtroom on the balls of his feet, hoping she kept her head in her hands. He hated the feelings the Crying Woman sparked in him, though he had no idea who she was. Some said she was mother to one of Marsden Hexcamp's victims, others said sister, or aunt; those asking questions or offering comfort were waved off like wasps.

The strange, heavily veiled woman quickly became invisible to the courthouse crowd, as familiar as the brass cuspidors or overflowing ashtrays. Never entering the courtroom during the three-week trial, she'd claimed the marble-columned halls as her parlor of grief, weeping from opening statements through last week's verdict of guilty. Believing her wounded by sorrow, the guards showed kindness, allowing the Crying Woman the run of the courthouse and occasional naps in an absent judge's chambers.

Willow took a deep breath and started to the courtroom doors, walking light as hard-soled brogans allowed. Her head lifted as he passed, the veil askew. It was the first time Willow had seen the Crying Woman's face, and he was startled by her eyes: tearless and resolute. Equally surprising was her youth; she looked barely out of her teens. He felt her eyes follow him to the door, as if riding his guilt into the courtroom.

He tried to rationalize his guilt – most often in the hours preceding dawn – telling himself he'd been an Alabama State Police detective for only two years, lacking the experience to understand virulent madness powered by intellect. He reminded himself of scrapes with departmental major-domos, trying to convince them the seemingly random horrors occurring in South Alabama were connected, that a full-scale investigation involving State, County and Mobile City police was necessary. Like his entreaties to higher-ups, the rationalizations failed, and Willow's pre-dawn sweats continued through the trial's daily revelations of the sexually bizarre and murderously horrific.

Willow nodded to the guard at the door, then slipped into the packed room. He excused and pardoned his way to his assigned seat in the gallery, against the railing directly behind the defense table. He didn't have time to sit. "All rise," the bailiff cried, and two hundred people in the courtroom rose like a single wave.

Only one person remained seated, a blond and slender man at the defense table, wearing jailhouse stripes with the élan of a man in a Savile Row suit. Marsden Hexcamp sat with his legs crossed, the upper bobbing to some lazy internal rhythm. A wisp of hair dangled down his forehead, drawing attention to his water-blue eyes. He turned his head to the gallery and smiled as if hearing the punchline of a lively joke. His eyes found Willow and for a split-second Hexcamp's smile wavered. The defense lawyer tapped Hexcamp's shoulder and waved in an upward motion, imploring his client to rise to the judge's entrance.

Marsden Hexcamp flicked his head sideways and spat into the lawyer's palm.

Willow saw the lawyer shiver with disgust and wipe his hand on his pants. No one else noticed this miniature drama, all other eyes watching Circuit Judge Harlan T. Penfield striding to the bench. Small in stature, Penfield compensated through a voice as deep as a country well and hawk-bright eyes blazing at any hint of misconduct. Penfield's eyes glared at Marsden Hexcamp, receiving a smile and lazy nod in return. The judge slipped on half-lens reading glasses and unfolded a sheet of paper with his sentencing decision, a conclusion reached by the end of the first week of trial.

"We gather today for the sentencing of Marsden Hexcamp," Penfield intoned. "And with it end weeks of such revulsion and dismay that two jurors could not continue, one still hospitalized with a nervous condition . . ."

Marsden Hexcamp's lawyer stood. "Your Honor, I do not think this is –"

"Sit," commanded Judge Penfield. The lawyer sat, looking relieved to be finished with his role.

"The toll has not only been on the jurors," Penfield continued in his rolling bass, "but on all who have smelled the brimstone rising from Mr Hexcamp like fog . . ."

Marsden Hexcamp mimed lifting a wineglass as if acknowledging a toast, the chains around his slender wrists ringing like chimes. Penfield paused, studied the defendant. "Your antics shall trouble this court no longer, Mr Hexcamp. By the power vested in me by the great state of Alabama, I sentence you to be conducted to Holman Prison, there, hopefully in record time, to receive the penalty of death by electrocution. And may God have mercy on whatever squirms inside you."

Penfield's gavel dropped as Marsden Hexcamp stood. He shrugged off his lawyer's hand.

"No last words for the condemned, Your Honor?"

"Sit, Mr Hexcamp."

"Am I not entitled? Does not sure and impending death allow a few final phrases?"

"Did you allow your victims a final say, Mr Hexcamp?"

Marsden Hexcamp paused and thought. Amusement flitted across his face. "Some of them spoke volumes, Your Honor."

"Bastard!" A coarse-faced man in the gallery stood and waved his fist. He appeared drunk.

"Sit and behave, sir, or be removed," Penfield said, almost gently. The man dropped to his seat, sunk his face into his hands.

Hexcamp said, "Well, Your Honor? May I speak?"

Willow saw Judge Penfield's eyes sweep the expectant faces in the crowd, pause on reporters aching to record the final public words of Marsden Hexcamp. Penfield tapped his watch.

"I'll grant you thirty seconds, Mr Hexcamp. I suggest a prayer for salvation."

Hexcamp's smile flattened. His eyes lit like flares. "Salvation is the province of fools, *Judge*. A vacant lot in empty minds. What counts is not where we go, but what we create while in the world's humble studio –"

"Murderer," a woman screamed from the gallery.

"Madman," called another.

Penfield pounded his gavel. "Silence! Ten seconds, Mr Hexcamp."

Hexcamp turned to the gallery. His eyes found Willow, held for a beat, returned to the judge. "It's the art of our lives that endures – moments captured like spiders in amber. But magically able to crawl. To bite. To influence . . ."

"Five seconds." Penfield dramatically stifled a yawn. Hexcamp's face reddened at the slight.

"YOU are a WORM," Hexcamp screamed at Penfield. "A wretched, despicable creature, a mere nothing, less than nothing, a vile insect risen in contempt against the majesty of ART!"

"Time's up, Mr Hexcamp," Penfield said. "Never let it be said you were at a loss for words."

Marsden Hexcamp angled an eye at the judge. Then, agile as a gymnast, he leapt atop the defense table. *L'art du moment final,*" he howled, spittle flying. "*C'est moi! C'est moi! C'est moi!*"

The art of the final moment, Willow thought, two years of high school French kicking in. *It is me.*

"Guards, seat that man," Penfield said. His gavel again rang from the sounding block.

A motion behind Penfield caught Willow's eye. He watched the door of the judge's chambers open slowly, saw the desk, bookshelves, low table . . . and then, framed in the doorway, the Crying Woman. She strode into the room and stopped at Hexcamp's feet, the crowd gasping. A large-bore pistol appeared from the folds of her dress. The weapon lifted, her finger tightening on the trigger.

She was crying again. She looked into Marsden Hexcamp's eyes.

Said, "I love you."

Willow dove across the railing, arms stretching for the gun. His foot caught the wood and he tumbled to the floor below the defense table. Thunder filled the room. Hexcamp's shirtfront gained a red button the size of a dime, but the back of his shirt exploded. He crumpled to the floor, landing supine beside Willow. Spectators hugged the floor or jammed at the doorway, screaming.

Marsden Hexcamp lifted his head and moaned, his lips forming words. Willow laid his ear over the man's mouth, listened. Hexcamp's eyes closed and his head slumped. "Stay with me," Willow yelled. He grabbed the man's shirt and shook, as if freeing words trapped in Hexcamp's throat. Hexcamp's eyes snapped open. He sucked in breath.

"Follow, Jacob. You've got to follow . . ." A scarlet bubble escaped his mouth. "You . . . have to . . . follow . . ."

"What?" Willow yelled into Hexcamp's glazing eyes. "FOLLOW WHAT?"

Marsden Hexcamp's eyelids fluttered. "The art, Jacob," he said, the blood now a red foam crawling down his chin. "Follow the . . . glorious art."

Hexcamp's eyes became wax, his mouth a frozen rictus. Willow heard a second roar of self-inflicted thunder. A body dropped to the floor six feet away. The Crying Woman became the Dying Woman.

CHAPTER 1

Mobile, Alabama,
present time

"Awards are dumb," Harry Nautilus said, aiming the big blue Crown Victoria away from the headquarters of the Mobile Police Department. "No good ever comes of stuff like this."

"Lighten up, Harry," I said, tightening my tie in the rearview mirror. "We're the Mayor's Officers of the Year."

"And I'm the state bird of Alabama. Tweet."

"It's an honor," I reasoned.

"It's a pain in the ass. And it ain't nothing but a politician's words."

"At least we'll get a free breakfast." I checked my watch; we

9

had an easy twenty minutes to get to the hotel where the Mayor's Recognition Breakfast was being held. I'd already cleared a space on my ersatz wall at work, a gray divider. I'd never had an award before.

"You think I should mention the folks at Forensics?" I said, holding out my arms and wondering if my navy blazer had shrunk since the last wearing, or if I was still growing at age thirty.

"What are you talking about, Carson?"

"My acceptance speech."

Harry growled, a low bass note. Government Street was under construction ahead, so we cut through the south edge of downtown, a poorer neighborhood of small houses and apartments. I was buffing my nails on my pants when a woman exploded into the street from an alley, arms waving, pink robe flying behind like a horseman's cape. She launched herself in front of the car. Two hundred and forty pounds of Harry Nautilus stood on the brakes. The robed woman held up her hands as if that would ward off a two-ton car. Tires squealed. The Crown Vic fishtailed. Our bumper stopped three inches shy of the woman's knees.

"They's a dead woman in that alley," the woman panted, clutching at her robe. She was in her thirties, skinny as rope, an Appalachian twang in her voice. "Got blood all up underneath her."

I called it into the dispatcher as Harry turned into the alley. A woman's body sprawled face-down on the concrete, arms above her head. Her blouse was white and I saw a crimson smear in the upper center of her back. Fearful of tainting evidence, we stopped the car short and sprinted to the body. We always ran, praying fast response and CPR might make a difference.

Not this time; seeing the amount of blood beneath her, Harry stopped running and so did I. We walked the last few steps gingerly, careful of the flood of red on the pavement. The blood was congealing and I figured the killer long gone. Sirens wailed in the distance. Harry knelt beside the body while I studied the scene: shattered glass, strewn trash, and other detritus of an inner-city alley. The concrete was bordered by dilapidated garages. Grass between them was yellow from scant rain. A bright object caught my eye: a plump orange nestled against a slumping garage twenty or so feet from the woman's outstretched hand.

Another Crown Victoria entered the alley from the opposite direction, followed by a patrol car and ambulance. Detectives Roy Trent and Clay Bridges exited the Crown Vic. This was their territory, District Two. Harry and I were District One ninety-nine per cent of the time, part of a special unit the other one per cent.

We gave Trent and Bridges a three-line synopsis of what we knew. Bridges took the woman in the robe aside to calm her for questioning. Trent walked to the body, looked down. He ran heavy hands through thinning hair.

"Damn. It's the Orange Lady."

"Orange Lady?" I said.

"Name's Nancy something. Lives in a group home a block over. Every morning she goes to the market and gets herself an orange. One orange. Does the same thing every night. I asked once why she didn't get two oranges in the morning, or buy a bag. Know what she said?"

"What?"

"The oranges liked being at the store because they got to watch people. At her place they'd just see the inside of the refrigerator."

Harry said, "This group home's for folks with mental problems, I take it."

Trent nodded. "Harmless types who need a little help getting by. Nancy might have been a tad disjointed in her thinking, but she was always happy, chattering at people, singing songs in French, whatever."

"There's the morning orange," I said, pointing it out. I crouched and looked between the woman and the orange, then dropped to my stomach, eyeballing the topography and the drain grate in the middle of the alley.

"You need water to swim, Cars," Trent said.

"And momentum to roll," I added, standing and brushing gravel from my palms. Trent studied the body, shook his head. "Who'd shoot her dead while she was standing in an alley?"

"Running in the alley," I suggested.

Trent raised an eyebrow.

"The orange is about twenty feet away. Slightly uphill. If she'd been standing or walking, the orange might have rolled a few feet. But the other way, toward the center of the alley. It's concave for drainage. The shot knocked her forward, of course. But I think it took added momentum for the orange to travel that far. Forensics'll do the math, but I'd bet a couple bucks she was running full-tilt."

Trent thought a moment. "If she was running, she knew she was in danger; recognized the perp, probably." He started to the patrol car to get the uniformed guys cordoning off the scene, then paused.

"Hey, did I hear the Mayor's making you guys Officers of the Year?"

"It's just a rumor," Harry said.

Trent grinned. "Officers of the Year doesn't quite cut it for you two. How about the Grand Pooh-bahs of Piss-it?"

Piss-it was departmental slang for the PSIT, or Psychopathological and Sociopathological Investigative Team, a specialty unit with a name longer than its roster: Harry and me. It was the one per cent of our jobs.

Harry sighed. "Don't start, Roy."

Trent thought a moment. "Or how about the Wizards of Weirdness?" He chuckled and started to invent another title, saw the look in Harry's eyes, remembered his business with the patrol guys and retreated.

Our bit part in a too-familiar drama over, Harry and I climbed back into the car. The Orange Lady's case would be cleared fast, we figured; the poor woman had pissed someone off and he or she had gotten revenge. Backshooting a fleeing woman in broad daylight was irrational, an act of emotion, not brains. Trent and Bridges would check the victim's acquaintances, find who she'd recently irritated. Nail the case shut.

Bang. Just like that.

The awards ceremony was at a downtown hotel. By the time we arrived, only carafes of tepid coffee remained on the banquet tables. Harry and I slipped to our table and nodded apologies. At the dais centering the front of the large, low-ceilinged room, an overdressed woman from the Sanitation Department clutched a plaque to her bosom, uttering immortal words about landfills.

"*. . . like to thank all the microbial organisms who work so hard at breaking down organic waste materials . . .*"

Mayor Lyle Edmunds stood beside her, a frozen smile on his ruddy face. The Sanitation woman finished her soliloquy and padded back to her table. The Mayor regained the microphone, but no words came from the sound system. He tapped the mic with a finger, was rewarded with a screech of feedback. Two hundred faces winced, mine included. The Mayor leaned forward, tried again.

"—esting, testing. This thing working again? All right. Once again I'd like to thank y'all for coming today, my chance to honor folks who've made a difference in the quality of life in the beautiful Port City, a year in which this administration also made a difference by . . ."

Most members of our table watched the dais, obliged to appear transfixed by the Mayor's oratory. At the head of the table – if a round table can have a head – was Chief of Police Burston Plackett. Plackett was flanked by four other members of the police brass. The lower-rent side of the table was Lieutenant Tom Mason, Harry, and me.

The Mayor wound down. He studied the table of awards beside him, lifted a pair of plaques.

"Two awards – it's us," I whispered to Harry. "What should I say in my acceptance speech?"

"Let the Mayor handle the speeching and preaching, Carson. Just grab the wood and beat your feet back to the table." Harry frowned at me. The frown said, *Don't go near the microphone.*

The Mayor tapped the mic again, leaned into it. "My next award goes to the Mobile Police Officer of the Year. This year I'm proud to recognize a team effort: two members of Mobile's finest, instrumental in tracking down the morgue killer a while back, as well as Joel Adrian a couple years ago. Together, detectives Nautilus and Ryder form a special team known as the PSIT, or Psychopatho-ological and Socio-socio-sociolo- . . . doggone, that's a mouthful. Let me just say that these two fine gentlemen are living proof that no city surpasses Mobile in the quality of its . . ."

The Mayor soared off on another flight of political self-indulgence spurred by the media. They huddled to the side, reporters, videographers, and a photographer from the *Mobile Register*. I saw the reporter from Channel 14 staring at me. When I stared back, she smiled and turned her gaze to the Mayor. I recalled her name as DeeDee Danbury. Trim, blonde, medium height, somewhat outsized features, eyes especially. When Harry and I'd been in the brief glare of camera lights, Danbury had the voice closest to my ear and microphone closest to my face. I didn't much care for either effect.

Two minutes of humid ventings later, the Mayor looked around the room, saw the slender white guy sitting beside the big, square-shouldered black guy.

"I'd like to introduce detectives Harry Nautilus and Carson Ryder. Come receive your awards, officers."

Applause rang out. I followed Harry's mustard-yellow suit to the dais. His shirt was lavender, his tie red. Harry liked color, but that didn't make him good at it. We stepped up, shook the Mayor's hand, took our awards. Someone yelled, "Hold for a photo." I angled my head, steeled my jaw, and did my best Serious Crimefighter pose. Cameras flashed. I tucked my plaque against my side and started from the dais. The microphone floated in front of my face and despite Harry's admonition I couldn't resist leaning in for a few words.

"First off, I'd like to thank the academy . . ."

The microphone squealed like chisels on sheet metal. Everyone winced, several people ducked. In the center of the room a startled waiter dropped a full tray of dishes, china shards skittering across the floor. Harry growled and jabbed his thumb into my kidney, propelling me from the dais and my moment of glory.

CHAPTER 2

The photo taken at the Mayor's bash ran the following day, Tuesday. I was off rotation and didn't see the photograph until Wednesday, coming in early to whittle at paperwork. Some wag had taped the clipped-out photo to my chair, attaching a Post-it scrawled, *Super Detective to the Rescue.*

In the photo, Harry and I clutched our plaques, the Mayor between us. Harry had a wisp of smile beneath his bulldozer-blade mustache. My Serious Crimefighter pose made me look like a cross between Cotton Mather and Dudley Do-Right. I shook my head, made a mental note never to accept an award again, and read the text:

OFFICERS OF THE YEAR HONORED – Mayor Lyle Edmunds presents Mobile Police detectives Harry Nautilus (left) and Carson Ryder (right) with Officers of the Year awards at the Mayor's annual Recognition Breakfast. Nautilus and Ryder are members of the MPD's elite Psychopathological and Sociopathological Investigative Team, or PSIT, and are considered authorities in the area of serial killers and other psychologically deranged . . .

"What you think? They get your good side?" said a molasses-slow voice from behind me. I turned to see Tom Mason smiling, or as close as his crepe-wrinkled face ever managed. "Interesting expression you got, Carson. Intense, I guess you'd call it."

I felt my face redden like a school kid caught with a girly mag and flipped the clipping on the desk. Tom said, "We just got a 911 about a body in a motel, the Cozy Cabins. I think it's got a little weird to it, maybe more than a little. I just got hold of Harry. He's heading that way now."

I stood, reached for my sport jacket. "Weird how, Tom?"

"Caller wasn't speaking real good English; I'll let you see for yourself. Medical Examiner's there, Forensics is on the way. I told everybody not to worry because I was sending the Officers of the Year. You can bet they got a kick out of that one."

The Cozy Cabins was a fading motel comprised of a dozen small units spread across four or five tree-shaded acres. Back in the seventies it had probably been charming, but the city's sprawl and clutter had metastasized, the units now surrounded by strip malls and bars and "We Carry Your Note"

18

car lots. These days the Cozy Cabins mainly catered to trysting couples, or Johns wanting to take their rented partners somewhere a little nicer than the back seat. I swung into the drive and saw Harry walking into the front cabin, a neon OFFICE sign in the window. I hit the horn. Harry paused in the doorway, turned.

I yelled, "What's up?"

Harry shook his head as if words were insufficient, pointed to the farthest cabin, and stepped inside the office. I drove back to the unit. Parked outside were ME and Forensics vehicles, plus a patrol car, Officer Leighton Withrow leaning against the fender and patting sweat from his bald head with a handkerchief. I pulled behind Withrow and got out. The day was a scorcher and my first non-air-conditioned breath about dropped me to my knees.

"What's up, Leighton?" I gasped.

He nodded toward the cabin. "You better git inside quick, Ryder. They're about to sing 'Happy Birthday.'"

"Happy Birthday?"

Withrow turned to watch the traffic on the highway, like it amused him. I walked to the unit, maybe twenty feet square, stucco, needing paint. Forensics supervisor Wayne Hembree stood in the doorway, his back to me. Hembree was a balding, 36-year-old black man with less meat on his bones than a race-bred greyhound. He turned to the sound of my footfalls, a sad smile on his moon-round face.

"Stuff like this makes it tough for me to eat by candlelight," he said, stepping aside so I could peek into the room.

Candles. Dozens of them. On the floor, on the scruffy

furniture, atop the bolted-down television. Tubular candles, square candles, octagonal candles, triangles. Some were scented and an olfactory collage thickened the air. Smaller candles had burned to pools of wax, while the bulk of them, larger and thicker, were topped by shivers of flame, bright points in the shadowed room.

A dozen feet away, centered on the red bedcover, a woman's naked body lay covered with wilted flowers. Her eyes were huge and white and poured from the sockets, tiny wormlike pupils in the center.

"Jesus," I whispered, wondering if her eyes had somehow liquefied. Stepping closer, the horrendous effect was revealed as melted-down white candles over her eyelids, the sockets overflowing with wax, burnt wicks forming her pupils. The wicks stared at me. Her lipstick-smeared mouth sagged open and seemed to be asking, *Why me?*

Hembree passed the camera to a Forensics tech, nodded for me to follow, and walked to the body between candles, moving as carefully as a man treading barefoot among glass.

Her hands crossed over her breastbone, barely visible beneath the roses and lilies and other flowers I couldn't identify. Cheap rings encircled both thumbs and most of her fingers. In contrast, her dark brown hair was short, conservative, clean; at odds with the rest of her. Wax drippings clung to her hair like petrified tears. Abrasions encircling the woman's neck suggested ligature strangulation, an angry red collar. There were no other apparent marks or signs of struggle. I smelled rot rising through the sweetness of the flowers. When we return to dust, it's not a pretty transformation.

Hembree looked at me. "What age you put her at, Carson?"

"I'll say late thirties, early forties."

The Forensics tech pressed an invisible button in the air, made a game-show buzzer sound. "*Bzzzzt.* Wrong answer. Try fifty. At least." He bent over the body and palpated a bicep. "Good condition, physically, muscle tone is balancing out the ageing. Or was. How many fifty-year-old hookers you see with muscle tone like that?"

I made a zero with my thumb and forefinger. Most street girls never made fifty, and if they did, looked eighty. I knelt and took the woman's hand from Hembree, seeing calluses across the palm and fingers. "Working hands," I noted. "Outside work, and I don't mean pounding pavement. Check the rings."

I slid a couple bucks' worth of pot metal and glass up the victim's digit. "Dime-store crap," I said. "If she'd worn it any length of time there'd be discoloration."

"Strange designs," Hembree said. "Some kind of knot on the one, a sword on the other. A moon on her other hand. And here's a pentacle."

"Satanic? Goth?"

Hembree lifted the hair behind the victim's ear. "Found an identifying feature here, Carson."

I saw a birthmark near the base of her neck, a quarter-sized splash of claret across the skin. Hembree aimed his penlight into the crease marks at the back of the woman's neck. There were thin, ruddy lines in the folds, like penstrokes made with rust.

"Look down here," he said, aiming the light at the crook of an arm.

"More of the same," I said. "What's the tint from?"

"Nothing's certain until we get it to the lab." Hembree wasn't big on guessing and having to later recant, though his accuracy made take-backs rare.

"Come on, Bree, give it out," I chided, mock-punching his vermicelli bicep. "I won't hold you to it. What are you thinking?"

He kept the penlight on the woman's arm, studying. "I'm thinking the perfect Officer of the Year wouldn't be such a pain in the ass."

"Maid find body," Cozy Cabins manager Saleem Hakkam was telling Harry when I opened the office door to a small room filled with smoke. "Maid scream into office, I drop coffee on floor, call 911. Much scream, maid."

Hakkam stood behind a chipped Formica counter sucking a filterless cigarette that smelled like burning shoeshine rags, occasionally tipping ashes into a Dr Pepper can on the counter. The portly Hakkam held the cigarette tightly with three fingers, like he was afraid it would get away.

"Can we speak to her?" Harry asked.

Hakkam took a deep drag. "Maid scream. Jump in car, drive. Scream down street." His words came out punctuated by smoke.

"When will she be back?"

Hakkam shook his head sadly. "Scream like that, no come back."

"Who rented the room, Mr Hakkam?" Harry asked. "They come in and register?"

Hakkam looked away. Harry sighed, seeing the picture. "Mr Hakkam, you're not in any trouble here. Unless you lie to me."

Hakkam's eyes blinked warily through smoke. "No lie at police. Phone call come yesterday after lunch. Want to rent cabin for Tuesday night."

We'd both seen this before. "And you don't know who rented the place?"

"No see. Come in late."

"Payment?" Harry asked.

"Caller say money in mailbox. I look. Money there. Caller say leave door open, key inside on table. The money good, why not do?"

"You see the vehicle?"

"No."

"You have the envelope the money came in?"

"Burn with trash."

"The caller – male or female?"

Hakkam shook his head and put his hand at forehead level. "Voice not up here like woman . . ." then dropped it to his groin ". . . not down here like man. In middle." He shrugged. I suspected the caller had muffled his or her voice.

Harry said, "How much money did you get paid, Mr Hakkam?"

"Five hundred dollar."

"About ten times going rate. You figured a dope deal, right? Drugs?"

Hakkam averted his eyes and sucked another chestful of greasy smoke. I figured his lungs looked like bags of mud.

"Job is rent cabins, not ask people's business."

He frowned, took one final hit and dropped the tar-soaked butt in the can. It hissed and died, a curl of brown smoke issuing from the opening, like the damned thing didn't want to give up.

We walked back to the cabin under tall longleaf pines, the shade meaningless in the heat. The conversation with Hakkam wasn't unusual in a failing neighborhood. Business was sketchy and he'd happily rented to someone paying a premium for privacy – dope dealers wrapping or distributing product, porn types taping a bottom-drawer flick. Hakkam did exactly as asked, hoping for repeat business.

We turned the corner to the front of the cabin. Harry froze, grabbed my jacket, and yanked me backwards.

"Buzzards," he said, pointing around the corner. "Pooling and drooling."

Harry had a rhyming tendency, though some days I'd call it an affliction. In the six years of our friendship, I'd learned to decipher half of what he said. But I'd seen these buzzards before. I peeked around the corner for confirmation.

Reporters.

Kept from the cabin by Leighton Withrow, they clustered near the entrance, alerted by police-frequency scanners, or some vestigial instinct that drew them to tragedy like June bugs to a screen door. There were a couple of television stations and radio outlets, a brace of print reporters.

Harry nodded dolefully. "I see Cunt and Funt from Channel 14 out there."

I gave Harry the raised eyebrow. While far from politically

24

correct, Harry wasn't fond of pejorative classifications. "Uh, who?" I asked.

"DeeDee Danbury from Channel 14, she's uh, the C-word lady. There's some squirrelly little camera guy usually with her; he's Funt. It's what they're called over at City Hall. By some folks, leastwise."

"Funt? That's the camera guy's real name?"

Harry peered around the corner again. "Used to be a TV show called *Candid Camera*. Folks'd go to stick mail in a box and suddenly a hand reaches out and grabs it, that kind of cheesy schtick. All the time the scene's being shot from a hidden camera. The guy who thought up the show was named Funt."

"The Channel 14 camera guy hides in mailboxes?"

"The way they work is Cu—, I mean, Danbury, zings in questions hoping to catch folks off guard, Funt shoots pictures of their confusion."

"How come you know this Danbury so well? You start watching TV?" Harry was the original Music Man, vinyls of old blues and jazz spreading through his house. He'd only recently – and grudgingly – started collecting CDs. The last time I saw Harry's television, a ten-inch black and white, it was a doorstop.

"She jammed me up three–four years back. I let slip a dead body was a heavyweight dope boy, tried to suck it back a minute later. She said OK, then later that night I hear the name on the news."

"And?"

"What I didn't know was DEA had a lock on this guy,

tracking a shipment to him from Colombia. When it hit the airwaves the guy was toast, the runners dove underground. Without the coverage, the shipment would have sailed into the arms of the feds."

I winced. "Ouch."

"I about got assigned to traffic control at tractor pulls," Harry said, peeking around the corner. "Still can't look at that woman without my teeth grinding. "OK, Carson, let's run it and gun it."

We came around the corner moving fast. The reporters dove at us the second we hit their sights.

"*Who's in there?*"

"No comment."

"*Was it a robbery?*"

"No comment."

"*Any ideas on motive?*"

"No comment."

We ran the gauntlet with heads lowered; eye contact increased their frenzy, blood to a shark. Answering questions wasn't our bailiwick anyway; the department had flacks to make up crap by the barge load – we always had our hands full dealing with the truth.

"*Is this a PSIT case, Detective Ryder? Is that why you and Detective Nautilus are here?*"

The last question caught me. I turned to the foam bulb of a microphone two feet distant. Behind it, big gray eyes highlighted a longish but compelling face framed in ash-blonde hair, Channel 14 reporter DeeDee Danbury. My feet stopped moving until I felt the nudge in my kidneys.

"Tell her no, for chrissakes," Harry whispered.

"No," I parroted.

She raised an eyebrow. "But aren't you two out of your regular district?"

Harry pushed me into the cabin. Hembree was watching the Medical Examiner's folks extricate the candles from the woman's eyes. He held up an evidence bag, several ruddy particles inside it. "Found these in the victim's hair. Similar to the substance in her neck and arm creases. Also found some under her fingernails, in her navel."

Hembree's tone was odd. I looked from side to side; no one but me and Harry were in earshot. "Come on, Bree, no one's listening. What are you thinking about?"

"Zombies," he whispered, an enigmatic smile on his face.

CHAPTER 3

Harry and I took the photos to nearby streets, checking so-called Ladies of the Evening. The "evening" part is a misnomer; most women selling their lives in ten-minute chunks depend on some form of chemical to get by, and addiction is hungry 24/7. We had plenty of girls – and one she-male – to talk to. Most glanced at the photo and shook their heads. A few pondered for a couple of seconds, always coming back with a "Huh-uh, not who I was thinkin' of," or the more popular, "Never seen her before. How 'bout you boys get gone so's I can keep workin'?"

Harry and I wore a few hours off our shoes and accomplished exactly nothing. When we returned to the department, Tom Mason headed us off at the door to the detectives' room.

"Chief's looking for you boys. He's waiting over in my office."

Tom didn't elaborate. Harry shot me a glance and we shuffled to Tom's office. Chief Plackett was bouncing on the balls of his feet and looking out the window over Government Street, his slender pinstriped back to us. A pink hand smoothed back perfectly tended black hair. A gold watch glittered from his wrist. He spun with a frown on his face, had it grinning by the time it got to us.

"There they are," the chief said, his hand reaching for mine as I stepped across the threshold. He gave it the politician's one-two pump, moved to Harry's hand. "Here are my specialists."

Harry made a soft groaning sound that only I heard.

"Specialists?" I said.

"The specialists of the Psychological and, uh, Sociological Team. I got word you fellas caught a weird one – hooker, candles, ritual stuff. You're putting the PSIT in gear, aren't you? Nip this craziness in the bud?"

I stifled a grimace. Originally created as a public-relations gimmick, the PSIT, consisting entirely of Harry and me, had one outing last year. Though almost everyone seemed against us, we were successful. But activating the unit – putting the PSIT "in gear" – turned out more complicated than it sounded, and created political and logistical problems neither Harry nor I wanted to face unless absolutely necessary.

"I don't think it's called for at this point, Chief," I said.

He raised an eyebrow. "Why's that, Detective?"

"There's evidence of a disordered mind at work. But one might argue that every premeditated murder is the product

29

of a disordered mind, since no orderly mind would risk the loss of freedom or life that detection would entail. That said, I'll note the scene had elements beyond the normal expectation of a . . ."

Like often happens when I start babbling, Harry jumped to the rescue. "What Carson's saying is, there's a certain ambiguity to the case as it stands, Chief. It's sort of borderline. For right now, we think the district guys should push it through."

Plackett looked out the window. "I'm getting calls from reporters, gentlemen."

We waited, our unspoken *And?* floating in the air.

"I think you fellas should handle this. If it's a psycho out there, it's best to say we had you in from the beginning. I don't want to get caught with our pants at half-mast."

After the morgue case, the brass took some flak, a few folks suggesting – not without reason – that PSIT should have been activated sooner.

"The problem, Chief," I explained, "is stirring up media attention we probably don't want. They'll dog our every step."

Plackett looked dubious. Tom, who'd been placating administrators for twenty years, clapped his hands. "Tell you what, Chief, if it looks like we need the more involving aspects of PSIT – giving Carson and Harry added autonomy, changing the command structure – I'll have everything ready. But for now, how about I reassign their current cases and make them leads on this one?"

Tom glanced at Harry and me. His raised eyebrow said, *This is the best I can do.* Plackett flicked a semi-satisfied nod and retreated out the door, leaving only a heavy musk of cologne in the air.

Harry and I headed back to our desks. "Damn," he muttered. "One day people barely admit the PSIT exists, the next we can't keep them from putting us in charge. What the hell happened?"

The photo from the Mayor's awards ceremony was on my desk. I picked it up and tapped it with a finger.

"We got validated, bro."

Though the air was hot and thick, I drove home with the windows down, trying to blast the day from my brain. I crossed Mississippi Sound at twilight, the dark water shining beneath the bridge, a few slow-moving pleasure boats returning to the marinas.

I live on Dauphin Island, a long and slender spit of sand thirty miles south of Mobile. Perched on high pilings and overlooking the Gulf, my home is a box in the air above an island, and my idea of the perfect sanctuary. It's a neighborhood far beyond my means, but when my mother passed away a few years back, I inherited enough to cover the tab. I'd initially planned to buy a single-wide on a cheap tract and let remaining funds spin a low-budget but work-free existence. But one day while fishing the Dauphin surf I saw my future home, its metal roof like polished armor, a wide deck facing the sea, the FOR SALE sign in the drive. The scant sleep I got that night was spangled with dreams. The house appeared as a boat, and I sailed it through what seemed safe waters. Two weeks later I dragged a couple hundred bucks' worth of used furniture into a four-hundred-thousand-dollar beachfront home.

I pulled onto a sand-and-shell lane leading sixty feet to my home, the center of three houses on a street truncated by a scrubby woods. John and Marge Amberly were my neighbors to the east. I saw an unfamiliar Hummer in the drive, Nevada plates. It was more cartoon than car: fire-engine red, outsized tires, lights mounted on the roof. Two figures were in the three dozen feet of sand between the houses. It was my property, but there were no signs and who cared anyway? The woman snatched something from the air. I flicked a wave and continued into my drive, John Lee Hooker raging from the speakers.

Many of my neighbors are reverse snowbirds who trade the stifling heat of summer for cooler northern climes, reducing the cost of their places by renting to vacationers. From May through September I have a steady stream of new neighbors, some for a week, some a month or more. The Amberlys, for instance, were somewhere up north for the summer, renting their elegant two-story home out in one-month minimums. About three times the size of my place, it went for two grand a week. My transient neighbors were good people, mainly, the rental rates prohibitively high for summer-break students and halfwits who fire up a grill in the living room because that's where the air conditioning is coolest.

Getting out of the car, I heard a voice behind me say, "Hey asshole, why don't you watch where you're driving?"

I looked up and saw a woman, mid thirties maybe. She

was attractive in a high-maintenance way: streaked, modelish hair that fell in tended ringlets, cream-smooth skin, an olive tan as even as a good airbrush job. The yellow sundress hadn't come from a rack, but appeared tailored to highlight outsized breasts, Dow Cornings, judging by the symmetry, the Showgirl series. Her only visual negatives were bowed legs and a mouth pinched tight with anger. She was swaying a bit, like maybe she'd had a few pops.

"Pardon me?" I said.

"You drove over our Frisbee," the woman said. "I yelled 'Watch out!' You kept driving. I watched you aim right at it, asswipe."

I studied a bent and flattened blue form in the road behind me. "No, ma'am. I assure you I did not purposefully drive over it. I've been meaning to get a bumper sticker saying, 'I Brake for Frisbees,' but haven't had the time."

"Don't you go wise-ass with my wife, buddy," a male voice said. "I don't like it."

A new player suddenly on the scene, hubby, judging by the matched wedding bands. He was six two or three, two hundred forty or so pounds, sucking in a paunch, difficult while being a tough guy. He had one of those silvery, short-bangs haircuts Hollywood sticks on Roman emperors. Like the woman, his tan was perfect, oak stain applied with a spray gun, even into the crinkly corners of his small eyes. He wore a brief black Speedo, not a good choice for a couple of reasons.

The woman picked up the wounded Frisbee and tossed it at me. It banged off my knees.

"You owe me six bucks," she commanded, opening her palm and gesturing with red-nailed fingers.

I'd met these folks before; their local equivalent anyway. They lived at the intersection of Big Money and Bad Breeding, a neighborhood that seemed to be spreading. They'd kiss up to anyone with more, belittle anyone with less, and proved "white trash" doesn't need the word *poor* in front of it. Their hobby was owning things, which was subconsciously sparking our current little drama. Though the pair probably had a net worth in the millions, I was supposed to shell out six dollars for their plastic toy, giving them sway over me, a psychological form of ownership. It had nothing to do with money, everything to do with my acquiescence.

Hubby said, "Better pull those bills from your wallet, buddy."

"And if that's not in my plans?"

He grinned and let his hands drift to his side, clenching and unclenching fists.

I had no need or inclination to interact with these folks, life was too short and my day had been too long. I thought a moment, then bent and picked up the mangled disc. I studied it, then held the Frisbee to my ear and cocked my head.

"What the hell you doing?" hubby said.

I put my finger to my lips. "Shhh. I'm listening."

"Huh?" hubby grunted, his tiny eyes crinkled in confusion.

"It's still alive," I told them, sad-faced, shaking my head. "It's in pain. Can't you hear it?"

"What the fuck are you talking about?" the woman cawed.

I set the Frisbee gently on the ground. Then, in one motion, reached beneath my jacket for the Glock, thumbed off the safety, racked the slide.

"Jesus," the woman said, her tan face turning white. Hubby started backpedaling, eyes wide. I knelt beside the Frisbee and patted it gently.

"I'm going to put it out of its misery," I said, taking careful aim at the plastic mangle. "Hold your ears."

When I looked up again, they were twenty feet gone and moving fast.

The light on my answering machine blinked two waiting messages. I peeled off my jacket and weapon, hung them over a chair, then slipped into running shorts and a tee-shirt. I was about to check my messages when a knock came to the door. Jimmy Gentry of the Dauphin Island Police was on the stoop. Jimmy was a couple years older than me, thirty-two or so, slender, red-haired. He was a good Baptist country boy who'd been with the Dauphin Island force for five years, still mystified people with money didn't spend more time thanking God for putting them on the champagne side of life. I waved him inside.

"Have a seat, Jimmy. Want a soda?"

"Just make me have to pull over to take a leak. I got a call, heard you pulled a gun on the Blovines."

"The what?"

"The renters next door. Woman's got a nasty mouth on her, don't she?"

I explained the scenario. Jimmy dissolved into laughter,

35

wiped his eyes on his sleeve. "I'll go suggest it's best they leave you be. When's John and Marge coming back?"

"Not fast enough. Mid October, I think."

"The Martins gone too?" The Martins were my neighbors to the west.

"Visiting the grandkids. North Dakota? South Dakota?"

Jimmy smiled. "West Dakota, maybe. Anyone renting their place?"

I shrugged and went to the window. The Martins' house was a modest single story with shining metal roof, a copy of mine, save for being coral with gray trim, mine white with green trim. The place was dark, blinds drawn. No car in the drive.

"No one there," I reported.

"Then you only got one set of neighbors to worry over," Jimmy said as he walked to the door. "Take care, Carson. And try not to shoot the Blovines. The paperwork'd be the death of me."

Jimmy stopped to talk to the neighbors. They didn't look happy when I wasn't dragged off in chains. Jimmy double-whooped his siren as he pulled into the street, telling me he was laughing. I chuckled and went to my answering machine, pressed Play.

"*Good evening, Detective Ryder, DeeDee Danbury, Channel 14 news. Listen, the victim in the motel today? You and Nautilus were out of your regular district there, right? If this is a PSIT thing, I'd like to be in the loop, maybe get a statement from you. By the way, I saw your picture in the paper; interesting expression . . .*"

I jabbed the Erase button and DeeDee Danbury disappeared. I waited for the second message.

A click of the mechanism, and the room filled with the voice of my dead mother.

"Cah-son? It's Mommy, son, calling from Heaven. My cellphone, that li'l thing I picked up a while back? It's getting mighty low on 'lectricity. Ah just found out Heaven don't have no phone rechargers. Now, Cah-son, what's a woman to do if she can't talk to her favorite son now and then? Ah have 'nother son, of course, but he's A PRISSY LITTLE DIRTBAG AND I WISH HE'D ROT IN HELL . . ."

I slumped to the chair beside the phone. It was my brother Jeremy. One of the many Jeremys. My mother's voice continued.

". . . ah recall some days I'd be tryin' my best to sew pretty dresses and THAT LITTLE SHIT JEREMY WOULD KEEP SCREAMING, 'HELP ME, MAMA – DADDY'S TRYING TO KILL ME – HELP ME, MAMA.' I declare Cah-son, how's a woman 'spect to get anything done WITH A SELF-CENTERED LITTLE MONSTER LIKE THAT AROUND? Ah me, such trib'lations as I been through. It's wunnderful in Heaven, Cah-son, they got sew-machines on ever' li'l cloud. And you can make your mama's time in Heaven even happier by calling on this very cell-estial telephone as soon's you get this message, tellin' her how she can get her very own phone recharger. She surely needs it fast. Thank you, and God bless us each and every one 'cept, of course, you can CONSIGN THAT LITTLE FUCKWAD JEREMY TO THE STEAMING BOWELS OF PERDITION. Please call me tonight, dearest

Cah-son. Give mah regards to that girlfrien' of yours, Miz Ava. Buh-byee, now."

The connection broke off.

My brother's call was an aberration; he wasn't supposed to have a phone. No one confined in that strange place was. But his hands were as swift with deceit as his words, and he'd slipped the phone from an orderly's pocket. I'd never informed the authorities about Jeremy's acquisition, and never quite knew why.

I erased my brother's message from the phone. No longer hungry, I went outside to lie on the deck and lose my thoughts in the blank hiss of the Gulf.

CHAPTER 4

The next morning I awoke to keening gulls and amber sunlight behind the curtains. Like most days I awakened a few minutes ahead of my 5.45 a.m. alarm, probably because it made an ugly sound, like a pig trying to chirp. I started coffee, slipped grudgingly into swim trunks, and walked to the water. I swam straight out for nearly a half mile, then turned and dragged myself back toward the cluster of beachfront houses. My standard four-mile beach run stretched to six as I tried to exorcise Jeremy's call. I slipped on a pair of faded jeans and white shirt, pulled on a beige thrift-store jacket to cover the shoulder holster, and hit the road north to Mobile.

When I got in, a half-dozen cops sat in their cubes, a couple discussing cases, most on phones. Harry was off at a meeting with the DA's office on a case in progress. No sooner had I sat than my phone rang. Calls to the detectives went through Bertie Wagnall.

"Guess what, Ryder?" Bertie said. "The local TV stations did a morning piece on that dead hooker. That Danbury bitch on Channel 14 talked about candles allegedly found at the scene. She's called for you twice, wants a statement."

"Candles, Bertie?" Harry and I'd requested all scene details be kept tight.

Wagnall belched; a liquid sound. "*Alleged*'s what she said. People been calling ever since, wanting to talk to you or Nautilus. They saw your picture in the paper and want to give you the benefit of their insights."

I sighed. "The usual nutcases?"

He chuckled. "I'm surprised at your cynical self, Ryder. These are upstanding citizens with important concerns. Here's a sample . . ."

"Bertie, I've got too much to do. Just take their numbers and –"

The clicking of a call transfer. Then a woman's voice, elderly, yelling over a television real close or real loud.

"Hello? Someone there? This the man what handles the lunatics? Weren't no crazyopaths killed that dead whore . . . that temptress got harvested by the sword of Almighty God, is what happened. Says right here in my Bible that . . ."

I set the phone down and massaged my temples. Last month Harry'd gotten called by a man who'd assigned numerical values to the letters in *Fluoridated Water*. The letters totaled 666. The caller was amazed we wouldn't arrest everyone in the Water Department.

After a minute I lifted the phone to my ear. Silence. I set it down and it rang immediately. Cursing Wagnall under my breath, I picked it up.

"Christ, how long you people keep citizens on hold?" a male voice said, strong, but with a sub-note of age. "Tell me about the hooker in the motel room, Cozy Cabins. I heard it on the news, the candles. But what about art? You find anything like that? I'm not talking covered bridges on the walls, I mean something small: a drawing, maybe, or paint on canvas."

"*Art?*" The woodwork seemed especially porous this morning.

"A-R-T. Maybe you've heard of it, bubba – pictures, color, shapes?"

I closed my eyes; it was looking like a twelve-aspirin day.

"Hello? I know you're still there, sonny Jim, I hear cops farting in the background. It's the lousy diet; fiber would help."

I affected my official voice. "No, sir. I personally inspected the room for over an hour. So did our crime scene people. No artwork was found. Thanks for you inter–"

"An hour ain't much. You're absolutely sure?"

"A hundred per cent, sir."

"That wasn't so hard now, was it?" my caller said. He clicked off the connection.

I hung up the phone and sighed. Somewhere across the room one of my colleagues broke wind.

Harry didn't know his ETA, so I headed to Forensics. Beakers bubbled. Printers churned out paper. Panels blinked.

The place smelled like bleach with a background scent of rancid meat. Hembree was beside a small centrifuge in the main lab. He popped the top and extracted a ballpoint pen. I wondered what ugly use the pen had seen.

Hembree dropped the pen in his pocket, winked. "Run a dry ballpoint at three Gs for ten seconds and you'll get another week of writing out of it, Carson."

I nodded like my life had changed for the better. "Get any print hits in on our motel lady, Bree?"

"To paraphrase the old joke, that was no lady, that was my Jane Doe."

"No hit?"

"Nothing in the system. Maybe she was just starting her career. I saw a news story last week about how folks in their fifties and sixties are going back to college just for fun . . ."

"Don't go there, Bree. Anything from the other prints?"

"Still got a bunch to process and run. Won't be long."

Hembree leaned his bony frame against the long white counter and smiled coyly. I'd seen it before, always an irritant.

I said, "You're waiting for me to ask something else, right?"

He jiggered his eyebrows. "Uh-huh."

"You got something on the candles?"

"Common, available at a zillion places. We did a burn-rate study last night. Looks like the candles still lit had burned for eight to ten hours."

He kept the coy smile on his moon face. More to come.

"How about the jewelry?" I asked.

Hembree whistled. A slender young woman appeared seconds later. In her late teens or early twenties, she had orange-blue hair and a wide assortment of piercings. There was a patch of unviolated real estate atop one ear, but maybe she was saving that for something special, like a Christmas ornament.

"This is Melinda. She's doing work-study with us this semester. Melinda, this is Carson Ryder. The Mayor's Officer of the Year, and he still can't figure out how to comb his hair."

"I like it," Melinda said, studying me. "Punk's retro, but cool on the right face."

"It's not a style," Hembree chuckled, "it's drying your hair by driving with the window down. Melinda, tell Detective Ryder about the jewelry on the victim."

"Cheesy junk. Stamped, not cast. Real low quality."

"The symbols mean anything?" I asked.

"A mish-mash. Some stuff is Goth, the swords, pentacles; some's more New Age, faeries and things. There's cross-over between the two, but not much."

"She wasn't making a personal statement, like a Satanist message?"

"If she was, she didn't know the language."

Hembree dismissed our ornamentation consultant. She walked away rather gingerly and I wondered what else she'd pierced.

"You've got one big question left, Carson," Hembree said.

"What was the henna-colored substance in the creases of the skin?"

"Bingo! That's the big question. What it is, Carson, is nothing more than red clay."

His previous reference to zombies suddenly made sense. I

said, "You're thinking this woman was buried and exhumed before coming to the motel?"

He grinned. "Some people can't make up their minds, I guess."

I returned to the office and told Harry the news.

"Freaky and geeky," he said, tugging on a tie so yellow it shamed lemons. "Candles and flowers, OK, the perp's got a thing for dressing a scene. But the back-from-the-grave bit jumps things up a level."

The phone rang and I grabbed it up. Hembree.

"The woman in the motel's still a cipher, Carson. But I got a print hit from the room. AFIS picked it up from a passport application three years back. Name's Rubin Coyle. Lawyer with Hamerle, Melbine and Raus. Blue eyes, brown hair. Forty-four years old. Five-ten in height, weighs one hundred and –"

"How'd you get all that info?"

"He's been listed as Missing. By the Mobile Police. You folks ever talk to one another over there?"

CHAPTER 5

"Frigging vegetables," Detective Jim Smithson growled, staring at a pale object resting on a napkin in the middle of his desk. He set his elbows on the desk and cupped his plump chin in his hands as Harry and I walked into the small office. A sign on the door said MISSING PERSONS.

"Excuse me, Jim?" I said. "Vegetables?"

Smithson shook his head, his neck-wattles shivering. "It's this freaking diet. Uncooked veggies and fruit." He pointed to the object. "How'd you like to wake up in the morning next to this?"

"A French fry?" I asked.

"It's a parsnip slice, Ryder. It's just a little brown. I guess it's an old parsnip. They don't date them."

"I didn't know that," I said. "I've never had a parsnip."

Smithson glared at the pitiful strand of vegetable. "This strip of parsnip, this one right here, is my lunch. Doc says to drop thirty pounds. I got the sugar, y'know."

"I'm sorry." It's all I could think of to say. Smithson wheezed, picked up a sharpened pencil, speared the parsnip, held it over his wastebasket and, wincing with repugnance, flicked it in the trash.

Harry spoke up. "It's not good to go without eating, Jim."

"Don't worry about me, Harry," Smithson said, "I've got a kohlrabi in my locker."

Smithson shifted heavily in his seat, his polyester-clad bottom squeaking against the vinyl chair. He was in his fifties, nosing hard toward retirement, putting in his time working the Missings desk with an occasional assist from one of the junior detectives. Smithson gave Harry a dyspeptic stare. "You boys here for a reason, or just come over to watch me eat?"

"You did that check for us on the woman we found in the motel, got nothing, right?"

He rolled rheumy eyes. "Yep. Brown and brown. Average height, weight."

"About fifty years old. You put that in?"

"Hell yes. What, you want me to call AARP?"

"Probably had hard work in her background. Outside perhaps, like I mentioned . . . picking, or maybe construction. Maritime even. You get that?"

"You told me all that. Nothing clicked." Smithson belched and pecked disconsolately at his keyboard. "To repeat myself . . . I got a nun reported overdue, but that's way up in Chilton County. Got an AWOL sailor; she's nineteen. Got about a dozen teen runaways. Got an insurance saleslady, a local, Bay Minette. Listed at 256 pounds –"

"There's another aspect," Harry said. "Seems a Mr Rubin Coyle's prints were among the hundreds that turned up in the motel room with the dead lady. We just found out he's a Missing. How long's he been listed?"

Smithson brought up another screen, squinted at it. "Six days back. He never showed up at his office, not at home. Reported by Lydia Barstow, a part-time paralegal at his office. She came in, did the report."

Harry scowled. "I didn't see a sheet on this Coyle. You forget to send a heads-up out on this?"

Smithson grunted, produced a Missing Persons report, waggled it in the air. "I sent a sheet out. It's probably buried somewhere on your desk, maybe under your stack of commendations."

I grabbed the report and angled toward the hallway. Smithson sighed, reached into his wastebasket, fished out the parsnip and flicked off the pencil grindings clinging to it. He was dangling it over his mouth when we retreated out the door.

The offices of Hamerle, Melbine and Raus were in an office building off Airport Road by USA, a five-story brown box with reflective windows. It had rained on our drive out, but storms blow through Mobile in the time it takes to count the change in your pocket, and the sun now pushed from the clouds. The traffic was thick on Airport, a stream of anxious metal. Exhaust mingling with evaporating rain turned the air into a poisonous brew and we hustled into the box.

The elevator deposited us on the fifth floor, opening to a hallway as hushed as a funeral parlor at midnight. We passed doors with signs boasting of the accountants, surveyors or financial consultants hunkering within. The last portal was the law firm, an office bathed in understated prosperity: satin wall-paper with a hint of floral pattern, beige carpet, gray-shaded lamps, abstract office-art in quiet pastels; even the trumpeter on the amorphous background pop was playing with a mute.

We announced ourselves to an elderly receptionist. Seconds later Lydia Barstow entered the lobby. In her late forties, I judged, green eyes in a round face, small nose, slender lips, hair walking the edge between brown and blonde. She wore a frumpish brown skirt and jacket, tan blouse, cream hose, brown flats. Muted. She walked with her hands wrapping her body, like the room was icy cold.

We asked Ms Barstow if we could meet in Rubin Coyle's office. She nodded, and despite her businesslike appearance, I noted the eyes of someone recently experiencing a near-miss by lightning. She led us past a long hall of lawyers in their kennels. Coyle's office was in a corner overlooking one of suburban Mobile's brick-encased communities. The requi-site diplomas were on the wall, alongside commendations from various charities and Rubin Coyle shaking hands with a variety of people, clients I figured.

"Do you have any word on Mr Coyle?" Her eyes were hopeful.

"I'm sorry, no. Detective Smithson probably told you –"

"There's not much you can do without evidence of . . . foul play. I understand. I was just hoping maybe . . ." She let the words trail off.

Harry apologized for repeating questions Smithson had asked, then revisited Coyle's disappearance. He'd been gone almost a week, with no calls, no e-mail, no messages of any sort.

I said, "No wife, right?"

"Divorced years ago. They don't stay in touch."

"Girlfriend?"

She paused. Her hands started to flutter, but she contained them in her lap. "I, that is . . ."

From her tremulous anxiety – and that she'd filed the Missing report – I figured she was closer to Coyle than a paralegal.

"Are you his girlfriend, Ms Barstow?" I prompted.

Her attempt at a smile didn't stick. "That would be me, I guess."

"You're uncertain?"

"He's so involved in his work. We didn't get much chance to go on dates, be together. Not like big nights out kind of thing, movies, dinner. We mostly, just, uh . . ."

She suddenly looked stricken, like she'd talked herself down the wrong road. Harry said, "We don't mean to pry, Miz Barstow. But the more we know, the better we can do."

Ms Barstow appeared on the verge of tears. "Mostly we stayed inside. It's what Rubin wanted to do." She looked away and bit her lip. I took it to mean Rubin Coyle was more interested in companionship than movies and restaurant dining.

"Did Mr Coyle ever mention, or take you to the Cozy Cabins motel?"

Pure puzzlement is one of the toughest expressions to fake,

the tendency being to overdo it, popped eyes, dropped jaw; Lydia's confusion looked real.

"Why?"

"He appears to have been there recently."

"I never heard him mention it."

"Did the routine of your relationship change any in the last couple of weeks?"

She took a deep breath. "The last time we . . . got together was Friday two weeks back. He seemed his usual self." She looked around the office, closed her eyes.

"Do you work solely with Mr Coyle?" I asked.

"I work for several lawyers. Truth be told, there wasn't a lot of work from Ru—, Mr Coyle. Typing, mainly."

I said, "We have to ask – do you know of anyone who would have reason to abduct Mr Coyle, wish to do him harm?"

Her head shook my words away. "Rubin . . . Mr Coyle is so – so, nice."

"No angry clients, cases lost, botched filings?"

"He never litigates. Negotiations are his specialty. And mediation. He always says, 'Lydia, if I have to enter a courtroom, it's because I've failed.' He feels successful negotiations are his calling – everyone leaves satisfied, or as close as possible."

Harry and I discovered nothing to mark Rubin Coyle as a target of anger. Indeed, he seemed almost an anti-lawyer, working to cement relationships, create effective settlements, broadcast harmony at every opportunity. On the seventh day he rested, now and then with Ms Barstow.

"How about the owners, partners, I guess they're called. Do they know anything?"

She shook her head. "Mr Hamerle's the head partner, the only person Rubin reported to, really. Mr Hamerle came in and tried to work today, but his angina flared up. He went to the hospital for observation. The poor man's seventy years old."

"What's Mr Hamerle think of this?"

"He keeps saying Rubin's taking a few stress days, he'll show in a day or so."

"One final question, Ms Barstow. The week before Mr Coyle disappeared, did anything set any kind of bell off? Don't think big picture, think small. Tiny. Anything stand out, good, bad or indifferent?"

A memory flickered across her eyes.

"A couple days before he . . . stopped coming in, Rubin was at a client meeting in Bay Minette. He got a package marked PERSONAL AND CONFIDENTIAL, no return address. Even when he's out, Rubin wants me to open everything. There was an envelope inside the package, thick and puffy. I opened it and found another envelope, smaller. It was like opening a puzzle. Inside that was bubble wrap. Inside the wrapping were pieces of cardboard taped together like a sandwich."

"Inside the sandwich was . . . ?"

She positioned her thumb and forefinger the width of three postage stamps. "An eensy little painting, or something like that."

I felt a tingle rise up my spine. "Excuse me, Ms Barstow," I interrupted. "Art?"

She nodded. "On canvas. The edges were torn, like it had been ripped off a larger work."

51

I heard my morning caller's voice rasping at me: *What about art? You find anything like that?*

But the caller had meant art at the scene, hadn't he? Very specific. I said, "What was the drawing or painting of, Ms Barstow?"

"Not any real image. More like swirls and shapes. The colors were breathtaking."

"No note or other explanation?"

"It seemed strange there wasn't a note with it. I put it in his inbox."

"You haven't seen it since?"

She shook her head. "He must have picked it up. He never mentioned it."

I said, "Is Mr Coyle an art collector, anything like that?"

A sad smile. "I made Rubin take me to the art museum once, a contemporary exhibit. He kept saying, 'But what does it mean, Lydia? I can't figure any of this stuff out.' We left after twenty minutes."

"Tell me more about the artwork from the mail."

"I'll never forget how gorgeous it was, the incredible colors, the way the shapes fit together. And yet . . ."

Her hushed tone made me look up from my note-taking. "What, Ms Barstow?"

"It had something strange about it. Something I could feel, but not see."

"Like what, ma'am?" Harry asked.

She gave us a puzzled look. "Like if I looked at it too long, I'd get bad dreams. Does that make any sense?"

CHAPTER 6

We left the law offices and revisited Hakkam. The office air was blue with smoke. Harry flicked through pages of check-in sheets.

"Looks like you're the motel of choice for the Smith and Jones family reunions," he said.

Hakkam shrugged. "No control what names people say."

Harry's forefinger traced the pages of the register, tapped an entry. "Here we go. Rubin T. Coyle. Signed in two weeks back. Correct name, address, tag number. Not hiding a thing. Probably the only true sign-in this decade. He say why he was staying here, Mr Hakkam, being a local and all? Painting, maybe?"

The oldest excuse in the world for folks staying at a motel in their town: *I'm painting my apartment, can't take the smell. Neither can my, uh, wife, out there in the car.*

Hakkam thought a moment. "He said he doing something with work. Research. Say he maybe make some business here, ask how long to reserve ahead to assure several cabins, seven or eight."

"And you said . . . ?"

Hakkam took an extravagant pull on the cigarette. "Twenty–thirty minutes."

We retreated to the car. I slid into the back seat, Harry the front. As he pulled away, I lay down, arms behind my head, watching blue sky and treetops flashing by. When I was a child and the dark things started in my house, I'd creep to our old station wagon and hide in the back seat. Rear seats remained a haven to this day, a good place to think. As an additional benefit, I didn't have to endure Harry's driving style. He loved piloting a car, but, like color, had never quite gotten the hang of it. We'd driven hundreds of miles this way and it was second nature.

"I don't think Coyle met Jane Doe," Harry said into the rear-view. "He was at Cozy Cabins twelve days before she appeared. Didn't hide his presence. Probably had a woman in the car. Or a guy. Coyle's not real wrapped up in Miz Barstow. She worships him, though. Naïve's what some might infer, me included. Maybe lawyer boy's having a mid-life meltdown. Take your pick of examples. How's Dale Bryson sound?"

Dale Bryson was a drably conservative 38-year-old civil engineer reported missing a few months back. When his credit-card path put him near a man killed in a liquor store, Harry and I got the case. Two days after putting Bryson in our sights, someone else confessed to the killing. Since we

54

were already involved, Harry and I tracked Bryson to an upscale motel off I-10, a shiny new Beamer convertible parked outside the room. We found him naked in a bathtub filled with five cases of forty-buck-a-bottle champagne. The bed was covered with teddy bears. He was embarrassed to his marrow, offering no plausible explanation, save that, "It was something I needed to do."

Bryson's case, though a bit extreme, wasn't unusual: today's white-collar, middle- and upper-middle-class males seem culturally programmed toward such events from mid thirties through mid forties. When they go missing, it's generally for a week or so, the prime danger being emptying their bank accounts buying a speedboat or sports car. Odds were, wherever Rubin Coyle was, he was safe. And had nothing to do with our Jane Doe.

"There's just one more thing, Harry," I said.

I felt the car swerve, bang the curb, correct. "What thing, bro?"

"I got a weird call this morning. Some old guy wanted to know if any art had been found with our Jane. Sounded like a crank. I blew him off."

"Nothing like that *was* found in the cabin, Cars."

"But a swatch of something artsy was delivered to Coyle."

Harry waved it away. "We don't know it was art. Hell, my first wife had samples of decorator crap coming in the mail all the time: wallpaper samples, swatches of upholstery, curtain material . . ."

"First wife? I thought you were married just the once."

Harry rarely mentioned his divorce and I'd never asked.

55

He blew out a long breath, scowled at some distant memory. "Yeah. But sometimes it felt like a lot more."

Harry dropped me at the morgue. Jane Doe's autopsy had been handled by a District Three detective two hours earlier, their last involvement. The case now shifted to Harry and me, and I wanted advance notice of what the preliminary might be, maybe influence it a little. Dr Clair Peltier was behind her desk in her spartan office, her furnishings scarcely nobler than those in the detectives' room. She'd done the procedure on Jane Doe and would be working up the report.

I stuck my head in her door. There was a vase of roses on Clair's desk, the only bright color in the room.

"Prelim in on Jane Doe, Clair?"

Everyone else called Clair "Dr Peltier". I'd used Clair from the moment of introduction and she let the faux pas stand, countering by using only my last name. Clair was director of the Mobile office of the Alabama Forensics Bureau, and my vote for Best Eyes in a Starring Role. In her mid forties, Clair had close-cropped anthracite hair and startling blue eyes that tended toward chill, but occasionally surprised with sudden warmth. I sat in the sole chair before her desk. Clair pulled her neck-strung reading glasses into place and scowled at the paper. The smell of the roses seemed dense enough to lean into, a red cushion of scent.

"I found postmortem abrasions that appear to be shovel strikes. Plus livor mortis markings that wouldn't be there if she'd stayed prone in a motel bed. Add the traces of clay on and in her body and we come to a pretty obvious conclusion . . ."

I nodded. "Buried and disinterred, I know."

"I looked at the Forensics report, of course – flowers, candles. What's your take, Ryder?"

I shrugged. "Candles are symbolic in several ways, flowers too. But I'm not sure if it's the work of a full-blown psychotic."

"Have you established that she was a hooker?"

"She was naked in a motel that probably gets half its income from one-hour stints."

Clair snapped the paper with a fingernail. "She didn't have prostitute's plumbing, Ryder. No lesions, scarring, signs of STDs past or present. No bruising or abrasions. Given her age, her genitals look like they're still under warranty. And no sign of sexual activity that night."

I tented my fingers, brought them to my lips. "Something else that's odd, Clair – she doesn't have prints in the system. New to the trade, maybe. Drugs make that sort of thing happen."

Clair shuffled through pages. "Let me read you the approximate timeline we're getting. Death by asphyxiation between midnight Saturday and Sunday afternoon . . ."

"I saw the ligature marks on her neck."

"What you didn't see was the internal damage. The ligature was tightened and released several times."

"Torture." I felt my stomach turn over. This was the kind of thing done by people enjoying themselves. Clair continued reading.

"The victim was probably buried shortly after death. Monday or Tuesday, she's unearthed. Washed."

I jumped in. "Tuesday night, she's brought to a motel room

rented hours before. Someone lights a lot of candles, throws some flowers on her."

Clair said, "You got nothing from the room?"

"Bree's running a trainload of prints. No latents on the candles, flowers. Nearby surfaces wiped. A careful perp. I doubt we'll find anything. Forensics vacuumed the carpet for trace evidence. I'd hate to sort through the dirt."

Clair raised a dark crescent of eyebrow. "Sounds like a tough one, Ryder."

I thought about the chief's concern, the media. He wanted us to look good, I wanted us to stay off the radar. But prelims were widely distributed internally and swiftly found back doors to the media.

"What'll you highlight in the report, Clair?"

"Ligature strangulation. Plus standard clinical findings."

"How about the candles over her eyes, her burial and retrieval? The torture aspect?"

She gave me a glance. "You don't want that disseminated?"

"Its absence now might help us later."

"It's conjecture so far. I'll leave out as much as possible."

"Thanks, Clair."

"I can hang a shroud over it only so long, Ryder. A week, maybe two. After that the public's going to get the full report. It could set off a sideshow."

I pressed my hands to my knees, stood. I got to the door when Clair spoke.

"Ryder? You hear anything from Ava?"

Ava Davanelle was a former assistant pathologist at the morgue. She'd been fighting alcoholism when she'd become

58

innocently involved in a case last year, almost dying in the process. We'd gone together for several months afterward, perhaps the happiest time of my life. Hers too, I'd hoped. A month ago – with no prior notice – she'd announced she was leaving Mobile, her job, her friends down here. Everything.

I was suddenly a part of her past.

Ava retreated to Fort Wayne, Indiana, where she'd grown up. She planned on acquiring additional schooling for hospital pathology instead of forensic pathology; to "work with the living and not the dead."

We'd spoken three times on the phone since she'd left. Our conversations had been stilted, falsely chatty, without any depth, like a conversation between Barbie and Ken dolls.

They broke up too, didn't they?

"Ryder? You there?" Clair's voice cut through my thoughts.

"I haven't heard from Ava in a week, Clair. Not a word. I hope she's happy. She deserves happiness."

Clair's eyes softened as she looked over her glasses. "And you, Carson? Are you getting . . . past it?"

The room shimmered. My knees felt oddly loose. I turned, waved over my shoulder, and retreated from the room as fast as possible within the bounds of civility. I stopped in the restroom on the way down the hall. Washed my face. Stared at my reflection until tired of it, two or three seconds. Took a deep breath and headed for the door. I was surprised to find Harry at the front desk. He turned from joking with receptionist Vera Braden and jammed his thumb toward the entrance.

"Buzzards outside, bro; thought you needed warning."

We walked to the door. Several reporters clustered outside.

It surprised me not to see the pair from Channel 14. Harry laid his big hand over my shoulder from behind. "Anything new in the post, bro?"

"Bad things," I said. "Torture."

I looked through the door, the faces of the media pressed against the glass, distorted, slavering for news, hoping it would be ugly enough to sell more papers, jack up the ratings to sell more commercials. I was suddenly sick of everything: the morgue, people who turned a woman's death into a carnival, women who left without warning . . .

And maybe sick of myself for being insufficient reason for Ava Davanelle to stay. I said, "Screw the bastards, Harry. Let's get out of here."

We strode into a wall of wet heat. Voices bayed simultaneously, like on a master switch, the shouted questions blending into an aural non sequitur.

How find is murder kind of weapon? do you think where circumstances? if you would there be a perpetrator? much the medical examiner can you determine the time of evidence any clues? be will you next notify of kin . . .

After a couple dozen feet they fell away. Harry and I jogged a hundred feet to the car. A door opened beside us. Danbury and Funt jumped from a black SUV. She aimed a mic our way. The diminutive, denim-clad Funt flanked her, the glass eye of the camera shifting between Harry and me, as if making up its mind.

"Well, looky here," Danbury said. "It's the pogobos."

"Pogobos?" I said.

"*Po*-lice *Go*-lden *Bo*-ys. Pogobos. How about an exclusive from the elite squadron? What are the autopsy results? Is this a case for the PSIT?"

"No comment," I grunted, additionally sick of people jamming faces, microphones and cameras into my life. Danbury pushed closer, the mic inches from my nose. "This victim, Detective Ryder, was there anything about her that concerns the PSIT? Mutilation? Strange markings? A pattern of –"

I slapped the mic away. It flew from her hand and smacked the sidewalk.

Her eyes widened. I said, "Go to hell. And that goes for your camera monkey, too."

"Carson," Harry cautioned.

The camera guy grinned into his viewfinder. "Testy today, ain't we?"

I retreated to the far side of the car. Danbury said, "Can you tell me why you're here and not someone from Third District?"

I glared at her. "You couldn't get a real job? How much you make as a grief pimp?"

"You got an anger-control problem, Detective," the cameraman said, the grin even wider. I wanted to jam the camera down his throat. Instead I got in and gave him the tight eye. He grinned back, winked. Harry fired up the engine. When he hit the accelerator, the car veered and fought and made the sound of a leather flag in a stiff wind.

"Uh-oh," Harry said. He braked and opened his door, looked at the tires. "Nothing here. Check your side, bro."

I jumped out. The front tire was a pool of flat rubber.

Harry pulled his phone. "Get in, Carson. I'll call the garage, get it fixed. Won't take but a few."

We were fifty or sixty feet from Danbury and the chimp. The video monkey sprinted straight for me. "Hey, Detective," he said, pushing the camera lens into my face. "A big smile for our viewers from the Cop of the Year. Be good publicity for the department."

"Move it," I said. Something happening in my gut that was more sound than feeling.

"Get in the car, Carson," Harry said, louder.

Danbury walked up. "Borg," she called to the videographer. "Cut. Leave it."

"Come on, Mr Ryder," the camera guy whispered, just me and him hearing it now. "Gimme that tough-guy face like in the paper. Your mama like the picture? How about your girlfriend? Oh, fuck me, baby, but first give me that *hard* look . . ."

"Carson! Get the hell in the car," Harry barked.

But it was too late. I had the video guy by the front of his shirt and was lifting his face into mine, explaining uses I might find for his camera if we could grab a quiet moment alone somewhere.

His pinched and simian face never stopped grinning.

That night I came home to a blinking light on my message machine. I knew it was Jeremy, maybe because it had been that kind of day. I pressed Play, was rewarded only with the knowledge of being right.

"Cah-son, Mommy's waiting for her new recharger," were the only words he needed. He sang them, like he didn't have a care in the world.

CHAPTER 7

I don't know why, but Chief Plackett had one of those fancy floor-standing globes in his office, a world the size of a beach ball. I stared into the blue South Pacific, wishing I was there. Plackett studied me from behind his wide and gleaming desk. The morning fog hadn't burned off, and the world outside his window was gray.

He said, "You stand what, Detective Ryder, height-wise?"

"Uh, six one."

"And you weigh what? One seventy, one eighty?"

"Somewhere in there."

"And you got into an altercation with a man who is –" Chief Plackett picked up a letter from his desktop, scanned it – "five six and weighs a hundred twenty-five pounds?"

The letter was from Channel 14 station management and

had been delivered first thing this morning. I gathered the chief had spent an hour on the phone with various folks from the station.

"Chief," Harry said from beside me, "in my estimation Detective Ryder was provoked into –"

Plackett cut Harry off with an upraised hand. "And not only did you threaten this man with bodily harm, you physically assaulted him."

"I gathered his shirtfront in my hand. Perhaps rather suddenly."

Plackett quoted from the letter: ". . . proceeded to lift him to his toes, holding him elevated until his face turned red."

"His face is naturally sort of red," Harry said.

"Not now, Nautilus."

"Yes, sir."

"Did you do this, Detective Ryder? Are these statements true?"

"Sir, I think the camera tapes might reveal the man in question verbally goaded me into –"

The chief threw the letter to his desk. "I don't give two hoots what he said to you. You're a cop. You've endured worse verbal abuse, right?"

I jammed my hands into my pockets, looked down. "He caught me at a bad time."

Plackett walked to his window, looked out over the morning traffic. "Luckily, the station is willing to let it disappear. I had to talk to people, call in some markers, make some promises. You understand?"

"Not really, sir."

"We owe them for not taking legal action. Or worse, airing a tape I understand is profane and embarrassing. This incident happens what – three days after you receive the Officer of the Year commendation? I don't have to tell you about the black eye if the Mayor got wind of this."

"I'm sorry, Chief." I'm not sure I was, but saying so was the protocol.

"I hate owing the media anything, Ryder. I shudder to think what the payback's going to be." He frowned. "You getting any closer on that case with the woman in the motel? The case that seemed to spark this confrontation?"

"It's proving to be difficult, but I'm hopeful we'll –"

"No leads? No tips? Nothing? This is your field, Detective. You're our specialist."

I paused, heard my mouth say, "We're pursuing a small conjecture based on a phone tip. Something to do with art."

"Is this a solid lead?"

"It's all we have at the –"

"Dismissed."

"Art?" Harry said as we retreated from Plackett's slammed door. "Are you talking about whatever-the-hell that dropped into the paralegal's palm the other day?"

"I was talking about the old guy that called, asking about art in the motel room."

"The lunatic?"

"He wasn't a lunatic. More like a codger. Did you want me to tell the chief what we really have, which is . . ." I zeroed together my thumb and forefinger.

"You got a point there, hairy and scary. I'm going to go

see what I can dig up from candle outlets. Maybe this freak bought himself fifty candles on a credit card, then used the same card at the florist. You think that happened?"

I headed to the front desk, where the phone logs could be accessed. The address was across the mouth of the Bay, on Fort Morgan Highway. My caller's name was unfamiliar, not surprising. I jammed the address in my pocket and hustled out the door.

After an hour's drive I turned onto a rutted drive cutting through vines and brush. Slash pines towered overhead. I drove two hundred feet to the rear of a cream-colored bungalow facing the Bay. I cut the engine and drifted up behind a dark-windowed Dodge Ram 2500 pickup, black, the diesel-engine job with twin chrome tailpipes like torpedo launchers. The truck had a rack above the bed, long tubes of PVC piping on the rack. Rod tubes, I surmised; a surf fisherman.

Seeing nothing threatening in the surrounding brush, I tiptoed to the front of the house. A glider hung on the small porch, its slatted seat and back shiny with wear. I heard boats on the Bay. Gulls above. The low hum of the AC. Water lapped the pilings of a dock stretching fifty feet into the water, a small runabout at its terminus.

A man's voice from behind me. "Freeze."

I froze. "I'm with the Mobile Police. I'm looking for –"

"Shush, sonny Jim. Move your hands away from your body, like you're flying. I got a .45 here. Blow a hole in your gut big enough to toss a cat through."

The voice of my caller, Art Man. *Where had he come from? The air?* I lofted my arms outward.

66

"Listen, Mr –"

"Ease out your ID, two-finger scissors. Move toward the weapon, you've bought yourself a headstone."

I plucked out my badge and ID, flapped it open, held it facing the rear.

"OK," he said. "Drop your drawers and fart 'Moon River'."

"What?"

I turned to find a man in his mid to late sixties, middle height, slender build. His eyes were pewter beneath a flop-brim hat. His short-sleeved shirt was plaid, his arms tanned even deeper than his face. Reading glasses hung from a yellow cord around his neck. Paint-spattered khakis fell to battered running shoes. He was leaning against a tree with his arms crossed. He didn't have a gun.

I felt my face redden with embarrassment and anger. "You were in the truck?"

"I heard you coming and jumped inside. A smarter fellow would have checked there." He shook his head. "You got a few things to learn yet, son."

"Your name would be one of them."

"Former Alabama State Police Detective Jacob C. Willow," he said. "Follow me, Ryder. You look like you could use a drink."

We went inside. He ambled to the kitchen and left me standing in the living room. It was bright and sizeable, a small kitchen-dining area to the rear. I studied a nearby bookshelf; tomes on fishing and boating mingled with a dozen or so biographies. Three running feet of shelf was dedicated to true-crime volumes, hardcover mostly. A thick accordion file nestled against a copy of *Helter Skelter*, Vincent Bugliosi's

67

account of the Manson Family murders. There was a low table between the couch and a couple of chairs. Willow reappeared with two glasses of lemonade.

"Sit yourself down," he said, pointing to the couch. "Don't wait on me to be polite."

Willow handed me a glass and raised a gray eyebrow. "I take it you're here because some old coot made a twenty-second call about a death in a motel, right? Are your leads that slim, Detective? Is it that kind of case?"

"Maybe I should ask the questions here," I said, fairly pleasantly, considering I'd been bushwhacked by an old coot.

He appraised me with his eyes, nodded. "Fair enough. But first let an old timer establish his credentials . . ."

He took the chair across from me. Jacob Willow was sixty-seven years old. He'd been with the State Police for twenty-five years, seven in uniform, the rest as an investigator, primarily in the lower third of Alabama. No one had ever offered an administrative position, knowing he wouldn't have accepted. His retirement party had been a dozen years back and he'd left after thirty minutes. It took him three minutes to sketch his background and he signaled completion by rising and beginning to pace. I cleared my throat.

"Art, Mr Willow. Remember? It's the word that brought me here. You haven't used it once."

"I wanted to establish my history, my credentials. It's important."

"I'm backgrounded. Now I need foreground."

"The news reports of the dead hooker mentioned candles. I needed to know if you also found a piece of artwork."

"I'm obliged to tell you nothing. I will tell you no art was found in the room."

"You're sure?"

"The best technician at the Alabama Forensics Bureau worked the room. Nada on the art side." I didn't mention the art that dropped into Lydia Barstow's hand, still considering it coincidence. "How about telling me why art is so important to you?"

He walked slowly to his window, looked over the Bay. A wavering strand of pelicans skimmed past his dock.

"I've been watching for things like this. Watching for years."

"For a dead prostitute tied to artwork?"

"For Marsden Hexcamp to resurface."

The name was familiar, but vague, like a faded notation on an old calendar.

"Hexcamp? Serial killer? Back in the sixties?"

Willow walked to the shelf and retrieved the accordion folder, pulling a file from it, thick with what appeared to be newsprint. "Hexcamp's first killing was a hooker. He left candles in the room. The similarity struck me."

"When was this murder, Mr Willow?"

"July 17, 1970."

I raised an eyebrow. "This Hexcamp, he still alive?"

"He was shot dead on May 15, 1972."

I resisted rolling my eyes. "Over a generation ago, Mr Willow. Maybe it's no longer rele–"

He tossed me the file. "A taste of poison from the past, Detective: news clippings from the Hexcamp days."

I politely studied a few articles, some with photographs.

Though headlines repeated words like *Maniac* and *Perverted*, Hexcamp looked as threatening as a model for The Gap. The final and largest headline was *Mysterious "Crying" Woman Kills Hexcamp, Commits Suicide in Courtroom*.

I said, "From what I see, the articles are long on speculation and short on fact. Sensationalism. Hexcamp and several of his followers do seem seriously deranged."

"The articles only hint at the madness. He killed slowly and with glee, claiming it was research into the last moment of life, the final beauty. And yet, he moved easily through society, having all the social graces, utterly charming, a gifted conversationalist, an artist who studied at a world-famous art school in Paris, the academy of something or other. The only American to win a full scholarship there, so I've heard. A fine mind powering an immense ego, horizon to horizon. Unfortunately, his charisma and good looks were in roughly the same proportion. He drew women and men like a flame pulls moths. But inside he was a dark force, a hellish mutation."

"Sociopathic. There's a lot of it going around."

"The newspaper articles don't come close to explaining the darkness festering in his brain, Detective. Or his effect on others. The effect may be lethal, even to this day."

I said, "Marsden Hexcamp is as dead as a sausage, Mr Willow. A difficult condition from which to be deadly."

Willow took a deep breath, dry-washed his face with his palms. "There's a rumor Marsden Hexcamp kept a collection of his thoughts and deeds. Like an artist's portfolio. A visual distillation of his thoughts on . . . death. It's rumored his artwork is highly prized and moves in a small circle of people who revere its message. It's hard to pinpoint – no one talks to the public about it."

"Twice I heard the word *rumor*."

Willow sighed, sat back. "There's no solid confirmation such a collection actually exists."

"People obviously believe it does. Do you?"

"I've heard people claim they held pieces from Hexcamp's portfolio. They were adamant."

"Folklore often blooms from psychotic killers, Mr Willow. Think of Jack the Ripper. Or Jesse James, society turning the venomous into the misunderstood. It adds to the mystique, provides a thrill."

"I know that. But I also knew something about these people. They were, are . . . afflicted, in their way, but not given to exaggeration."

"Who are they?"

"Collectors of serial-killer memorabilia."

Such folks weren't unknown to me. My haphazard college career took me at last to the Psychology Department at the University of Alabama, where part of my study involved traveling to prisons and mental institutions throughout the South, interviewing some of the most horrifying psychopaths and sociopaths on the face of the planet. Nearly every one of them had a "fan club": sick men and women who clamored for communications and souvenirs from celebrity murderers.

"I've met a couple of them," I admitted. "A guy who collected scribblings from incarcerated crazies. A woman who not only did the same, but proposed to every killer who sent

71

her something. They were small, pathetic people. Sick, but harmless."

Willow nodded. "That's the bulk of them. There's another contingent – no less sick, but far wealthier, able to indulge themselves, to collect more esoteric and expensive memorabilia."

"Like what? David Berkowitz's high chair?"

"Items from the scene. Or used in the killing itself. A bloody hammer. A ligature. Clothing is big. If it stinks with shit from a death-released sphincter, so much the better."

I studied Willow's face. "You're not kidding, are you?"

"I wish."

The typical homicide scene came to my mind: all involved items bagged, tagged, and locked away in the evidence room.

"There can't be much of that stuff around," I said.

Willow shot me a crooked smile. "Making it all the more valuable."

"Where does it come from?"

"The trial ends, the evidence goes to a property room. Money changes hands. Pieces slip out."

I checked my watch; I'd put two hours into this already, another hour before I'd be back in Mobile. I stood, said thanks for the hospitality, jiggered the stiffness from my knees, and headed outside. Willow dogged my heels to the car and watched me climb inside. He stared through the open door, waiting for me to say something. I settled on the truth.

"I don't particularly know how to end this conversation, Mr Willow. It's been interesting."

He frowned. "Interesting is what people say when they don't want to call someone crazy."

I fired up the engine. "I'm not downplaying anything you've told me. All I could do today was listen. You were a detective. What would you do in my shoes?"

"Keep an open mind," he said, pushing the door shut.

I stopped in Willow's drive just short of the road and called the department. No news on our Jane Doe. Harry'd found nothing on large candle sales; not surprisingly, he added, since, "every fourth store in the world sells the damn things."

I turned west on Fort Morgan Highway and drove to the ferry, catching the timing perfectly and pulling on board just before the ramp lifted. The ferry went from Fort Morgan to Dauphin Island, crossing the battleground of the Battle of Mobile Bay. Wreckage from that fierce conflict still ghosted the waters beneath the waves, and no matter how hot the day, I never made the crossing without suppressing a shiver.

I'd had my own form of passage over the Bay as well. Three years back, long after Jeremy had slain our father with a hunting knife, I found the weapon hidden in our family's basement. I tucked it beneath my shirt and rode the ferry across the Bay. Midpoint in the journey I tossed the knife overboard, figuring the water had seen so much violence, one more small memento of horror would not be noticed. I'd felt better from that moment on, somehow cleaner.

In my dreams I have thrown that knife away a hundred times.

Since the ferry landed less than a mile from my home, I went to grab lunch before taking the strange tale of Marsden

Hexcamp to Harry. Turning the corner to my place, I saw a car in my drive, white and nondescript. Someone was sitting on the picnic table beneath my house, staring out at the long blue of the Gulf.

I knew that form. It was Ava.

She'd returned.

Her eyes startled when she turned to the sound of my wheels over shells. My heart dropped; it was evident she didn't want to see me. The half-hearted wave confirmed it. I got out, walked beneath the house.

"I thought you were in Fort Wayne," I said.

"I flew down to finish a few chores, legal things. I'm renting out my house down here until I . . . decide what to do with it. I rented a small place in Fort Wayne. It's small, but windows everywhere, light. It's by a place called Lakeside Park . . ."

She was trying for cheery and up-tempo. I stared the notion away. "You weren't going to tell me you were in town?"

She closed her eyes. "Not this time, while we're –"

"While we're what? Breaking up? Having a trial separation? What are we doing? Tell me."

Her eyes watered. A tear fell down her cheek. I wanted to reach out and brush it away, feel the warmth of her face, her hair. I had never felt this way about a woman; it was a foreign land and no one had taught me a word of its secret language. And yet somewhere deep within, I felt a sense of betrayal at her having kept me distant while she made decisions I'd thought were ours, not just hers.

I said, "I can't make sense of this, Ava."

"Maybe there isn't any. Yet."

"I know you have horrible pictures in your mind. They fade. It takes time."

"Nothing's fading, Carson. It's getting louder. It terrifies me."

"A madman fixated on you. That was the sum of your involvement. Fate selected you and you can't change it. No matter how fast or far you . . ." I caught myself, but not fast enough.

"You were about to say 'run', weren't you? No matter how far or fast I run?"

"It doesn't matter."

"Yes it does."

I jammed my hands in my pockets and watched the waves fall and retreat. "It's not important."

"Don't patronize me. Tell me the truth." There was a note of anger in her voice. If she wanted the truth . . .

"Here today, gone tomorrow. Sounds like running to me."

"That's cold, Carson."

I felt a hard prickle of anger in my gut. "Cold is telling me you were leaving after you'd already decided to. Cold is cutting me out. Cold is showing up here when you were sure I wouldn't be home."

Three days of frustration burned from my mouth so fast I didn't hear it until it was over. "Just what was between you and me, Ava? A handy-dandy little pick-me-up? An extended nooner? Do I look different now you're off the bottle? Hi, I'm Carson Ryder. I'd like you to meet my girlfriend, Ava Davanelle, but she sobered up and ran away."

I wanted to provoke anger from her, hard-edged and

visceral, a volcanic eruption of emotion that might carry with it a moment to understand, an explanation. Instead, Ava looked at the sea. Her eyes were greener than wet emeralds.

"I'm leaving now," she said. Her shaking hands started to cross between us, wanting to hug, to hold. Needing understanding, or just comfort.

I kept my hands pocketed and turned toward the water, like there was something more interesting in the waves. She started crying and I listened to the sound of her retreating footsteps and the closing of the car door. I turned when she was a block gone and moving away.

"What did you come here for?" I yelled. "Just to look at the damned water?"

And then even the sound of her engine was gone.

CHAPTER 8

While a child I became a mental compartmentalizer out of necessity; good things up front, bad things in back. I jammed Ava into a far corner of my head, put on my work face and met Harry at the department. The tire on our regular ride was fixed, and while he drove us to the motor pool to exchange vehicles, I described my visit with Willow.

He snorted. "Art coming back to haunt people, kill them? Sounds shaky, Cars."

"It's a distance thing. It sounds strange here, but he makes it kind of interesting."

Harry dodged a bicyclist, drove up on the curb, banged back down. "Did he tell you who was doing this killing? People from the past, maybe?"

"No. Most are dead, the important ones anyway. Willow

thought it might have something to do with collectors of serial-killer memorabilia."

"Scrawled pages from prison, twisted little drawings? We've both seen that stuff."

"Willow's talking about folks who collect grimmer stuff, like relics from crime scenes. Or bizarre, but high-caliber, art."

"Like this Hexcamp supposedly made."

I shrugged. "I guess."

"Yet there's no solid proof, no evidence whatsoever, of anything. It's just this old cop's theories. Theories based mainly on rumors, no less. What's the tie to today?"

"Hexcamp's first vic was a hooker. Evidently he and his jolly campers left her strangled to death in a candlelit motel room."

Harry gunned the engine, blew by a beer truck so close I could have snatched a six-pack. He said, "That's what set the old cop off?"

"I think so."

"It's candles, Carson. Not real rare, right?"

Ritual killers were often attracted to candles for various symbolic reasons. They were also, unfortunately, attracted to prostitutes, whose lifestyle made them among the easiest human targets on the face of the planet.

"No," I admitted. Willow's tale was starting to sound eccentric to me, too.

"It's obsession, Carson; at least that's how it feels so far. A case gets in a guy's blood, goes unsolved, or he thinks it didn't fall right. When he retires it turns into his life, just keeps replaying it."

"You don't think anything's there?"

"I feel for the old guy, admire his devotion. But it sounds like obsession, pure and simple."

We pulled into the motor pool and went inside to pick up the car. It wasn't much cooler inside than outside. Ranks of cruisers and unmarkeds waited in various stages of repair. The smell of paint and solvents soaked the air. The workers had pneumatic tools, painfully loud, a jackhammer concerto. A fiftyish black man with a blue uniform walked over, rubbing his hand on a rag. Embroidered across the pocket of his shirt was *Rafael.*

He said, "Hey, Harry, whatcha need?"

I said, "We have the sky-blue Maserati with the flame decals behind the wheel wells. You were putting in the microwave oven."

Harry sighed from beside me, gave the man *look-what-I'm-burdened-with* eyes. "It's the dark blue Crown Vic that came in yesterday, Rafe. Flat tire."

Rafael nodded my way. "Your partner there, Harry – he make a lot of enemies being funny, does he?"

"Don't know. No one's ever heard him say anything funny. Why?"

Rafael come-hithered a forefinger at us and walked away, skinnying between two cruisers masked for painting. "Walk on over thisaway. Be careful not to rub up against any of the Maseratis."

We followed carefully, avoiding paint, stepping over various pneumatic tools and hoses, making our way to the rear of the cavernous building. An unmounted tire was propped up on a workbench. Rafael spun the tire toward us, slapped it with his palm.

"Tire was cut in the sidewall. The slit's about as wide as a hunting knife."

I leaned in to check the incision, thinking about how Harry drove. "Maybe we bumped off a curb or something," I ventured. "It was sharp and cut the tire."

Rafael turned to Harry and shook his head approvingly.

"Now that's funny," he said.

We returned to the department and gathered our call slips at the desk. I threw away two from Danbury. I found a flagged slip from Smithson in Missing Persons the same time Harry found his. I pulled my cellphone from my pocket, dialed Smithson's number.

"He's right upstairs," Harry said.

"You want to see him eating again?" I said.

Harry winced. I heard Smithson pick up. "It's Ryder. I heard you're looking for –"

"Listen, Ryder, I've been checking on some stuff here. The woman in the motel – you got the autopsy prelim didn't you?"

"The basics, Jim. And I was there."

"There any major physical identifications on her? You know, like maybe a –"

"There was a small port-wine stain on the back of her neck, about the size of a quarter."

"I think there's a problem. Y'all may want to stop by here pronto. Pray I'm wrong, Ryder. There's a reason I'm using those words."

* * *

80

"She's a nun?" I said, incredulous.

Smithson pushed back the artificially black strands of his wispy comb-over. "Sister Anne Mary, real name is, or was, Marie Gilbeaux. There's a convent up in Chilton County, like a farm community or something. They make and sell goat cheese and peach preserves and suchnot. She'd supposedly been traveling to the south 'bama and 'sippi area to check stores that sell the wares. Remember, I mentioned her when you and Nautilus stopped? We didn't pick up on it, naturally; who'd expect a body in a sleaze-bag motel would turn out to . . ."

Harry picked up the report, leaned against the wall, read. "Birthmark, approximately three centimeters in diameter, left rear neck just below the hairline . . ." He looked at me. I nodded. "Pretty conclusive."

It suddenly all fit. Farm work was hard, physical, outdoor labor, and would account for her rough and callused hands and sturdy, taut-muscled legs and arms.

Harry said, "We've got to let the convent folks know what's happened. I suppose we could call up there. But it's the kind of thing really needs a personal visit."

"We could call the Chilton cops, have them handle it."

"We could. That would be easiest, right?"

I thought of the body in the bed, the tiny candle-wick pupils, the *Why me?* mouth slack with agony. She'd died on our watch, and we owed her.

"I'll bring the car around," I said.

CHAPTER 9

Harry said, "How long had Marie Gilbeaux been with you, Sister?"

Sister Beatrice looked off into the distance. Her eyes glistened with tears.

"Thirty years, give or take," she said, wiping a cheek with the palm of her hand. "How quickly it passed."

Sister Beatrice was the head of Villa Madonna convent, and probably in her early seventies. Her eyes were green as the leaves of the oak above us, her skin weathered in a way that added a sense of agelessness. Her hair was short and silver, a bright cap. If I hadn't known she was a nun, the baggy, faded Levis and white cotton work shirt might have led me to believe she was a retired Texas cowgirl. When we'd arrived fifteen minutes ago and our faces told our story before we did, she'd said, "Let's go outside. I don't want sad moments trapped in the walls."

She'd led us through the large main building and out back to a porch beneath a slatwood awning. There was a flower garden past us, wildflowers, an untamed palette of whites and yellows and purples. Beyond, a large meadow swept to a grove of peach trees. In the distance two women repaired a fence, one steadying the post, the other nailing up wire. A herd of goats gamboled around them. I watched the goats for a moment; there were perhaps a dozen of all sizes. They seemed happy, I guess, as far as goats go.

"I don't know how such things work," Harry said as we let Sister Beatrice wind us through Marie Gilbeaux's years at the convent. "Did she join you from high school or college?"

Sister Beatrice sat in a rocking chair, Harry and I on a large wooden bench. Every few moments Sister Beatrice closed her eyes, as if blotting out the madness we'd visited upon this peaceful retreat.

"She was a foundling, Detective Nautilus."

"An unclaimed baby? Like left on your doorstep?"

"Found on our doorstep, yes. But she wasn't a baby; not chronologically. She was twenty-two the day I opened the door to her crying, desperate face. But Marie was as lost a little girl as you'd find in the slums of Rio or Calcutta. I asked her why she'd come to us. You know what she answered?"

Harry leaned forward. "What?"

"She said she followed the light. She was serious."

Harry nodded. "Hard to turn someone like that away."

"She started as a volunteer. We provided quarters in

exchange for work. She worked like a mule, nonstop. I'd say, 'Slow down, Marie, take a break. The work will be here tomorrow.' She'd push even harder, as if she had to keep in motion because she couldn't stand stillness. She later confessed constant work quelled her memories."

"Memories of what?"

Sister Beatrice turned uneasy eyes to the meadow. The two women moved to the next fencepost down the line; the goats followed.

"We talked over everything before she embarked on her studies. But any conversation we might have had is between us. Her life . . . was never meant to be public."

Behind the words, I sensed her need to talk. "I respect that, Sister. But it's possible something in her early life caused her death. Whatever turned her into that lost little girl so long ago."

A flash of anger lit Sister Beatrice's green eyes, hardened her voice. "She was abandoned at birth, Detective Ryder. Her father was a wealthy, depraved man who flaunted his lifestyle. Her mother was distant and indifferent. Marie was an accident, unwanted, and her parents whipped her with that fact until they drove her into the streets at age seventeen."

Harry sighed and looked at his shoes. Tales that started like this rarely ended well.

Sister Beatrice continued. "Marie was a confused, yet intelligent young woman, and first found the freedom an adventure. But castaways always seek a surrogate family. She found it in a slightly older group of students at an art academy. They became a —"

84

"Paris?" I interrupted, a cold blade tracing my spine. "This academy was in Paris, wasn't it?"

Surprise from Sister Beatrice. And suspicion. "How did you know that?"

"Would you know if one of those students was named Marsden Hexcamp?"

Sister Beatrice stood abruptly, leaving the rocker clicking on the floor. "What do you know about this?" Her voice was a whisper.

"Little more than the name. And some of the deeds. Like murder."

"Marie hurt no one, Detective. She followed the group from France and by that time Marsden Hexcamp's teeth were eating her soul. Some of Hexcamp's followers were murderers, I know that. Others were onlookers. Hexcamp, a bloom of evil, enjoyed various . . . erotic entertainments. That was what Marie was used for, to view and participate in these activities, not the darkest aspects of this man's evil, the killings."

"She told you that?" I asked.

"She gave herself to God. After that there were no secrets to hold. She looked from the eye of evil to the eye of God. It allowed her to cast off all shame. She spoke freely to me, because she was free."

I leaned forward. "This will sound strange, but it's important: had she ever been a prostitute?"

Sister Beatrice regarded me curiously. "Not in the classic sense. Her father paid her a large allowance to stay away from home. It was access to money that initially made her attractive to the student group. She didn't sell herself to strangers for money. But she referred to having been 'a whore for Hexcamp'. In that manner, I think, she felt herself a prostitute."

"How were her last few days here?"

"Up before the sun and working like she had for three decades. It was her love, gardening, putting up the preserves, feeding the baby goats. As always, she was excited about her trip, talking with our retailers, meeting new people. And then she was gone with no word back after two days."

Harry said, "May we see her room, Sister?"

"Of course."

We followed Sister Beatrice through the building, past the wide doors of a quiet chapel with hardwood pews semi-circling a large crucifix. Sun poured through a stained-glass window, its rays tinted scarlet by the glass. Christ was looking down, eyes averted, rigid with his own passion. I found myself on tiptoe until we were well distant, walking a long hall with doors to either side.

"This is, was, her room."

It was serene inside, windowed, dust motes crossing a yellow band of sunlight. There was a bed, a large bookcase, a chest of drawers, a desk and chair. A small woven rug centered the floor. Above the desk was a crucifix, a small version of the one in the chapel. I admired the detail, the crown the size of a wedding band, each bright thorn sharp as a pin.

Harry said, "Have you found anything to explain her disappearance?"

"I looked across her desk, found nothing. The county police were in a few days ago, but that was before she was . . . found . . ."

Sister Beatrice broke down. Harry steered her to the chair, helped her sit. I studied the bookshelves. Tomes of dogma and biographies of saints nestled against books on gardening and animal husbandry. There were several mystery paperbacks. Sister Marie's closet revealed work clothes, a few dresses and suit-pant combos, and two habits. I found nothing untoward in her chest of drawers, Harry managing to stand between Sister Beatrice and me as I pawed through Sister Marie's unmentionables, sturdy and unadorned. I checked beneath the bed, between mattress and boxsprings, nothing.

I looked at her desk. A small stack of envelopes, junk. And a small brown envelope with only the address. The lettering was in ink, block-lettered.

"Is that her mail, Sister Beatrice?"

"From the past couple of days."

"Do you mind if I . . ."

"No, please, do what you think best."

I pulled latex gloves from my jacket pocket and plucked the brown envelope from the desk. It was about a quarter-inch thick, postmarked in Mobile on Wednesday, the day after the room at the Cozy Cabins had been rented. I opened it, shook out the contents.

Another envelope. Brown. Like Lydia Barstow had described arriving for Rubin Coyle.

Harry said, "Why do I think I know what's coming?"

I opened the second envelope, shaking into my palm two

pieces of cardboard, lightly taped together. I separated the sandwiched cardboards, flapped them open.

A swatch of bright color fell into my hand. Paint layered over torn canvas scarcely larger than a postcard. Reds and whites and blues were overcoated with glazes that gave the swatch striking depth and reality. It was beautiful, striking. But looking closer, I saw a white slash that could have been a shard of broken bone, pulpy marrow dripping from within. What looked like gilded worms squirmed over the surface. Sister Beatrice walked to the swatch as if drawn by a magnet.

"It's beautiful," she said, transfixed. "And yet . . ."

Harry looked at his watch. "We're three hours out of Mobile," he said. "Why don't you give this Willow a call, tell him company's on the way."

CHAPTER 10

"A week after Hexcamp was jailed I took up residence at the farm where he and his band of mutants lived." Willow paused to sip from his bottle of beer. "A half-dozen evidence techs had found nothing. But I had been tracking the monster for months. Once I saw him in the flesh, sat in the shadow of his monumental ego, I knew he'd have something. I was thinking souvenirs of the killings. Photos. Some type of memento. He'd need them."

I drifted in the glider; Willow sat across from me on a wicker chair. Harry leaned against a porch support. Cumulus scudded across the Bay, bronzed by fading sun. A western breeze made the air tolerable.

"I ate there. Kept my clothes in his closet and my food in his refrigerator. One morning I was in the barn, converted to what he called his studio, sitting at the table where he worked. Nature called, and there being no facilities in the barn and the house a couple hundred feet away, I headed to the outhouse. It hit me that a warped man wanting to hide something might find a good place for it beneath a pile of shit. I got a flashlight and found a strand of clear, high-test monofilament running down the chute of the old two-holer."

"How was the fishing?" I asked.

"Caught me a waterproof case. Inside were rolled canvases I figured destined for the collection, works in progress."

"What did they look like?" I realized I was whispering.

"A brilliantly rendered skull, a rib cage with flesh rotting from it. Several pages of philosophical musings – dark, bleak stuff, created while under the spell of tracking and taking his victims. A poem about the beauty of the final moment, beautifully worded ugliness."

Harry whispered, "Jesus."

"Jesus was never anywhere near Marsden Hexcamp. He burrowed out of hell."

Harry said, "If you'd kept these works you'd be showing them. Or copies at least."

He shook his head. "I took them to the Mobile cops for safekeeping and they disappeared two days later. Presto, gone. Luckily, they weren't needed for the trial; he'd left a wide red path. Not long later Hexcamp was shot dead in the courtroom. There should have been much more sensation following the events, but if you know history, you know –"

I nodded. "Hexcamp was sentenced in the morning, Governor George Wallace was shot that afternoon."

Willow nodded. "The shooting was a wave crashing over everything. Marsden Hexcamp was washed from public attention."

"And you?"

"I went undercover to investigate the murder of a union leader. Years passed. But I never got those pieces out of my mind. Hexcamp's last words were spoken to me, Detective Nautilus. He said, 'Follow the art, Jacob.' Then the little son of a bitch rolled over and died."

Harry said, "So that's what you've been doing for over thirty years – following the art?"

Willow caught the allusion to obsession. His eyes tightened, but his voice stayed even. "What I've been doing for the past thirty years is pretty much same as everyone else, Detective: working, shopping, paying taxes, fishing when I get a chance – the sane and standard stuff. But now and then a case brought me into contact with people on the fringe, sado-maso-scato-whatevers. You know them – the people without souls."

I could only nod my head. When you know these types, no words are necessary. Or sufficient.

Willow said, "Some of them talked about the collection, of having seen it. Stuff like that got me wondering about Hexcamp for a while, then another case'd be added to my workload and he'd go to sleep in the back of my head again."

Willow took a deep breath. "The piece of art, whatever, you found at the convent – you couldn't bring it along?"

I shook my head. "Left it with the Chilton County cops,

their jurisdiction. They'll send it to the AFB in Birmingham, we'll find out anything as soon as they do."

Harry said, "What about this woman that shot him, then ate the gun herself?"

"The Crying Woman; name was Cheyenne Widmer. From what we pieced together, she was Hexcamp's main lover – though they all bounced between one another like rabbits, one big happy family: sex and love and death."

"Sounds like the Manson clan," Harry said.

Willow nodded. "Hexcamp enlisted others in his crimes, made them proud to serve him. But Manson was a pox-brain druggie, Hexcamp a genius – Van Gogh with a homicidal heart."

Harry frowned. "Assume – *assume* – for a moment this big chunk of whatever is out there. Why would someone kill for it?"

Willow snorted. "Status. Telling others you have it; being admired for it. The only difference is, with serial-killer memorabilia, you're important in a smaller crowd. But these people make up for size in devotion. Worship even. Some are run-of-the-mill spookies, sure. People stunted in adolescence. Others are as serious as people who collect Ming vases. And some are rich, *big* rich. Owning the Hexcamp collection would, for these people, be about the same as owning the *Mona Lisa*."

Harry said, "Let's break this down, start at the beginning, see if we can get a sense of where this crap got to."

"Probably the best place to start is with the stuff you found in the outhouse," I said to Willow. "Where it might have gone."

Harry thought a moment. "If it disappeared from the property room, there probably weren't a lot of folks who could have made that happen. Know anyone who might . . ."

Willow narrowed his eyes. "I've suspected someone all along."

Harry said, "Someone tied to Hexcamp?"

"Someone tied to the need to make a buck." Willow looked at me. "Remember how I told you money pulls stuff out of property rooms . . . if the right person's in charge of the room?"

"It's been thirty-something years," I said. "This person still around?"

"Ambrose Poll. Haven't seen his name in the obituaries," Willow said. "Not that I ain't been hoping."

CHAPTER 11

I awakened several times in a toss-turn night, fought back to sleep until seven, then jogged the beach. Though it was Saturday, a day off rotation, Harry and I had decided to brace Ambrose Poll this afternoon. We'd also elected to take Willow along.

I ran an almost-deserted beach, most vacationers waiting until the sun is high to wander from their rentals. I'd always found it strange, since the beach was cooler and more amenable in the early hours. I passed a few die-hard surf anglers, long rods tucked into sand spikes, plus the occasional beachwalkers, walking slow and looking for shells. The Alabama coastline is known for sugar-white sand, not shells. Specimens cast aside on Sanibel Island are keepers here, just being whole is noteworthy. Entire families will *oooh* and *aaah* at an unbroken sand dollar the size of a quarter.

I came inside and ate a couple of sausage biscuits at the counter, then swept the sand out the door, made a grocery run, did two loads of laundry, and greased the squeak from the bathroom door. I was folding towels and counting the hours until I met Harry and Willow for the trek to Ambrose Poll's place. Hearing a crunch of shells, I glanced through the curtain and saw a silver Audi pulling into my drive. I heard the door open, but couldn't see who exited. Footsteps climbed the stairs.

I opened the door to DeeDee Danbury, knuckles poised in mid-knock. I almost didn't recognize her. She wore a sleeveless blue denim work shirt tucked into multi-pocketed khaki shorts with a webbed belt. Her hair was bundled in a neat ponytail and tipped-back sunglasses rode the crown of her head. A pair of compact field glasses hung around her neck.

"It's OK," I said, "I'll let you closer than that."

A flash of puzzlement, then she looked down. "Oh, the binocs. I wear them so much I forget they're on. Some girls probably say that about diamonds, but what the hell."

I waved her to enter and she looked around at my decor of posters and driftwood. The furniture came in a box from Sweden and had looked better in the catalog, but it was comfortable.

"Helluva place, pogobo," she said. "You get a commission on the big solves, or what?"

"It's an inheritance, basically," I said. "What brings you here, Ms Danbury?"

She seemed not to have heard, wandered to the deck doors and looked out. Without the TV make-up, designer clothes, and camera-bred intensity, she looked relatively human. Danbury lifted the binoculars to her eyes and scanned the beach.

"If I had a view like this," she said, "I'd never make it to work."

"The binoculars part of journalism? Or window peeping?"

The glasses dropped to her chest. "Birdwatching. It's how I relax."

It didn't seem appropriate; I'd have figured her for collecting poisonous plant species. She said, "I was out this morning on the inland side, then thought I'd come over here, see what's in the air."

My hand swept toward the beach. "Pelicans, gulls, sand-pipers, herons, now and then a frigate bird . . ."

"I mean like what's up between us. After that little tussle at the morgue the other day."

"I explained myself to the chief. I don't have to explain anything to you. Now, if you'll excuse me . . ."

"I didn't tattle to management, Ryder. All part of a day's work is what I figure. Borg can be an asshole sometimes. No, all of the time. If it means anything, I told management there was another side to the story."

"I don't need your help, Ms Danbury."

She walked toward the living room. "I found it curious the sound on Borg's camera cut out when he might have been talking, but was recording when you were explaining the various proctological possibilities of a videocam."

"Is that what I did?"

"It was wonderfully colorful."

"What really brings you here, Ms Danbury?"

She nodded at the couch. "Mind if I sit?" Without waiting for my response, she sat, settled in comfortably. "I know how you work, you and Nautilus. I've studied it."

"How about blessing me with a synopsis, Ms Danbury?"

She leaned back and crossed her legs. The economical knees counterbalanced the extravagant calves. "You guys have selective gravity or something. The strange cases pop up, look around until they see you, then run over and jump in your laps. Half the time you don't seem to know what you're doing, then *Bang-Hallelujah*! The case is cleared, your faces are in the paper, and everyone's running up to bask in your sunshine."

"Maybe it's just luck."

"Luck is dice coming up hot when you need it. They could just as easily sit cold. It's statistics. Statistically, you and Nautilus are full-time hotties when it comes to crazies. Magnets for freaks."

"I disagree. Either way, I'm not sure how it affects you."

"I think there's a story cooking here. Give me a peek in the kitchen. It'll be a trade. I'll tell you how I know what little I know, keep filling you in as I learn more. I'm going to learn more; you know I will. It's what I do."

"It's not my place to keep you informed of anything, Ms Danbury."

She raised an eyebrow. "I said I researched you and Nautilus? I concentrated on you. Nothing you've done in the department has been typical. You cut your own path, usually through the backcountry. I remember the Adrian case, how they shut the door in your face, so you kicked in the wall. Don't go by-the-book on me now, Ryder. Give me a taste of what's happening. I'll keep you up on what comes my way. What do you say to that?"

"No comment."

She started to speak, then shook her head slowly. She stood and walked to the door, pulled it open. She stepped toward the stoop, but stopped and turned. Danbury lifted the binoculars, reversing them to study me through the front lenses rather than the eyepieces.

"Isn't that interesting," she said. "I could have sworn you were a lot bigger."

CHAPTER 12

I hadn't noted DeeDee Danbury's perfume when she was in the house; only after she'd left did it appear. There was delicacy to it, floral, with a base note of spice, something dry and exotic, like clove or cardamom. I walked slowly through the living room, sniffing, detecting where it seemed strongest, wondering how long it would take to dissipate.

I suddenly felt foolish and looked out at the beach. It had grown crowded during my conversation with Danbury. The Blovines were out as well, she sunning with her top strap undone and her pumpkin boobs squishing out the sides, him trying to fish. He'd backlashed the casting reel, and was tugging at the snarled line. Picking out backlashes takes patience, and he finally gave up and tossed the rig in the sand.

The clock rang noon and I headed off to meet Mr Ambrose

Poll. Harry and Willow were at a diner in mid Mobile and we drove the last few blocks in Harry's department car. Poll lived on a tree-lined street of bungalows built in the forties, tended flowerbeds, safe, boxy cars in the drives. No children playing, no sports cars in sight. A man on the porch eyeballed us over a paper he was pretending to read. Next door, an elderly woman with silver hair hosed water over dogwoods.

Willow nodded at the man with the paper. "That's Poll."

"Let's face him and brace him," Harry said.

"Hey there, Poll. Ambrose Poll," Willow called when we'd walked halfway up the drive.

Poll squinted. "Willow?"

"It's me, Ambrose. A ghost from the past. Boo."

Poll frowned as he studied us. He had a ruddy, vein-spidered face and a prognathous jaw; he thrust the jaw at Willow like a defense. But his eyes flickered nervously.

"What's going on here?"

Willow strode the steps to the porch as if it were his own. "These are detectives Ryder and Nautilus, Ambrose. They're looking into the Hexcamp case. They'd like to talk to you about it."

"Hex who? What the hell you talking about?"

"Stow the amnesia, Poll. You remember the case, no one could forget it. What I especially can't forget is how everything I found in his house turned to vapor two days later."

"I don't know nothing about pages from Hexcamp."

"I gave them to you. They disappeared."

Ambrose Poll shrugged and spat off the front of the porch. "That was a long time ago."

Harry spoke up. "Ancient history, Mr Poll. So it shouldn't matter if you fill in any blanks we might have."

Poll scooted the chair forty-five degrees away from us and stared into the street. The woman watering her lawn moved closer to the porch, her ear cocked toward us as she tried to eavesdrop.

Harry said, "You were the property-room clerk for a long time, Mr Poll."

"I was good at what I did. You do good in a job, you keep it."

"Back then property room was a job for guys too tired and fat for the street, or on the outs politically. You started in the job before you were thirty, and worked there until you retired. Must be a record."

"What I did was my business, and you can take yours elsewhere."

Harry peeled off his burgundy jacket, draped it over his arm, and sat on the porch railing, a relaxed man. He took his time looking up and down the street.

"Pretty little neighborhood here, Mr Poll, neat and sweet. Lots of retirees, I'll bet. Like that lady watering her lawn. Or that fellow across the way looking through the curtain."

"It's a nice place to live. Be even better when you leave."

"I'll bet they love to hear your cop stories. Nailing the bank robbers, breaking the big cases. Ambrose Poll, the scourge of criminals everywhere. How many times did you almost buy it in the line of duty, Poll?"

"I got no idea what you're blabbering about. I think you're crazy's what I think."

"Do you tell people you were the original blue knight? Or a detective to rival Sherlock Holmes? Or do you tell them the truth: that you spent twenty-something years as a clerk?"

Poll stiffened. "I don't lie to no one."

I sauntered over and smiled at the woman, who had now turned off her hose and was fiddling with a myrtle five feet from the porch.

"Morning, ma'am, how're you?"

She lit up at the notice. "Just fine, officer. You're a policeman, aren't you? I can always tell." She pointed to our ride. "You folks drive the drabbest cars. The Navy drives gray ships and police drive drab cars." She peered between the posts on the porch. "Morning, Ambrose. I watered your tomatoes."

Poll looked stricken and forced a smile. "Thank you, Myrna."

She arched a penciled eyebrow at me. "Is he helping you on a case? I know he still does that. Detective Poll probably has a lot to teach you younger fellows."

"I guess, ma'am," I said, nodding. "Trouble is, he's just so doggoned humble, we can barely pry a story out of him."

"Well you just ask him about the time he rounded up that cat burglar, chased him clear across a rooftop like in that movie with Cary Grant and Grace Kelly."

I produced a quizzical face. "Cat burglar? But all those years I thought Mr Poll worked in the –"

"Hey there," Poll barked. "No need to go into all that." He sighed and looked down. "Come on inside. I'll tell you a story or two."

Poll slumped into the house, Willow and I in his wake. Harry brought up the rear. He paused at the door, then leaned out to look at the woman. "Mr Poll's an amazing resource, ma'am. I don't know what we'd do without him."

She beamed.

Poll's house smelled like coffee and fried ham. We sat around his dining-room table, a pile of scissored-out coupons centering the table. Poll said, "I didn't give a shit for all that street stuff. Car air conditionin' wasn't like now and half the time you'd spend all day in a rolling sweathouse. One day I allowed to the old dep'ty chief I'd do near anything to be done with it."

Harry said, "You bought the job."

Poll's mason-block jaw jutted defiance at Harry. "I kicked back twenty per cent every payday. I didn't care, it was a good job, and needing doing."

"Twenty per cent is a big bite, Mr Poll."

"I'm an economical man, I made do."

"How much you make on the retail side?"

Poll started to protest but Harry held up his hand to cut him off. "Let's turn off the fiction machine, Mr Poll. Nothing bad's gonna happen if you tell the truth."

Poll slumped in the chair, studied his hands. "Hell, there were guns and stuff in there went back fifty years. Closed cases. Nobody'd ever miss a little something gone now and then. I just moved enough to make back the twenty per cent."

Willow leaned in, his eyes hot but his voice cool. "Hexcamp's possessions, Poll. What about them?"

Poll squeezed his hands together, stared at them. "That was

something different. I got a call that night. Said if the stuff you brought in got misplaced there'd be five hundred bucks in it. You know what five hundred bucks was then?"

"Over two grand now," Willow said. "At least you weren't a cheap crook."

"Fuck you," Poll said, but his venom had been replaced by resignation. I saw Harry eyeball Willow, *Ease up*.

"Where'd the stuff go?" Harry asked gently.

"I was told to take the package out back one night. Every piece, nothing held back. A car come along and we traded packages."

"What'd the guy making the pickup look like?"

Poll pressed his hands into his eye sockets as if it helped light his memories. "Wasn't a man," he said, so softly we had to lean closer. "It was a woman, beautiful. She looked like an angel."

We left Poll staring at his hands. "The beautiful woman?" I asked Willow as we walked to our cars. "One of Hexcamp's followers?"

"Just because their heads were scrambled didn't make the women ugly. Some of the prettiest women you ever saw would have gone a month without food just to wash Hexcamp's feet."

"What happened to them?" Harry asked.

"Most just drifted away; disappeared. A couple of the girls eventually went to prison on lesser raps. As you read, the Crying Woman shot herself after she put a bullet through Hexcamp's belly. There were a couple of men as well, I heard, but not in for the long haul. There is one woman from the day who you can talk to."

"Name?"

"Carla Hutchins. Lives in the country outside Chunchula. Be in her early fifties now."

"You've not spoken with her?"

"I approached her twice. She wouldn't talk and no way I could make her. I got the impression she didn't want to relive those days."

"She do time?" Harry asked.

"No evidence of direct involvement in the killings, a follower type. She was one of the sanest of Hexcamp's groupies. Probably not saying a lot."

CHAPTER 13

Carla Hutchins lived out where the phone poles held two fraying wires. As Harry drove, I reclined in back staring at the ceiling and thinking, loosely speaking. Clouds piled up above us, darkened, broke with fast hard rain, and the storm blew by like an afterthought. A quarter mile ahead a copse broke the fielded landscape to reveal a small gray house tucked in the trees. Coming closer, we made out a woman hanging laundry in the side yard.

"That should be Hutchins," I said, noting the number on the mailbox. Harry edged the car into the dirt drive. Hutchins glanced at us with little interest. I figured she probably spent a fair amount of time directing people back to the main road. She plucked a pair of jeans from a basket at her feet and shook them out, *whapwhapwhap*, counterpoint to the hiss and burr of insects in the fields.

"Excuse me, Ms Hutchins?"

She turned, startled at hearing her name. She wore a simple blue dress and a white pocketed apron. Her feet were bare in the grass. She was slender to the point of skinny, her angular face long, framed by straight hair falling to her shoulders, blonde hair going gray, shiny with a recent cleaning. She wore no make-up or jewelry and could have blended into any Depression-era farm community in Oklahoma.

"Yes?"

"I'm Carson Ryder, a detective with the Mobile Police. This is Detective Harry Nautilus. I'd like to ask you some questions about . . ." I didn't know how to complete the sentence.

Harry jumped in. "About a long time ago, Miz Hutchins. When life wasn't so peaceful."

Hutchins turned back to hanging laundry. The pins in her apron pocket rattled when she moved. There was just enough breeze to waft the clothes and I smelled whatever she'd washed them in, something with lemon.

"Please go," she said. "I'm clean now."

Harry said, "I'm sorry, Miz Hutchins. I don't understand."

"I'm clean. I used to be dirty, but I'm clean. Talking about back then makes me dirty again. Please leave."

Harry reached up his finger and touched a line as if seeing if it were really there. "Lord, it's hot as a sauna today," he said, wiping his brow with the back of his hand. "Rain feels so nice when it's falling and ten minutes later it's gone straight to steam. Are you thirsty for something cold, Miz Hutchins, Carla? Can I call you Carla?"

"I don't know. I mean, yes, I'm thirsty. But there's nothing I can offer you but tap wat–"

Harry flicked his head down the road. "Go down to that store we passed, Carson. Get us some cold drinks. I'll take a diet RC, Co-cola they don't have it. You, Carla?"

"You really don't have to . . . an orange soda? Is that all right?"

When I returned a few minutes later Harry had clothes-pins in his mouth and was hanging clothes alongside Ms Hutchins. I passed out bottles, opened a bag of boiled peanuts, and sat atop the picnic table, chomping like a draft animal and listening as Ms Hutchins spoke in a dusty drawl surpris-ingly refined in diction and vocabulary.

"I don't know where his work went, Detective Nautilus," she said, clipping a sleeve of a pink blouse to the line. "I don't know much about it. Maybe that seems strange, after living there for over a year, but only a very few saw it all, the totality. Calypso did, certainly. Terpsichore perhaps. Persephone."

"Strange names," Harry said.

"We were given names from art or mythology. M-Marsden's idea."

Harry clipped the other sleeve to the line. "What was your name?"

Hutchins paused. I watched her shape a silent word with her mouth, then add breath to it. "M-Maja, after the Goya painting. It feels strange to say it; I haven't said it in years. Sometimes I hear it in dreams. I've learned to force myself awake."

108

"Why didn't he let you see the art?"

"I'm not sure it was his idea to be so secretive. I'm sure it was Calypso's idea. We saw pieces. Had special viewings. We'd study it, praise him, the beautiful work. There was always a viewing and reading before an . . . affirmation."

"Affirmation was when someone would die?"

"When someone was selected."

Harry said, "How did this happen, how was it determined?"

"It was simply announced. The planning started, then, several weeks later, the event. Calypso was in charge."

"Was the group in on the event?"

"Everyone had roles. I was never chosen for a major role. I was a lookout, just one time, in a phone booth, supposed to call if anyone came along. I could have called . . . someone. Told what was about to happen." Her hand started shaking and she dropped a pin. Harry retrieved it from the grass.

"Easy, Carla," he said. "It's all in the past, dead and gone. There's nothing in front of you but real and honest life. You're safe."

She turned to Harry. A ragged sob tore from her throat and she stumbled toward him, fell into his arms. She cried almost without sound. They stood like that for a full minute, until she slowly pushed away, palming tears from her cheeks.

"I'm sorry, Detective Nautilus. I'm . . . all right now. I guess I need to hear that more often, that the past is dead."

Harry produced one of his cards, took her hand, pressed his card into her palm. "Take it, Carla. Keep it somewhere close. You ever need to talk, call me. Day or night, twilight or dawn."

She closed her hand around the card. "You never sleep, is that it?"

He winked. "It's overrated."

We turned as a green Subaru wagon passed by, a man at the wheel, a woman in the passenger seat. The driver wore a Stetson, the woman a long-billed ballcap. They were turned away, as if focused on something in the opposite field, fallow, filled with dry vines. When the car was only dust in the air, Hutchins walked slowly to the basket on the table and refilled her apron pocket with clothespins.

Harry said, "Who was the woman crying in the courthouse? The one who killed him."

"Calypso," Hutchins said. Her voice was stronger, as if she'd absorbed some of Harry's strength.

"She must have been either very high or very low on the totem pole, very dispensable or very honored."

Hutchins glanced toward the sun for a moment, turned away. "She was iron, Detective. In mind, spirit, body. His total protector. Cross Calypso and she'd slap your eyes half out of your head, or shred your heart with words. It was her idea, the courtroom scene. He knew he'd be sentenced to die and didn't want death at the hands of the government. His original plan was to be smuggled poison, to take it in the courtroom. He'd make his speech and die magnificently, artistically."

"But Calypso concocted plan B?"

"She'd dress in mourning clothes, wear the make-up of an older woman – she was in her early twenties, though I swear that woman was born a hundred years old, she knew so much.

With the dark veil she'd be hidden. A woman shows up in a black dress and veil at a murder trial crying her eyes out – one of many grieving family members, extended family, friends of deceased – what guard's going to search her? And she was an incredible actress as well."

"Sounds like she knew people, how they think."

"She knew *systems*. She saw us, his followers, as a system for his self-preservation. She saw the courthouse as a system that gave a wide berth to grief."

"But braving detection on a daily basis? I see what you mean about iron."

"It excited her. There were just a few of us by that time. The cops were all over the farm, and we'd moved to a rented house not far from the courthouse. She'd return and need sex. Again and again. Maybe she figured, since she was going to die, she'd better get in a lifetime's worth."

"A hungry woman."

"You could smell the hunger on her. Hunger for every-thing, especially . . . him. For caring for him, keeping him working. Passing us out to him in public, but keeping his totality to herself in private. They spent most of the days together in the studio, a converted barn. The rest of us stayed in the farmhouse. They had their own little world out there. Now and then someone from the elite would take food or drink out to them. Calypso created wild jealousies among the rest of us. I think that was part of the purpose: channeling our anger against her, increasing our reverence toward him."

"She truly loved him, obviously, to die for him."

"We all would have, sad little girls, needy little girls, willing to do anything for *him*, to die for him, convinced it would keep us together for eternity. He never challenged the idea, of course."

Harry shook his head. "Today they might be suicide bombers. I can't conceive of the kind of power Hexcamp held."

Hutchins shook her head. "I would have burned myself at the stake for a promised kiss from Marsd— . . . him. Does that tell you anything?"

Hutchins's back was to me. I looked at Harry and mouthed *Willow*.

He nodded with his eyes. "Did Hexcamp ever mention a cop by the name of Willow?"

"He was the one who figured it out, put the pieces together. Too late for so many, of course. M-Marsden hated Jacob Willow, which is to say he respected him. Anything worthy of an emotion as potent as hate also demanded respect." She paused. "Jacob Willow came here a year ago. And a few years before that. I stayed inside. He stood out here a long time."

Harry said, "Tell me about the art."

"He kept his work in the studio, the barn, which was always locked. Locks the size of apples. When he was taken to create – that's how he said it, 'taken' – he was like a man in a trance. Calypso was always with him because he had to be fed. Only Calypso or those few could take him food and supplies. Wash his . . . his soiled clothes. He'd get carried away and mess himself. When he finally finished working, he was exhausted for days."

"All that work but he never sold pieces?"

"It was to be his gift to the world; his 'legacy', he some-times called it. Not the world of the ordinaries, but the world of us as we thought ourselves – those knowing how to inter-pret it, to use it. He said if you put words and pictures together perfectly, the effect was greater than any individual pieces. Something he'd said he started to discover while at the Institut des Beaux-Arts . . ."

Harry said, "The what?"

"A famous art academy in Paris. He won a full scholarship there; he was proud of that, never stopped talking about it. Sometimes he spoke in French."

"Anyone else speak the lingo?"

"One other girl, Persephone. I gathered they met in Paris, while he was at art school."

"Was there anything special about her?"

Hutchins shook her head. "Calypso wouldn't allow us to be special or distinctive. Persephone, I recollect, was one of the ones permitted – can you believe it, *permitted* – to enter the barn and haul out his shit. We all thought she was special, y'know." Hutchins shook her head slowly, laughed without humor.

"There were levels? Like a caste system?"

She thought a moment. "Not a whole system. There were two or three allowed into the studio to bring food, remove his shit can, clean the place. Persephone was among the elite, as far as it went. Maybe because she'd come over from Paris. But that's all I really know of her. We never spoke of our pasts, or our futures, only of . . . him."

Apparently that's all there was on Persephone, who could

113

only have been Marie Gilbeaux. Harry said, "You were telling me his feelings about the works he created."

"They would shift the earth on its foundation, Detective Nautilus. His words. The art would make him famous forever."

Harry said, "You haven't seen any of these pieces of art recently have you, Carla? Not in the mail or anything?"

She was blindsided by the question, eyes wide in sudden fright.

"My God, no. Why?"

Harry waved it away. "Nothing, just thinking out loud. But these earth-shifting works, Carla. This collection of pages and paintings and whatnot. You have no idea where it went after his death?"

Hutchins's hands balled into fists. Her eyes lit with distant fire. She turned to Harry, her voice a ragged whisper.

"I hope it drilled itself into the ground and went straight back to hell."

On that note, we headed south to compare notes with Jacob Willow.

CHAPTER 14

It was dark when we got to Willow's. There was a breeze and the three of us walked to the edge of his dock and looked into the sweep of Mobile Bay. The western shore was a chain of glittering light. Waves lapped the pilings and Willow's boat thumped against the bumpers.

"Hutchins saw the damned thing," I told Willow. "Or what went into it, like a collection of individual pages. Some art, some text, some a combination."

"Like the pages I found," Willow said. "What Poll slipped out the back door."

I said, "Hutchins reiterated the nightmare lifestyle of sex, servitude, and predation. Hexcamp had an aide-de-camp, or perhaps gatekeeper from hell. Her name was –"

"Cheyenne Widmer. Aka Calypso, aka the Crying Woman,"

Willow interrupted. "Never got much background on Widmer, though she ended up dead on the courthouse floor after eating a .44 hollow-point. Same path as the others, I'd think. She followed him over from France."

"Same path?" Harry said.

"Runaways, girls mainly, drifters from busted-up families, rejects from the drug culture. No pasts. There were a few males, but they drifted on, probably too hard to compete with Marsden."

"Hutchins said interactions between Hexcamp and the others went through Calypso. Except you spoke of how cool and calm Hexcamp was. Hutchins has a slightly different picture. The Hexcamp she describes sometimes retreated to his 'studio' and arted his heart out for a couple of weeks. Barely ate, crapped himself, basically fell apart."

Harry sighed. "Thirty years later, the stuff this guy painted in the middle of a shit fit sells for thousands of dollars."

Willow said, "That's individual pieces, Detective Nautilus. The collection itself, offered as a single purchase, would be worth a lot more."

"Guess," Harry said.

"A half-million dollars. At least."

A ship's horn sounded and we turned to watch a bulk carrier out in the ship channel, a shadow against black, its lights no more than fireflies. We watched it push south toward the mouth of the Bay, using the moment to gather our thoughts.

I turned to Willow. "Poll gave us nothing but history. Is there a way to connect with these people you were talking about? People who might have hard information on this collection . . . where it is today."

"Major collectors of serial-killer memorabilia," Willow said. "A tight band; you need to know someone to know someone."

"They're all over the country, right?" Harry said.

"There are a couple of collectors in the area, and one of the country's biggest dealers lives in Spanish Fort, a squid named Giles Walcott."

"You know this Walcott personally?" Harry asked.

Willow kicked at a piling. "Can't get near him."

I said, "Cops looked into him before?"

"There's nothing illegal about obtaining objects associated with killers. Walcott keeps tax records, all the aboveboard stuff. Doesn't consort with active killers. He brokers pieces from people dead or in prison, or pieces with pasts so clouded he can't be nailed for receiving stolen goods."

"How would I manage an audience with this Walcott geek? As, say, a new collector on the scene."

"Impossible. It takes years to make the connections, get known."

"At the intersection of greed and money," I said, "anything's possible. How could I force the issue?"

Willow stared at the sky and scratched his chin. "You'd need a major piece, a signature piece, to tempt Walcott past his caution."

"Signature piece?"

"Something personal to the killer. Directly involved in the crime, physically or psychically. You've heard of Willy Palemountain?"

I nodded. Palemountain was a predator who wandered between southwestern Indian reservations in the forties. Before dispatching his victims with a hatchet, he dressed in buckskins and a feathered headdress and loaded his head with peyote. There'd been a movie based on his life.

Willow said, "Five years back a headdress of Palemountain's went for over a hundred grand. That's an example of a signature piece."

"Feathers from a killer's head?" Harry said. "People want that in their homes?"

"The Nazis murdered millions of human beings, Detective Nautilus, turned Europe into a bloodbath. People laughingly trade Nazi memorabilia at swap meets."

I walked to the end of the dock, stared into the shimmering black water.

"I might come up with something."

"Carson," Harry cautioned, "we can make something up. A fake."

Willow shook his head. "Tough to do. You'd have to construct a plausible chain of how the item got to you. Anyone can spatter a shirt with pig blood and claim it was Jeffrey Dahmer's favorite dinner-party shirt. Fakes are everywhere. That was Poll's ace in the hole; stuff he sold came with evidence tags attached, authenticity verified by the MPD. Collectors demand verification by an authority. Blow it, and Walcott's lost to you."

"Don't go there, Carson," Harry said.

I said, "Walcott wants a major piece, I'll find something to make his heart go pitty-pat. I guarantee it."

"Where would you find something like that?" Willow asked.

Harry whispered, "Carson, *no*."

"I've got connections," I said.

The old cop was smart enough to stop asking questions. Harry turned away, shaking his head and watching the carrier move from Mobile Bay into the horizonless black of the Gulf beyond.

I walked in my door at nine-thirty. A single message waited on my machine. I pressed the button. Two bars of Ellington played in the background before I heard Harry's voice.

"Don't go down this road, bro."

The machine clicked off.

I went outside, but the breeze had died. I waved mosquitos from my face and ears and looked down the beach, the high moon making the sand appear to glow. To the east, the Blovines had at least two televisions cranked to chain-saw volume. I took a final swipe at the insects and retreated inside to the phone. Jeremy kept his hidden away in a manner time-honored among prisoners. I dialed the number and was directed to voicemail.

"Jeremy, call me back," was all I said. I sat and waited for seventeen minutes.

"Carson," my brother trilled, "I knew it was you. Either that or my butt left a wake-up call."

I pictured him in his room at the institution, almost a dorm room – bed, desk, chair, chest of drawers, the Mylar mirror that skewed reflections, like watching yourself in mercury. But there was no campus outside, only guards and succeeding rings of cyclone fencing topped with razor wire.

"You've got to find a more comfortable hiding place, Jeremy."

"I did. I was just teasing."

"Good," I said.

He cackled wickedly. "A friend hides it for me. What do you need, Carson?"

"I was calling because of your call to me."

"THAT WAS TWO DAYS AGO," he screamed. "I TOLD YOU TO CALL BACK AND YOU DIDN'T." He did a sad little boy's voice. "Why din'cha call me back, bruvver? Don't you luuuv me?" His voice shifted back to reasonable, pleasant. "Hi Jeremy, how are you doing? Are the creamed peas to your liking? Are the toilet seats sanitary? Can I send you a case of MoonPies? WHAT MAKES YOU TOO BUSY TO CALL YOUR ONLY BROTHER?"

My brother alternately screamed, sang, whispered, spoke in hauntingly perfect impressions of other voices, or talked rationally. With Jeremy you never knew which was coming, or when. I decided to get to the point, hoping my odd request would evoke one of his more rational characterizations.

"It's a case I've been assigned, Jeremy."

"DETAILS, CARSON. Gimme, gimmee, gimmeeeee . . ."

"It's not . . . your kind of case, Jeremy. But I need something special. You won't have it. But maybe you can get it."

"Something special? Oh suh, you do set mah bones all a-tingle. WHAT IS IT, CARSON?"

"An item used in an . . . event."

120

"An event?" he mused. "You mean like the Fourth of July? You want me to get you a pack of sparklers?"

"An event like the ones that put you there."

"OH-HO! You don't want spark-LERS, you want spark-LEEEEES . . . the other bright things that have lit up many a lonely night. Is that it, Carson, you're looking for some spark-lies?"

"Can you get something like that? Or tell me where something might be found?"

He did his little-girl sing-song. "I know what you're do-ing, I know what you're do-ing. You're baiting a tra-ap, you're baiting a tra-ap."

"No. I'm simply using this item to walk through a door."

"Who's behind that door, Carson? An adventurer? ARE YOU HOLDING BACK?"

Adventurer meant a psychotic killer; in Jeremy's twisted world, that equated to *friend*. I said, "No, not an adventurer. Just a regular man." Or whatever this Giles Walcott was.

"You're showing me three cards," he hissed. "What's behind the fourth?"

"I'm telling you the truth, Jeremy."

I could almost hear my brother measuring my syllables; he was a Truth Machine, and no one could slip a lie past him.

He finally crooned, "Tell me what you need."

"Like I said, an item used in an . . . adventure."

"There are categories. Are you talking about A: something in the general area, B: something in the immediate vicinity, or C: something that . . . tasted the syrup?"

I closed my eyes and shook my head.

"It's probably C, Jeremy. I need something major."

"C and major. C major . . . HA! You want a chord? GET IT, CARSON? A CORD?"

I was silent. He tittered, a musical note, high and sweet. "You're losing your sense of humor, brother. I recommend a high colonic. Maybe telephones will wash out. They would around here."

"You can do it, Jeremy?"

"You're SURE you're not using it to trap an adventurer?"

"I'm simply trying to walk through the door of a man who sells such items."

"SELLS THE STUFF? THAT'S SICK, TWISTED, PERVERTED. HEARING THAT MAKES ME WANT TO VOMIT DOWN MY . . . What are the profit margins, Carson? What are the start-up costs? Can it be done mail order?"

"Have you heard of such folks, Jeremy?"

"Brother, if I could slip things out of here, I'd need an agent to screen the offers. But let's cut to the matter at hand: you need something unusual, I need a phone recharger. Are you seeing a pattern here?"

"I'll get you what you need. What do I get, Jeremy?"

"I DON'T KNOW, CARSON. It's not like I'm sitting in a fucking Toys'R'Us. I have to bring the subject up at kaffeeklatsch. I'LL GET BACK TO YOU ON THAT ONE, HAVE MY GIRL CALL YOUR GIRL. Speaking of the girlies, brother, how's that lovely little cut-up friend of yours, Miss Ava?"

"She's in Fort Wayne, Jeremy."

"My, my. That's what? A thousand miles away? Did she

betray you, Carson? Run out on your love? You gave and gave and got nothing but a face full of spit. Did she hawk it from so far it was cold by the time it hit your eyes?"

"Give it up, Jeremy, you can't make me –"

"Women always betray our love, don't they, Carson?"

A sound of satisfied laughter. He hung up.

CHAPTER 15

My phone rang at 7.12 a.m. I was jogging up the steps, returning from my morning run. I noticed someone had rented the Martins' place to the west. There was a red Toyota sedan under the house, a couple of beach towels hanging over the deck rail in back, two pairs of flip flops, large and small. A few pieces of clothing hung on the line beside the house – a woman's blouse, shorts. Beside them were several men's tees, X-large at least, trumpeting Auburn University.

I strode across my floor and grabbed the phone, still catching my breath.

Jeremy said, "I think I've done myself proud, Carson, with that little request of yours. Naturally it's not here, but I know where it is . . ."

"Where . . . is what . . . Jeremy?"

"You sound out of breath, brother."

"I just finished running."

"You sure you haven't been marching the old soldier? Now that li'l Ava skipped out on you, it's probably a regular occurrence, right? WHOOPS, IT'S SEVEN FORTY-THREE, TIME TO FLOG THE DOLPHIN! WHOOPS, IT'S EIGHT NINE-TEEN, TIME TO MILK THE MAMMOTH. WHOOPS, IT'S NINE OH-TWO . . . Eat to keep your strength up, Carson. And switch hands to help avoid carpal tunnel."

My brother's sense of sexual innuendo had been frozen in the adolescent phase, about the time he murdered our father.

"Can it. What have you got, Jeremy?"

"It's bigger than a breadbox, sharper than a hound's tooth, and oh, the things it has seen in its short lifetime . . ."

"Come on, Jeremy, I don't have time for —"

"The final mask of Trey Forrier."

I froze. Trey Forrier was a serial torturer and killer locked away in the same institution as Jeremy. Like many psycho-pathic killers – Hexcamp among them – Forrier preferred the personal involvement afforded by a knife. It wasn't known how many victims he'd truly murdered over the years, there having been several unsolved killings with similar method-ology.

Forrier's delusions had reached a strange point where he created a crude mask before each attack. Whether he wore the masks himself or preferred them to watch during the savagery was never known. Evidence at his small basement apartment indicated he'd created four masks, but only three had been found at murder scenes. No one knew what had become of the final mask, and Forrier only smiled wearily when asked.

He'd been caught perhaps seven years ago. I was in college at the time, studying psychology, and followed the case. Forrier had worked for years as a sort of itinerant dishwasher and low-level restaurant help, and was described as a "total loner" and a "daydreamer". He had no friends. I recollected that he had some form of physical malformation, but couldn't recall it exactly. I also recalled his vigorous initial protestations of innocence, but when the death penalty had been lifted in return for life at the institute, Forrier acquiesced, smiling and avowing to whatever crimes the prosecution assigned him. It had been an odd case and I suspected the mask of Trey Forrier, wielded properly, would secure my entrance into the world of big-time collectors of serial-killer memorabilia.

"You can't be serious, Jeremy," I rasped, my breath dry in my throat.

"Brother, I am as serious as a shark in a kiddie pool. See you soon."

The phone clicked dead. I blew out a long breath and started to slump until I heard an insane shrieking outside my window.

I bolted for the door, the sound outside horrendous. The door opened to a wheeling cloud of gulls, keening, swooping, diving. I heard a chuckle and looked down to Danbury's Audi. She was sitting on the hood, a bag of bait shrimp in one hand, pitching shrimp into the air with the other. The birds were frenzied.

Danbury tossed the rest of the shrimp, provoking a final shrill battle, then slid from the hood.

"A familiar sight," I said, stepping down the stairs.

"You feed the gulls too?" She pulled off her sunglasses and dropped them into the pocket of a white linen shirt. Her blonde hair floated on the breeze.

"I meant shrimp pecked apart by hungry, screeching critters."

She thought a moment, smiled. "Like the media on the attack? Goodness, that's a metaphor, pogie. You never cease to amaze me."

"I'm real busy, Ms Danbury," I said. "If you'll excuse me, I've got things to do."

"Can I come inside?"

"No."

She wiggled her fingers at me. "I've got shrimp hands, Ryder. You'd make me drive all the way back to Mobile with my hands reeking of half-rotted shrimp? You're more of a gentleman than that."

I pointed beneath the house. "There's a hose beside the fish-cleaning table. A bar of soap, too. Good talking to you, Ms D."

Unruffled, she walked to the table, washed her hands. "Did you find out anything new on the woman in the motel? I hear she's a nun. This case is turning weird, Ryder."

She looked at me for reaction. But I'd heard yesterday that Marie Gilbeaux's name was being released by the authorities upstate. That was standard; it couldn't be held tight anymore. The press conference was scheduled for this afternoon. I tried to look like a man stifling a yawn. "Everyone's getting that news today. Your source didn't give you much more than squat. Again."

Danbury finished washing and shook water from her hands. She studied the grungy towel hanging from a nail on the table, then wiped her hands dry on her walking shorts.

"It's out of my control, you know. What information I'm given. Or fed."

She looked at me for a comment. I wanted to ask, *Fed? What do you mean?* Instead, I stretched my back, said, "Where's Funt?"

"Funt?"

"Your video monkey. Shouldn't he be here taping all this exciting news?"

"His name's Borgurt Zipinski. Borg's not my videographer, he's the station's. Freelance, really, but on retainer. The day I rate a full-time videographer is the day I blow out of Mobile with stars in my eyes. Besides," she said, smiling, "you'd probably make Borg do something colorful with his camera."

She walked to her car; it was a good walk. "We need to have a tête-à-tête soon, Ryder," she said through the open window, dropping the sunglasses to her eyes. "Talk about this funny little case." The white teeth smiled at me. "No comment, right?"

"No comment."

Danbury slipped the car in gear. "You're getting good at that no-comment action, pogie, making an art of it. Art. Now there's an interesting word."

She laughed and sped away in a spray of sand and shells.

CHAPTER 16

I was twice stopped for speeding on my way to the institute – tucked away in the countryside west of Montgomery – but badged my way clear. I arrived before one p.m. and pulled through the outer gate, the guardhouse breaking the circling monotony of fence and razor wire.

The main building was a brown, single-story concrete rectangle. The front third contained offices and kitchen facilities and had windows like slitted eyes. There were no windows in the "residential" section. A small exercise yard stood to the side, boxed in by walls topped with heavy mesh fencing. In the corner of the yard, facing the cream-colored wall, a tall and slender man stood with his back to me, appearing to conduct a symphony orchestra. He heard the sound of my vehicle and looked up. There was something wrong with his face, off-kilter. I passed by and pulled into the lot.

Dr Evangeline Prowse met me at the door. In her middle sixties or so, Vangie – the only name she'd acknowledge – had a serene face beneath a neat cropping of silver hair. Her eyes were dark and shiny as polished walnut. She had the loose-limbed gait of a retired marathoner, and a handshake hard and tight as a brick.

"Great to see you again, Carson. Jeremy's been very calm of late, maturing, perhaps. I've been pleased to lift some of the restrictions on him, allow him more television, guests in his room."

We walked the long hall to her office. Every fifty feet or so a button was recessed into the wall at shoulder height, the word EMERGENCY stenciled beneath it. It wasn't referring to fires.

Vangie's office was high ceilinged, with shelves bowed under books. There was another shelf behind the door, holding pieces of statuary, several drawings, a few pages in Plexiglas frames, a figure constructed of twisted pipecleaners.

"I don't recall these," I said, picking up a crude eye-like shape seemingly made of hardened Play-Doh.

"My curio shelf. Items created by residents."

The eye was uninteresting. I set it down to read from a framed poem scrawled in thick black pencil. It rambled about a dog and a carrot and a red sky. I held up the poem.

"You've heard of folks who collect such things as a hobby; business, even?"

Vangie said, "We've had collectors trying to get our

130

employees to smuggle out items from the residents. More often than you'd imagine."

"What do you do when they try that?"

"It's not illegal to solicit such items. Our staffers tell me they're being pestered, I contact the people making the requests, if I can, and imply legal action. The naïve are scared off, others just laugh."

"Ever heard of a fellow named Hexcamp?"

She thought a moment; nodded. "Marsden Hexcamp, of course. Serial killer, ran with a band of outcasts? Mansonesque kind of communal set-up, if I recall."

"You don't know much about him?"

She smiled. "He died before being incarcerated any length of time. When they're out and about, they belong to you folks. When they get to where they can be mentally dissected, they're mine."

"You ever hear of something called the Hexcamp collection?"

She shook her head. "Doesn't ring a bell. What is it?"

"No one seems to know. Something to do with art, I suspect."

Vangie picked up the pipecleaner figure, something an elementary schoolchild might create.

"Most of what these folks call art is this kind of thing, Carson – simplistic, almost stunted, from an aesthetic point of view."

"Stunted like their personalities."

"Art is emotion, right? When you don't feel normal emotion, you don't create compelling art. These folks don't create art, but mimic what they think art is. There are exceptions, of course. Now and then you'll find a sample that's interesting. I imagine there are a few pieces that are truly stunning – powerful, even."

"But they'd be rare?"

Vangie set the twisted figure back on the shelf. "Oh my, yes, Carson. Extremely, I'd think. Are you ready to see Jeremy?"

A guard escorted me to the rear of the building. The doors were thick metal, with small slatted windows of mesh-encased glass. We stopped before Jeremy's door. I looked through the slat and saw him sitting on his bed, reading. Jeremy showed no sign I was outside his room, but I knew he had heard our approaching footsteps. My brother had been endowed with alert senses, and each progressive year of incarceration honed them further.

"We want privacy," I told the guard, meaning to keep the window slat closed. He nodded and opened the door.

My brother sat on his made bed, appearing absorbed in the text of his book. His neatly combed hair was the color of straw. Jeremy had our father's delicate features and pale skin, but lacked our father's size. Though Jeremy was six years my senior, I suspect most people would have made him for about my age, if not younger.

"What are you reading, Jeremy?"

He turned a page, not looking up. His light hair fell across his forehead and he brushed it back with pale, slender fingers.

"*Black Sun*. About a man and woman who destroy one another. It's a comedy."

132

He read another page, finger following the print. "How are things at the house, Carson? Your house on the beach, the one you bought with the money Mama left you."

My heart sank. When my brother brooded about our respective places in life, it never boded well. I tried to wedge a smile into my voice.

"Things at the house are fine, Jeremy."

He turned another page; I knew he was no longer reading the book. "No termites or structural problems? No sagging roofline or dry rot of the pilings? It does sit on pilings, doesn't it? So you can look down on people?"

"Yes, Jeremy, it sits on pilings. Like all of the houses on the beach."

"Do you think Mama left you the money to buy the house because you sat with her while she died?"

"That's probably part of it."

He threw the book aside, aimed the full fire of his blue eyes into mine. "Then tell me this, Carson: YOU WATCH ONE WOMAN DIE AND GET A HOUSE ON THE BEACH. I WATCH FIVE WOMEN DIE AND GET STUCK IN HERE. WHAT'S WRONG WITH THIS PICTURE?"

"Jeremy —"

"BY ALL RIGHTS I SHOULD HAVE FIVE HOUSES ON THE BEACH."

He grabbed my wrist, yanked me beside him on his bed, patting my hand while speaking in our mother's voice.

"Thank you so much, Cah-son, for watching me die, it's been so en-tuh-tay-ning. Heah's a big fat wad of money yo daddy made befoah he came home and beat the living shit out of Jeremy. Why don't you buy yourself a nice house on the beach an' if you ever get the chance, dear, dear Cah-son, please go piss on your brotha Jeremy for me. Bein' dead ah won't get the chance no more."

Jeremy jumped from the bed and paced the small room. He caught sight of himself in the soft Mylar mirror, his image imprecise, shivering. He winked at his reflection, then spun to me.

"Tell me about li'l Ava. Why did she spit in your face."

"You know what happened last year. It was stress. She needed to get away for a while, Jeremy. That was all."

He grinned. "She was your first, right? I don't mean the –" he pumped his hips at me like a hunching dog – "*hunh-hunh-hunh* kind of first: OH MY GAWD, HONEY, *hunh, hunh, hunh,* YOU'RE BETTER THAN A FISTFUL OF VASELINE! *Hunh, hunh, hunh.* I mean she was your FIRST LITTLE LOVE? Two hearts squishing together as one, all that stuff."

"We were close, Jeremy. We're . . . still close."

He dashed across the room, jumped on the bed, sat cross-legged beside me. "But if it's really LOVE, how could she forsake you like that? AH SURE DO LUB YOU, CARSON, BUT GOSH A WILLY I SURE GOT A NEED TO SEE FORT WAYNE BEFORE I DIE."

He leaned over, cupped his hands around my ear, whispered, "They betray our love, don't they? If she loved you she wouldn't have left you. You know it, Carson. IF THERE WAS ANYTHING TO YOU, SHE WOULD HAVE STAYED."

He was twisting our family horrors, using his blind and misdirected hatred of our mother.

"Screw you. You don't know love."

"I know BETRAYAL. Here's all LOVE IS, Carson —" He jumped from the bed and stood in front of me, frantically jerking his hips as his head lolled to the side.

"*Hunh, hunh, hunh, hunh . . .*"

"Stop it, Jeremy."

". . . *hunh, hunh* OH GAWD, BAYBEE, *hunh, hunh . . .*"

"I said to stop it." I felt anger flash through my cells like electricity, fighting it, not willing to let him do this to me again.

". . . *hunh, hunh, hunh,* OH PLEEEEASE, CARSON, *hunh, hunh, hunh,* I WANT TO COME ONCE MORE BEFORE I GO, *hunh, hunh, hunh . . .*"

I stood and grabbed his shoulders, shook him. "You little bastard, I'll . . ."

I heard the door open and looked over. On the threshold stood the man I had seen gesturing in the air in the exercise yard. His face looked like he'd been pulled from his mother's womb with Vise-grips, the left cheekbone indented where it should have projected. His skin was coarse. His hair was thick and black and uncombed. He stared at me like we knew one another and made a wet, amorphous sound.

Jeremy squirted from my grasp, took the man's elbow, pulled him into the room. "What perfect timing, just as Carson and I were discussing COMING, here comes my good friend. Carson, this is one of our most talented residents, a man you should meet . . . Trey Forrier."

The guard stepped through the door. "Earlier this morning, Mr Ridgecliff requested Mr Forrier be brought down for a visit. It's a reward we allow your brother, since his behavior has improved the past couple of months. If you don't wish Mr Forrier here, Mr Ryder, he doesn't have to be. He's never acted out in any way, if you're concerned."

"Never acted out" was the guard's way of telling me Forrier wouldn't try to kill me the minute the door closed; a distinct possibility with many of the residents.

"No," I said. "It's fine. Let Mr Forrier stay."

The guard nodded and closed the door. Forrier continued to stare at me. I got the impression he stared at a lot of things.

Jeremy said, "Trey, this is my brother, Carson, who I saved from Hell."

I held out my hand and said, "Pleased to meet you, Mr Forrier." He didn't seem to notice.

"Trey keeps to himself a bit, Carson. Don't you, Trey? You keep your own counsel?"

Forrier's mouth quivered and bubbled out a string of wet sounds.

"Is he saying something?" I asked Jeremy.

"He's saying you have the face of a man who is kind. Trey's very attuned to faces, to shapes. His is, well, somewhat unusual. Not greatly, I mean, it's not like he's the Elephant Man or something. I think he makes too much of it."

Forrier did the strange motion again, like waving a baton for an orchestra. "Did he ever conduct?" I asked, observing the ritual.

Jeremy grinned. "Some say he conducted several rather artistic little adventures."

"What does he say?"

"That he likes it here. He has no hunger. And on that note, brother, I'm hungering for my little gift."

I looked toward the door. "The guard . . ."

"Is down the hall. He walked away a minute ago. Gimme, gimme."

I reached into my pants and extracted the recharger, a black plug scarcely larger than a matchbox and a couple feet of coiled cord. Jeremy spun away, adjusted his bedding for a second. When he returned the device was gone. He looked down at my belt, where my cellphone was affixed.

"Let me see yours, Carson. I think it's nicer than my model. I'd show you mine, but it takes a little time and a lot of grunting."

I handed him my phone. He dandled it in his hand, pushed a few buttons, shined it on his shirtfront. He did a commercial-announcer's voice. "And you call anywhere and everywhere for one low monthly fee. Bet my plan's better."

"How *can* you use a phone, Jeremy?" I asked. "The charges?"

"I think it's illegal, a clone or whatever." He jiggered his eyebrows, winked. "Probably why it was never reported missing." He flipped my phone back.

"You have your end of the deal, Jeremy," I said.

He raised his eyebrows, perfect innocence. "There was something more?"

"A location."

Forrier was staring at me. When I looked at him, he turned away. Jeremy walked to the mirror, studied his splayed reflection, finger-combed back his blond hair.

137

"Sometimes life doesn't work out as it's planned, brother. Sometimes you get what you want. Sometimes you just get *hunh, hunh, hunh.* It's my nappy time. Trey, say goodbye to Carson."

Jeremy's games seemed endless, but I resisted the useless urge to protest. There was nothing to do but return to Mobile and hope he had a change of heart. I was a half-hour south when my cellphone chirped.

Jeremy's voice was loud. "It works so much better with a full charge, Carson. I could probably call all the way to heaven, say hello to dear Mama. Not that she'd take the call, of course."

"Something you want, Jeremy?"

"You don't think Trey was going to send his mask into the hands of just anyone, do you, brother? He wanted to see you, make sure you were the type to understand. He likes you, a rare honor."

"He wanted to see if I was the type to understand what?"

"History, brother. You got a pen with you? I've got some directions you might enjoy."

Ninety minutes later I carried a pick into a brushy field thirty miles north of Mobile. The skeleton of an ancient farm implement rusted away in the weeds. Insects rasped in the tall grass. Per my instructions, I found the concrete foundation of an old house, and walked south, counting steps to a small cairn above an old well. Sweating hard in the sun, I began levering away rocks with the pick.

Twenty minutes later I brushed dirt from an old leather suitcase. I felt like weeping, but did not know why.

At home I sat the case on my table and stared at it through

the span of two beers before finding the nerve to open it. The lock was corroded and I slit the brittle leather with a linoleum knife. Inside was a succession of sealed plastic bags. The final bag was padded with scraps of red tissue paper. I reached through the paper and freed the mask.

Larger by half than the normal human face, the nose was a sharp ridge, the cheekbones exaggerated and protruding. The finish was glossy, anthracitic black. White-painted shards of broken glass formed the teeth and bordered a red wound of mouth. The eyeholes were circled in white, giving the mask a look of insane anger. A trick-or-treater wearing the mask would reap baskets of candy, anything to get that kid off the porch.

The foundation of the mask was, surprisingly, papier-mâché. In the fifth grade my class had built a piñata, and I knew strips of paper had been soaked in a flour-and-water glue and overlaid, building the mask to an approximate one-inch thickness.

For a split second I considered bringing the mask to my face. But it occurred to me that evil might be less action than essence, a dark and infective poison needing only a deep breath at the wrong time. I pushed the mask into a waiting box, closed it tight, and crept to bed. Sliding beneath the covers I noticed a lamp left burning in the living room. *I'm too tired to get up and turn it off*, I told myself, knowing it was a lie, that with the mask finally free of the earth, the house needed all the light it could muster.

CHAPTER 17

"Good morning, Walcott Imports and Collectibles."

The voice was deep and polished, the syllables individually savored, a man enjoying the sound of his voice. Figuring he'd have some form of caller ID, I'd phoned from a booth on Government Street.

"Mr Walcott?"

"Yes. Who's calling, please?"

A first-timer would be nervous, and I made my voice hesitate. "My name is . . . Carrol Ransburg, sir. I'd like to talk to you about getting an appraisal."

I selected the first name on the theory that any male choosing a false moniker wouldn't opt for a name generally associated with women.

"On an antique?" Walcott said.

"No. Another kind of item . . . a more special sort."

Utter silence, no TV or radio in the background, no traffic outside. "First, how did you hear of me?" It was more command than question.

I said, "From . . . a friend. No, not really a friend, a person I met. He suggested you'd be the one to do this thing. The appraisal."

"What's the name of the person who *suggested* you contact me?"

"He wouldn't want me to say. He's . . . very private."

Walcott's defenses slammed into place like a portcullis. "I'm sorry, I only do business on known referrals."

"I promised his name would remain unspoken."

"Then my response can only be, good day, sir." The voice grew distant as he moved the phone from his mouth.

"I'm calling about Forrier," I yelled. "Trey Forrier."

I heard the phone return to his ear. "What did you say?"

"Trey Forrier. I have something of his. A mask."

"Impossible. You're lying."

I gave him a precise recounting of its look and construction. There was a long pause. When he spoke I heard a pitch-rise of concealed excitement.

"How did you come up with this . . . item?"

"I was on the team that evaluated Forrier's state of mind after he was captured. I'm . . . was, a psychologist." I didn't know if Walcott knew anything about psychology, but I could babble the jargon if necessary. The character I'd selected was Fallen Psychologist; I'd seen a couple of them.

"Go on . . ."

141

"I worked as a clinical hypnotician, a forensic hypnotist. On a project basis."

"Trey Forrier never said anything noteworthy under hypnosis."

"I never *reported* he said anything. There's a difference."

"You've had this piece for years. Why do you want me to see it now?"

I added shame to my voice. "I . . . know it might be worth some money. I could use money, Mr Walcott. Times haven't been good, I lost my license to practice. A problem with . . . substances."

A long pause. Walcott said, "I don't know what such a piece would bring, Mr Ransburg. The market's been depressed. We all suffer from a weak economy. There's been a glut on the market recently."

Just like that he turned from suspicion to camel merchant. I backpedaled, hoping it would set the hook. "You're probably right, Mr Walcott. Maybe this isn't the time. I'm sorry for disturbing —"

The command returned to his voice. "Bring it by tonight. At nine. Be precise. You're in the Mobile area? Here's my address . . ."

Giles Walcott's home seemed normal for the upscale neighborhood: pricey landscaping, lush carpet of lawn, a ludicrous but expensive fountain featuring a leaping dolphin squirting water through its blowhole. I noted a camera tucked in a tree and one above the door, hidden in a cast bronze eagle with spreading wings.

Deadbolts withdrew electronically. The door opened to a large and chandeliered foyer. Beyond sat high-ticket antique furniture in rooms with twelve-foot ceilings. It seemed more museum than home.

"This way, Mr Ransburg," a deep voice rumbled. "Down the hallway, turn right."

Suspecting surveillance, I paused as if fighting panic, tucked the box with the mask to my chest, and walked to a dimly lit room. A deep indigo carpet cushioned my footfalls as I entered. A man appearing to be in his early sixties stood behind a massive desk. He looked less born than extruded, head and neck almost the same circumference, broken only by a flat length of nose and a half-cup of chin. Thinning black hair stretched across his scalp in shining strands. His shoulders sloped to a tubular body in a dark suit, adding to the sense of extrusion.

"You're Mr Walcott?" I said, not extending my hand. He nodded, not offering his, and looked at me curiously.

"Is something wrong?" I asked.

"You remind me of someone, but I don't know who."

I shrugged and looked away. On his desk lay a ceramic representation of the male genitalia, crude and outsized. I couldn't help staring. Walcott raised an eyebrow.

"Do you know what that is, Mr Ransburg?"

"I have a passing familiarity."

"I mean do you know who created it. No? It's a Vaughn Ray Bodie original. He created them while he was . . . working. Primitive but very expressive, don't you think? It's dated behind the testicles. May fourteenth, 1959. His fourth . . .

143

event occurred on May sixteenth. It's the only Bodie phallus not currently in a private collection."

Vaughn Ray Bodie was a serial rapist and murderer finally dragged down in the early sixties. I suppressed a shudder and forced interest into my eyes.

"It's quite rare, I'd imagine, Mr Walcott."

"Six victims, six phalli. I'm reserving it for auction. I expect it to generate something in the low six figures. Another item I'm auctioning is a tee-shirt worn by Vincent Canario when he was journeying with Terrance Swann."

"Journeying" was Walcott's euphemism for Canario's abduction and violent cross-country run with the terrified fourteen-year-old Swann. Neither survived.

"What would such an item bring?" I asked.

"I'm anticipating something in the eleven to fourteen thousand dollar range. He wore several shirts on his way, so its value is diminished."

"A pity he packed to travel," I noted.

Walcott nodded mournfully. "The mask – let me see the mask."

I set the box on his desk and removed the mask. Walcott held it beneath a lamp and magnifier combination, switched on the light. He inspected the mask from every angle, checking various measurements with a small ruler. Twice he stopped looking at the mask, studied me, then returned to his labors.

"The paint appears to be oil-based, not overly unharmed by time. The eyeholes are the correct width. The glass teeth are carefully fitted into bored sockets. There's a craftsman at work here, Mr Ransburg. Some people do things right. Look here –" Walcott used his thumbnail to flick at a loose end of the composition material. "It's a combination of cloth and paper instead of paper alone; rather like money. One of the reasons it's in such fine shape. And one of the reasons I know it's not a forgery."

"There are forgers in this business, Mr Walcott?"

"There are forgers in every pursuit where money can be made through forgery." He smiled as he dropped the ruler back in the drawer. "I'm in favor of them, myself."

It took me a second to catch on. "Because it makes you more valuable; you provide authentication, right?"

"Within the boundaries of my experience and knowledge, yes." His tone implied that he found few boundaries to his expertise.

"Then you'd know what the mask is worth."

I caught him staring at me again. This time something seemed to click and he frowned. "Excuse me, Mr Ransburg," he said, and left the room.

My inclination was to rifle drawers and search closets, but wary of unseen surveillance, I remained in front of the desk and let my eyes roam the shadowed room. I discerned no other attendants of death.

Walcott returned, a large envelope in his hand. He picked up the mask, sighed, then returned it to the box. "Is it really yours, sir, the mask? Or is it perhaps the property of a police department somewhere?"

My heart paused. "I don't understand, Mr Walcott."

"I think it's simple. You're not who you say you are."

145

I forced myself to breathe normally, look nonchalant. "Who am I, then?"

A smirk danced at the edge of his mouth. He tapped the envelope. "Not long ago I came across a piece of information I thought might somehow be useful – a couple of fellows who wander at the edge of my business."

Walcott slipped a scrap of newsprint from the envelope and held it up to me. It was the photo from the awards ceremony.

"It appears you've a double at the Mobile Police Department, Mr Ransburg. A brother, perhaps?"

That damned picture. I said, "I am here as a researcher, nothing more."

He narrowed a dark eye. "I've done nothing wrong. You must leave. You unsettle me."

"*I* unsettle *you*? A guy who keeps a plaster dick made by a serial killer on his desk?"

"It's ceramic. And I do not *collect* such items, I *broker* them. I'm but a humble dealer in limited commodities, that's all. Much like rare stamps. Or coins, perhaps."

"Coins don't take part in murders."

He smirked. "If you believe no one has died over gold doubloons, you hold a naïveté perhaps beyond cure."

I produced my badge wallet and set the black leather square on his desk. "If I open that, there will be a badge in the room. It will drastically alter the complexion of our conversation, Mr Walcott."

"I doubt it, since I've done nothing wrong. Do I need to phone my attorney and have him explain that to you?"

"Your lawyer has no reason to be here, Mr Walcott, unless he's interested in research. I simply need a historical perspective on certain items. Surely that's not too much to ask."

"What is this historical perspective?"

"I want to know about the Hexcamp collection."

He walked to the window, looked out into the dark woods behind the house, and stared into the trees. When he turned to me, his eyes were oddly disengaged, as though focused an inch above my pupils.

"There is no such thing, sir. It's a myth, a gorgon."

"For something that doesn't exist, it gets a lot of attention."

He returned to his position behind the desk, putting four feet of gleaming wood between us. "In philately, there is a stamp called the Scarlet Angelus. Some say it exists, some say it never did. But that doesn't prevent people from seeking it." He paused. "In every form of collection, there must be a ghost piece, an entity to make the spine tingle. To give people something to whisper about."

"Who whispers about Hexcamp's collection?"

He smiled, his teeth tiny wet chisels behind his lips. "The collecting community as a whole."

"What does this community say about it?"

"The community's opinion doesn't matter; the collection is a pocketful of dreams . . . until pronounced otherwise by someone in a position to know."

"Like yourself?"

"In this matter, even I lack the proper qualifications."

"My research must continue, then. I need the name of a major collector, Mr Walcott. Local, if possible."

He rotated his tubular head. "If I were to tell you, my record of confidentiality would be broken. I'd be out of business."

"Give me several names to use as reference; I won't mention yours. No one would know who sent me."

He tapped the crystal of his watch. "I'm sorry, sir. Our time together is up."

"This is important, Mr Walcott. I need to know –"

"My patience is wearing thin, sir. I'm afraid if you're not out of my home in ten seconds, I'll phone my lawyer."

He put his hand atop his phone and studied me calmly. I had no leverage over Giles Walcott. I expected he recorded all sales, kept accountant-quality figures, everything necessary to remain above reproach with governmental entities.

But with the public?

In spending so much time with killers who giggled when caught, pimps proud of beating their women, dope-boys driving mink-upholstered Beamers, I sometimes lost sight of people's sensitivity to public opinion. Walcott's prissily attended yard, crafted suit, attention to financial detail, all bespoke a man who wouldn't wish his neighbors to know he sold relics from abattoirs.

I reached to the desk and picked up the ceramic phallus. He frowned. "Careful with that, it's quite –"

I flipped it in the air, caught it.

"I think you should call your lawyer," I said. "I'll phone the Spanish Fort constabulary. Let's have a coming-out party for Walcott Collectibles."

His voice dropped to a whisper. "What do you mean?"

"When the local cops know what you do, it's bound to leak into the community. How's it going to be, pulling into the Winn-Dixie and hearing the whispers? 'That's him, Giles Walcott. He makes his money from death.' You ready for that, Giles? Or how about the low-level crazoids who'll line up at your front gate, drooling for a chance to sniff Vincent Canario's tee-shirt? Get ready for the parade."

The phallus took flight again, grazing the ceiling. I had to reach out to make the save. "You know what you're lacking in here, Mr Walcott?"

"Careful! What?" Sweat beaded his face. I cocked my hand, ready to toss.

"One of those signs."

"What – put that down, *please* – what signs?"

"You break it, you bought it."

He lowered his head. His hand retreated from the phone. "I think we can work something out, sir," he mumbled. "Please put my penis down."

I left with Walcott's promise of a suitable entrée into the world of his buyers. I planned to continue as Carrol Ransburg, now a man with some ready money and newly hot for the idea of acquiring serial-killer memorabilia. As I walked from his house he called to my back.

"One thing, Mr *Ransburg*. The mask. It is the property of a police department somewhere, isn't it? On loan?"

I turned and let my eyes say there were no lies left in them. "No, Mr Walcott. The mask resides at my address."

I felt his confused stare long after the door fell shut.

CHAPTER 18

The next day Walcott delivered the name of a local collector, Marcella Baines, "a proper woman with exquisite and discerning taste". When I expressed surprise a woman was involved, Walcott accused me of gender bias.

Baines lived in a high-rise beachfront condo in Pensacola, far enough from Mobile, I hoped, that she hadn't seen my photo in the *Register*. I checked in at the desk and after the security guard found my name on a list, he overrode the elevator control, allowing me to reach the penthouse.

Not knowing what aspiring collectors of serial-killer mementos considered fashionable dress, I'd hauled out the black suit reserved for funerals, weddings, and other somber occasions, lacquering my hair flat with something Ava left behind. I stood in a small entryway and smiled warily at a camera above the door, speaking with the clipped precision many associate with intellect.

"My name is Carrol Ransburg. I have an appointment with Ms Baines. Is she . . . ?"

The door opened to a bright room expected of a moneyed dowager: delicate furniture, pretty paintings on the walls, a broad window overlooking the Gulf. Marcella Baines appeared from behind the door. In her mid sixties, I figured, wearing a white chef's apron over a simple blue pantsuit, a lone strand of pearls around her neck. She was five ten or eleven, with short hair bobbed and dyed to a uniform auburn tint, the color at contrast to her pale skin. Outsized earrings dangled from her lobes like small chandeliers. Ms Baines's mouth was extraordinarily wide, her smile a wondrous display of dentition. Her green eyes crinkled with delight, as if I was precisely what she'd wished for this morning. Her hand took mine and drew me quickly across the threshold. "I'm so happy you're here," she said. "The toast is stuck."

"Pardon me?"

I followed her to a four-slot toaster on the marble counter of a copper-appointed kitchen. She frowned at the device.

"The toast simply refuses to come out, Mr Ransburg. I can't figure how this happens, but it's going on more and more lately."

I fiddled a moment and discovered a bent wire in the toast rack or whatever. A few deft manipulations and presto, toast. She applauded, teeth beaming like a spotlight.

"Thank you so much, Mr Ransburg. I was hoping to have

some caviar and then this problem with the toaster. Please have a seat, it'll just be a second."

I went to the living room and sunk into a gray leather couch. A minute later she returned sans apron and sat a serving plate on a low mahogany table between us: chopped eggs and scallions, toast points, lemon wedges, and a mound of gray-black caviar.

"Eat up, Mr Ransburg. Bon appétit."

We ate fish ova, sipped champagne, and discussed the weather for several minutes. Her eyes turned to me, studied my mouth.

"You have a speck, an egg, right there at . . . I'll get it."

Her finger brushed at my lip as I resisted the urge to draw away. Her hand smelled of fish and lemon. "There," she said. "A handsome man is tidy again." She leaned forward in her delicate chair, knees primly together, hands crossed in her lap.

"I understand you're quite new to collecting. How long have you been in it?"

"A year. Less, maybe."

She leaned back, crooked a finger beneath her chin. "Are there any celebrities whose work you admire?"

"Celebrities?"

"Even a newcomer must have favorites. Tell me, whose work do you gravitate towards? Whom do you admire?"

I mentioned several serial killers and rapists I'd interviewed in prison. She listened with a series of facial reactions; one name got a twitch, another pursed lips, one a raised eyebrow, another a satisfied smile. She reached over and patted my knee.

"Ah, but they're all relatively new players on the field, all in the recent past. You must also study the classics."

I did the dog-ate-my homework look. "I'm with a group of developers, we've been very successful, but success is a thief of time. I haven't dug into the classics just yet."

"Tell me who truly fascinates you; who you feel a kinship with beyond all others."

My selection was determined by the word *kinship*. There could be only one fitting that description, my only kinsman, my brother. Although we'd shared childhoods, we no longer shared a name. While in college I tried severing ties to my past by replacing my surname with that of an artist renowned for paintings of small boats on raging seas. It had worked about as well as changing my hairstyle.

I said, "Jeremy Ridgecliff."

Baines stood abruptly and crossed the room to lean against a large buffet. She studied me through unblinking eyes. "Tell me why you've selected Jeremy Ridgecliff," she said, a note of challenge in her voice. "That's a most interesting choice in a day of Dahmers and Coronas and Gacys."

"He was so different . . . so artful with his arrangements, I've heard. And his method of, uh, acquisition so unusual. There seemed a sensitivity in his manner."

I saw a moment of sparkle in her eyes, a ghost of a smile shimmer across her lips.

"Do you recall Charlie Chaplin, Mr Ransburg? His Little Tramp character, beautiful and puzzled and delicate, all rolled up together?"

"Yes. From film festivals."

"I picture Jeremy like a sweet little Chaplinesque tramp, shuffling between parks and libraries and the lobbies of elegant hotels, sitting quietly and waiting for his mother to come, so blissfully patient, his cherub face the perfect combination of sorrow and longing."

She was talking about our mother – Jeremy wanting to kill her for not protecting him when my father had wild explosions of violence that ended in Jeremy's room. But killing our mother would have consigned me to a foster home or institution, so my brother sought surrogates.

I said, "I've heard that, to certain women, he was irresistible."

"Tender-hearted, poetic ladies in their early forties. One look at Jeremy and the maternal instincts bloomed like hothouse flowers. They probably started lactating. Finally, a motherly type, just the right age, just the right look, crossed to him, laid a gentle hand over his neck, said, 'Can I help you, son? You seem so troubled. Is there anything I can do?'"

"Much of this is new to me," I lied.

"And later, while he worked, expressed himself . . . Do you know what Jeremy would say to them, Mr Ransburg, his would-be benefactors?"

"That I don't know, Mrs Baines." Another lie – I knew exactly what Jeremy said to his victims, what he *sang*.

Baines put her voice up a register, made it light and shimmery.

"You're too late, you're too late, you're too late . . ."

I kept my eyes fixed on the deep red carpet. Marcella Baines walked to me. "You're beautiful, Mr Ransburg. You *feel*. I

154

watched your eyes when I spoke of Jeremy, saw anguish, respect, that elusive sense of kinship. Your selection of Jeremy Ridgecliff tells me much about you. Only those of subtle taste can discern his true glory."

"Ms Baines, I'm not sure why I selected –"

"Shhh, Mr Ransburg. You're young, fresh. New to this bright and shiny world. But there's one thing I know about you – you don't collect because you want an interesting investment; you collect because it's in your soul."

She strode to the far side of the room, pressed a panel and a mirror slid aside, revealing a doorway. She laughed, a rinkly-tinkly sound like an old-time piano.

"Come back here, Mr Ransburg," the wide mouth said. "Let me show you where I really live."

CHAPTER 19

I stepped through the doorway onto a plush black carpet. The expansive room resembled an art gallery: framed photos, shadowboxes on the walls, display cases, shelves, track lighting.

"Over here, Mr Ransburg. Let's start with the photographs."

She gathered me by my forearm as though we were a beach-walking couple, escorting me to a wall of framed photos. They were exclusively male – a clown-suited man blowing out candles on a cake; a man sitting naked on a dirty bed, surrounded by rifles; a man glaring from an old truck. I saw a gilt-framed photograph of a grinning, heavily tattooed man with jumper cables clamped to his nipples. I saw pinched faces, eerie smiles, drooping lids, Methadrine eyeballs . . .

Marcella Baines's smile was so wide it seemed the only thing above her neck. "They're my fellas, Mr Ransburg."

"You certainly have a lot of them, Mrs Baines – fellas."

She pointed to a black-and-white photo of a man with porcine eyes and dried spittle in the corners of his mouth.

"Charles Osland," she said.

Osland was an infamous murderer of the fifties who dispatched five women through ligature strangulation. Tina Caralla was his most famous victim, a TV reporter working in Memphis.

While I studied the photo, Baines walked to a display case, removed something, returned. She offered me a zip-bagged length of rope.

"The clothesline Charles used to confine Tina to her bed," she said. "Go ahead. Open it."

"It's not neces–" I had no need to touch the ghastly thing.

"It's all right," she said, patting me on the shoulder as if encouraging a child. "It's part of your new world."

I lifted the bag. *It's just ordinary rope,* I told myself, *woven strands of fiber.* I opened it.

"Now sniff," she said.

I held the bag to my nose and whiffed. Nothing. Marcella leaned her head over the bag and took a long draught. She leaned back, a drowsy smile on her face. "Spins your head, doesn't it? Chanel Number 5, the perfume Tina wore. She dabbed her neck with it, her sweet, swan-like neck."

"It's . . . lovely," I said, starting to close the bag.

"Take one more," she urged. "Please, I insist."

I closed my eyes, feigning a deep intake of breath. For a

moment I sensed the dark scent; not perfume, but the odor of violent death. She said, "Two of the strongest moments in a pair of lives, captured forever on thirty inches of cotton rope."

"How much?" I asked, closing the bag.

She patted my hand. "It's not for sale. It's a personal amulet, one I use for fortification."

"But if it was?"

"Let's not prattle over concerns of the marketplace, Mr Ransburg. We're here to enjoy."

For the next half-hour I attended a reliquary of savagery – scarves used for bondage, tools employed in obscene fashion, more lengths of electrical cord than I wish to remember. At one point she handed me a small plastic box with simple thumbtacks rattling within. When she told me how the tacks had been deployed, I wanted to flush them down the toilet, keep flushing all afternoon. Instead, I shook the box, raised a discerning eyebrow and said, "Quaint."

After I'd been shown all the visible objects, she said, "What did you collect previously? Everyone who comes to me has collected something before this."

"The usual, I suspect. Stamps. Coins."

A sympathetic smile. "I tried stamps; they were too distant for me, though I collected coins for several years. Not mint, used. I wanted to see the wear, feel the hands jingling the coins in a pocket, judging their weight. It made me a laughing-stock in the coin world, my insistence on grubby, used coins. But then I came into a collection of coins from Merle Banton. You know of him?"

"A bit." Banton was a brief horror in the thirties. A railroad

158

bull, he savaged a dozen rail-riding depression wanderers, leaving them strewn beside tracks from St Louis to Santa Fe.

"Suddenly the coins came *alive*, Mr Ransburg. I discovered Mr Banton often put his coins in his mouth, swooshing them from cheek to cheek. I wondered, had he coins in his mouth when he felt the need to . . ."

She seemed lost in thought for several seconds. "What started you collecting?" she finally said. "What was the first?"

I searched my past: third or fourth grade, running through a meadow with a homemade net, cheesecloth pinned around a wire clothes hanger.

"Butterflies," I answered.

She smiled. "So many of us do. Start with Lepidoptera, that is. I loved the Monarchs best. When I was girl I found a chrysalis hanging in a bush. It was like a small ornament, precious and vulnerable. I plucked it from the branch and brought it home. As the days passed I watched how it seemed to sense the events ahead, its tiny heart beating against the green casing. Then, of course, the inevitable, the tearing from confines, wings unfolding. Flight. That very day I decided to preserve that moment forever, collect others. I still have that collection, Mr Ransburg. Would you care to see it?"

"I would be honored."

She stooped low to open a drawer in the credenza and removed a glass-covered display box. She pursed her lips and blew dust from its surface.

"They took several years to acquire," she said, handing me the box. "But each one is perfect. It's the timing, you know."

I looked down. In three rows of four, a dozen green

chrysalides, green-brown wrappers as delicate as parchment, sides rent. From each tear, a butterfly was half emerged, wings beginning to unfold.

"Beautiful," I murmured.

She looked away to allow me a personal moment with the collection, then returned it to the vault. She again took my arm, walked me back toward the residence.

"I have collected far and wide, Mr Ransburg. I have some beautiful things, some improbable and magical things. I can be your mentor, if you let me."

I let my mouth drop open, mock-astonished at her generosity. "That would be incredible, Mrs Baines. I don't know how to thank you."

"We'll improve each other – you will learn, and I will enjoy watching you, as though starting the journey again."

Marcella Baines turned and pressed her lips to mine, her kiss light and chaste. She drew back, looked at her watch and smiled sadly. "We have much time to learn from one another, Mr Ransburg. But now I'm late for my bridge club. Boring old ladies with lives as gray as their hair, but one must keep up appearances. Shall we meet again soon – say Friday?"

"That would be wonderful."

"There's so much for you to learn. And this is an incredible time in collecting, a golden age. Have you heard of a man named Marsden Hexcamp?"

"I, uh, just a little. Rumors."

She smiled a thousand watts in my direction. "Here's something to add to your rumor chest, Mr Ransburg: Marsden Hexcamp is almost alive again. How about that?"

CHAPTER 20

There were only two dicks in the detectives' room, Wally Daller and Burke Madigan. Wally was across the room running a comb through his thinning hair, studying the result. Madigan was on the phone. Harry looked over the gray cubicle wall to the next set of desks, making sure no one was crouching there.

"She *what?*" he said, eyes wide.

"Believe me, Harry, it wasn't my idea."

"You mean like on the mouth? That old woman?"

"Closed mouth. Closed tight." I jammed my lips tight and pointed to them. "I hit that condo lobby running. I was afraid she was on my heels."

Madigan hung up. He ate a fistful of antacids, belched into his palm, and walked to the restroom. When the door swung shut, Harry said, "Kissy-face aside, Cars, what's she know about Hexcamp?"

"That's all she said; that he was coming alive."

"You think she's the type to really know anything? Or is she just trying to sneak a few drinks from the Fountain of Youth?"

"Harry, the back half of her penthouse is like a property room from hell. She even had a box of thumbtacks Tommy Dean Murgatroyd used to –"

"I'll pass on the details. You go back Friday?"

"That's when I'll find out what she knows about Hexcamp. Press her about the work."

"She's probably gonna press too, press your ass right down into the mattress, ripping and stripping. You're gonna get some of that geri-action."

I took another swig of black coffee, wiped my mouth for about the fiftieth time since leaving Baines's aerie; the eventuality was too grim to think about. Harry's cellphone sang from his pocket. Somewhere he'd managed to find the defining melodic pattern from "Spoonful".

"That spoon . . . that spoon . . . that spoon-ful . . ."

"Nautilus."

He listened for a moment, frowning, the scowl growing darker every second.

"No. Not at all. Listen to me, ma'am, there's no way my partner would do that. Right. Especially not with her. You said, 'No comment,' right? Good. If she comes back, I suggest locking your door and pulling down the blinds." He sighed and hung up.

"Remember how I gave Carla Hutchins my card, said to call me? That was her. Seems Cunt and Funt just left. Danbury was trying to ask questions. Ms Hutchins, well, she ain't real happy with you, Carson."

"Me? Why?"

"Danbury kept dropping your name, like you and she were old friends. Hutchins kinda got the impression you sent Danbury."

"I'll deal with it," I said.

I paced and stewed for the hour I figured it would take Danbury to return to Mobile, then called Channel 14. The woman at the switchboard took a deep breath. "Welcome to Channel 14, home of the Action 14 news and Mega-Doppler Weather, a member of the Clarity Broadcasting Network."

"You have to say that every time you pick up the phone?" I asked.

"I do," she replied, not sounding happy about it.

"I'd like to speak with DeeDee Danbury. This is Detective Carson Ryder of the Mobile Police Department."

"I'm sorry, sir. She was just here, but took off again. Let me try her cell."

The connection clicked to Hold. I waited in the vacuum.

"She's not answering, sir. She's hard to catch unless she wants to be caught."

"How about Funt, can you catch him?"

"Who, sir?"

"Her usual camera guy."

"Borgurt Zipinski." She sounded like she smelled something bad when she said it. "He's all yours."

Back on Hold. Two minutes ticked by before the phone picked up.

"Hey there, Detective," came a voice sounding like it had just been oiled. "S'up?"

"I need to get in touch with Ms Danbury, pronto," I said. "You can do it, you're her Panza a lot of the time, right?"

"Her what?"

"Her sidekick. You can connect even when she's off the radar?"

"She pretty much does her own thing, sport. I mean, uh, Detective." He was having a good time.

"How 'bout this, Sancho," I said. "Take down this number and get it to her. Tell her I'm not a happy camper."

"Oh, that'll give her goosepimples for sure." Zipinski chuckled as he wrote down the number.

I stared at my cellphone, unable to do anything else. Ten minutes into my stare, she called.

"Hi, pogie. What's up?"

"Ms Danbury, I think you may be following Harry and me. And you're upsetting people that don't need to be upset. I'm also beginning to suspect you may be withholding information vital to a case, which is illeg—"

"White or red?"

"Excuse me?"

"I'm pulling into a wine shop now, picking up a bottle. You prefer white or red? In this kind of heat I tend toward

164

white, but since we're consuming it on your premises –
sevenish? – you decide."

"Listen up, Ms Danbury, there's no way –"

"Silly me," she said. "I'll just get one of each."

She broke our connection.

CHAPTER 21

"Red or white, Ryder?" Danbury said, standing at my kitchen counter with a sommelier-style corkscrew in her hand. "Or I could mix them together. Is that how they get pink zin?"

I held up my bottle of Bass Ale. "I'm good."

Danbury had arrived a few minutes before seven, two bottles clinking in a paper sack. Before I could speak, she'd charged into my kitchen and was opening the wine.

"I brought a corkscrew just in case."

"I actually own a corkscrew, Ms Danbury."

"A real one, or does it fold off your Swiss Army knife?"

I winced. She winked and bustled back into the living room, sat, perched her wineglass on a bare knee. The TV uniform had been replaced by ragged, sun-bleached cut-offs

166

and a white tee-shirt with the logo of the Mobile Bay Birder's Project over one modest breast.

"I confess," she said.

"Confess what?"

"How I knew about the candles, that the victim was a nun, that Carla Hutchins was involved. I confess that I don't know how I know. That is, I don't know my source."

"You're . . ." I caught myself.

She leaned back and sipped her wine, unconcerned. "Lying? No. I rarely lie, Ryder, though you may not believe that. Sometimes, when I can't get a story any other way, I'll bend the truth –"

"Shred," I corrected.

"Twist," she refined, smiling. "Your move."

I leaned forward. "Why don't you know the source? He-she-they send messages in a bottle?"

"I get fast little phone hints. Why and who, I have no idea."

"Male or female?"

"The voice is muffled or filtered. Neither and both."

It stopped me. Hakkam, the manager at the Cozy Cabins, had described the caller who rented the room almost the same way:

Voice not up here like woman . . . not down here like man. In middle.

"Tell me what they say."

She rose, walked to the deck door, stepped outside. I shook my head and followed. She was leaning against the deck railing and studying the flat and shimmering Gulf.

"Danbury? Hello?"

She set her glass on the rail, turned. "Remember my barter offer? We're two-stepping into teamwork. Who's going to lead?"

"Teamwork? You're out of your mind."

"They're real interesting messages, Ryder. Coy, almost. Tantalizing little drops of information. But I get the feeling I'm being played. Everybody plays reporters, of course, that's the object of Spinworld. But there's something else here. I can't quite put my finger on it. Maybe someone more experienced with such things could figure it out." She batted her eyes at me, twisted a lock of hair, and affected the voice of Scarlett O'Hara. "Maybe someone jus' lak a big, strong policeman."

I didn't want to smile, but couldn't help it. "You're a piece of work, Ms Danbury."

She picked up her wine, sipped. A light breeze floated her hair as she studied me.

"We're alike in many ways, you know."

"How's that?"

"We see the seamier side of life. I cover murders and car crashes and suicides because that's what people tune in to see. I'm there as an observer, you as a participant. And it's going to continue no matter what – your participation, my observation. Let's drop the walls between our functions, just a bit, and see if it doesn't make things better for both of us."

"You're no longer an observer, Ms Danbury. If you're receiving information about the case, you're a participant."

She raised her glass to me. "Touché. But since the lines have already begun to blur, let's see where it goes. I'll start by

168

telling you about my source. Remember my last news bit, when I mentioned the candles in the victim's room?"

"I remember."

"No other station had that, the *Register* didn't. I knew because at three a.m. I got roused from my beauty sleep by a voice that said, 'Ask the cops about candles in the Cozy Cabins.' Click, that's it. Weird voice, blocked number. The next night the information got refined. Two-thirty a.m.: 'Ask about candles on the eyes.'"

"That's it?"

She held up three fingers. "Scout's honor, I didn't hear another peep until Saturday night."

"That the victim was Marie Gilbeaux."

"Of course, all the stations had the news that afternoon. It wasn't much of a scoop. Then, last night, I hear. 'Carla Hutchins in Chunchula.'"

"And you raced up to Hutchins's place. Used my name."

"I used it because I truthfully could: 'Ms Hutchins, I'm a reporter for Channel 14, and an acquaintance of Detective Carson Ryder. We're both looking into the circumstances surrounding the death of Marie Gilbeaux.'" She looked at me. "Is it true?"

"It's the truth," I admitted. "Bent and hobbled and walking on crutches, but it's the truth."

"I don't guess you ever did anything that lame in your work?"

I winced again. Danbury smiled a *gotcha* smile. "Like I said, we're not too different. Back to my question: Why is someone giving me little tastes of info about a dead woman and a live one?"

"All this could be coming from inside the department. Your own sources. You're just making up the late-night calls to yank my chain."

"I do have a few sources there, but I'm positive it's not them. You've done a good job of keeping them hushed. What's the tie between the women?"

"I don't know anything."

"Another 'no comment'?"

"Guess so."

"We'll find out, pogie. We're just getting started."

"We'll? We're? What's with the plural?"

She turned away and looked out over the blue water. She took a deep breath before turning to face me again.

"I was hoping you'd agree on your own to give me a little assist. Since it's going to happen anyway."

"Pardon me?"

"I didn't start this thing. You lost your cool with Borg. And I really did stand up for you with the station management. But the rest was my idea."

"What are you babbling about, Danbury?"

"This afternoon my station struck a deal with your chief. You're supposed to keep me in the loop on this case. Now that we're partners, Ryder, how about telling me what's really going on?"

She smiled hesitantly, waiting for my explosion of anger. I couldn't help it; I started laughing.

"You made a rotten deal," I said. "No one has the slightest idea."

CHAPTER 22

"You brought this on yourself, Ryder," Chief Plackett said, demoting me from detective to surname. He turned from the window behind his desk to face me. It wasn't a happy face.

"It came out of the blue is all I'm saying, Chief."

He put his knuckles on his desk, leaned toward me. "I didn't know the reporter would contact you so early. I was going to call you in this morning, give you the news about the agreement with Channel 14."

I glanced down at the globe, saw Siberia, looked away. "You didn't expect that the first thing she'd do would be to –"

"I'm not happy with the entire situation. I'm even less happy that you're trying to shift the emphasis from you to me."

"I didn't mean to, sir."

"Nor did you mean to manhandle the camera guy –"

"Videographer."

Plackett narrowed an eye at my correction. Where was Harry when I needed him? He would have heard what I was about to say, faked a sneeze halfway through the first syllable. Or simply punched me. The chief would probably have jumped Harry to lieutenant. Instead, Plackett turned back to the window, as if the oily morning mist was more attractive.

"Here's the way it's shaken out, Ryder. The station is forgetting you attacked one of their personnel. In return, one of their reporters – this Danbury woman – gets in the door. She wants first shot at a story on this case, and that's what we've agreed to allow her. Don't give away company secrets, but don't be prickly about sharing the other info. And make sure Nautilus is singing off that page, too."

"She's already stuck her nose where it didn't belong. If she does it again, it might –"

He spun back to me. "Zero," he snapped.

"Pardon, sir?"

"Your argumentation allowance on this, Ryder. It's zero. With a zee, as in zip your damn lips and keep them that way."

I nodded. He glared at me like he thought I nodded too loud. He jerked his thumb toward the door. I did the quietest nod possible, then crept out. I headed back to the detectives' room. Harry stood in Roy Trent's cubicle, Roy sitting long-faced with his arms crossed over a pile of files. When I walked up, Roy pushed back dark hair falling to his eyebrows, pointed to his brow.

172

"How's my forehead look, Carson?"

"Uh, looks fine, Roy. Why?"

He let the hair fall back. "I've been banging it into walls for a week. That backshooting ten days back, Orange Lady? It's not panning out the way I thought. We're missing something."

"You got our sympathy," Harry said. "But we got our own bucket of worms to untangle."

"Wanna trade buckets?" Roy asked, only half-joking. "Fresh perspectives, all that?"

"On one condition," Harry said. "There's no art involved, right? You didn't have any art laying around the body, did you? Shiny little pictures?"

Roy shook his head sadly. "Nope. Only thing near my vic's body was a pool of blood. And an orange."

Harry and I made our way back to our desks. It was quiet on the floor, a couple guys on phones, the rest out on individual trails of misery. Summer's heat was near peak, which always upped the homicide quotient. It didn't help that Plackett had assigned our open cases to the other dicks, letting us full-throttle this one – not that it was making a difference.

"The chief bang on your head a little?" Harry asked when we were out of Trent's earshot. "Thump you and lump you?"

"Shat on me and spat on me."

He mulled it over. "Not bad."

I said, "You no doubt heard rumors of an unholy alliance . . ."

"If you mean us and a certain lady reporter, I heard. We'll keep her inside just enough to make her think she's inside, but really . . ."

I shot a thumbs-up. "She won't get to know jackshit."

"There you go."

I looked up and saw my desk a dozen feet ahead of me. The desktop was a paper junkyard: files, folders, sticky notes, timelines, interviews, photos. But nothing had sparked that Aha! Moment – finding the single fact that pulls one event into alignment with another, then another and another . . . and the sound of falling dominos is like a twelve-string guitar set on High Anthem Rock.

All I saw was a silent pile I'd swam through a dozen times from six different directions. If I sat in front of it again, I'd drown.

I stopped dead in the middle of the floor.

"Carson?" Harry said. "You all right?"

"I need to see water," I said.

We were on the causeway fifteen minutes later, and I felt better than in days. A slender strip of land crossing northern Mobile Bay between Baldwin and Mobile counties, the causeway borders on holy. Wider stretches are home to fish camps, crab shacks and ramshackle bait shops. Here and there, vehicles park beside the two-lane, pickup trucks and station wagons predominant. Somewhere near the vehicle you'll see an old fisherman – black more often than not – kicked back in a lawn chair, rod in hand, hoping for a little luck. Sometimes entire extended families fish together, generations drawn to the water, to the causeway.

Another reason I love the causeway is that it bends to the whim of nature. Scant feet higher than the waves, the causeway occasionally gets flooded over. For a few days, it's home to flounder and specs and scuttling crabs. When it dries, we humans get sway of it again. Still, now and then, a big gator crawls from the Bay intent on taking a walk on the pavement. Traffic slows or stops until the sheriff's department sends someone out to relocate ol' snaggletooth. I love such moments.

Paralleling the causeway is the Bayway, an elevated conduit built to facilitate the passage of workers and goods to and from Mobile with the greatest possible dispatch. No floods, no gators, no families relaxing with a line in the water. I drive the Bayway only when speed is necessary or the causeway is closed. Like many contrivances designed to outwit nature and expedite commerce, it's a soulless creation, the antithesis of the causeway.

Harry pulled in behind an old junker either abandoned or awaiting repairs. We were at one of the wider pull-offs, a good twenty feet to the high reeds at the water's edge. The low waves slapped the shore. A pair of crabbers were pulling traps a couple hundred feet out in the Bay, dragging the rectangular baskets to the surface, checking for blues. They followed a rigorous pattern: check a trap, pull a few draughts from their beers, putter twenty or so feet to the next trap. I admired their methodology.

Harry and I leaned against the side of the car, drank convenience-store coffee, and stared at the crab fishermen. The sun was pushing higher and the water sparkled. I said, "I had to get away from my desk, bro. I'm getting sucked under by details."

Harry sipped, thought. He studied the abandoned wreck

down the way, pasted with bumper stickers: *I'm On the High Road to Heaven, Jesus Saves, Read Your Bible.*

"Strip it down to bumper stickers for me, Cars." He said, pointing at the junker, "Just like that."

"Do what?"

"Leave out the details. Tell me what's gone down in the fewest possible words."

I studied the crabbers and gathered my thoughts. "In 1970, Marsden Hexcamp kicks off a killing spree that lasts almost two years. He creates a collection of paintings and drawings based on at least six murders: his 'Art of the Final Moment'. Fast-forward to approximately two weeks ago. A man named Rubin Coyle is –"

"How big a bumper you got?" Harry said. "Edit."

I did some mental Cuisinarting, said, "Two weeks back, negotiator Coyle gets art in mail. Disappears shortly there-after."

"That's better. Keep going."

"Marie Gilbeaux killed the following Saturday or Sunday. Buried."

"Good," Harry said. "Then, on Monday –"

"We're made Officers of the Year," I joked.

Harry shot me the eye. I said, "Sorry. Monday or Tuesday, Marie Gilbeaux is dug up. Tuesday night her body is left in the Cozy Cabins. A strange and carefully crafted scene. Body found Wednesday, the same day someone mails art to her at the convent."

Harry popped the lid from another coffee, poured in three packets of sugar, two of cream, stirred it with his little finger.

"Art possibly created by the same artist who killed a half-dozen folks thirty years earlier. What else?"

"If you mean facts, that's all there is."

Harry shook coffee drips from his finger, sucked it. "You know, Cars, with all the loose wires cut off, one thing screams at me."

"Yeah," I said. "The exhumation. It makes no sense. Marie is dead and presumably hidden underground. Why call attention to the crime?"

"Exactly. And somehow, Carson, we're supposed to think this is being driven by thirty-five-year-old paintings from a guy who couldn't control his bowels."

"Rumor has it."

Harry laughed, a high and improbable warble.

"You know, Carson, without the dead bodies, this'd be a damn joke. Come on, let's go stare at some paper."

We stared until eight that night. Nothing happened.

CHAPTER 23

The bedside phone rang somewhere in my head. I looked at the clock: 4.24 a.m. I grabbed for the phone, dropped it, retrieved it from the floor.

"Rrrdr," I grunted.

"Cold water," the voice said.

"Hnnf?"

"Cold water, pogie. Go splash cold water on your face, then come back to the phone. It works; do it."

I stumbled to the kitchen sink, splashed. The pipes on Dauphin Island weren't deep and the heat seeped everywhere; the water was tepid. Still, the motion to and from the sink brought some blood to my brain. I stumbled back to the bedroom and picked up the phone.

"Danbury, if this is some kind of joke . . ."

"Who's Heidi Wicky?"

I searched my sputtering brain; the name didn't touch anything.

"I don't know a Heidi Wicky."

A pause. "That's strange. You knew Carla Hutchins."

"Are you working toward a point here?" I grabbed the pillow and blotted drips from my face and neck.

"I just got a call on my cell. That same plastic voice said, 'Heidi Wicky in Elrain.' That was all. Elrain's in Florida, right? The Panhandle?"

"Not that far," I said. "Two and a half hours, maybe less."

"Who's driving, partner?"

"So Danbury got another of these messages," Harry said as I left my car in front of his house and climbed into his. It was 5.45 a.m. I'd called him directly after receiving the alert from Danbury.

"Something's changed," I said. "It's an unknown name."

He paused; thought. "Right. It's been us knowing the thing, the info then going to Cu—, I mean, Danbury. Now things take a reverse spin."

"Or maybe we missed something somewhere."

Harry jammed the car into gear. "So we're heading over to Elrain, check out this woman, that's the plan?"

"Uh, one stop first. Got to grab a passenger."

Harry made a sound I'd never heard before, like a dying trombone.

Danbury lived in a well-kept brick two-story downtown near the Oakleigh Garden District. It surprised me, expecting

179

her to be a condo-in-the-burbs type. Bright flowers encircled the base of a foot-thick magnolia tree in the front yard, a half-dozen bird feeders hanging from its branches. Azaleas and myrtles bordered the house. Danbury was on the front porch sipping coffee when we rolled up. She wore a knee-length khaki skirt and a simple white linen blouse. White socks and running shoes provided a utilitarian air. I opened my door and stepped out.

"Sit up front," I said. "I prefer riding in back."

She gave me a strange look, bent to look in the door. "Is that Nautilus in there? Hi, Harry, been a while." He moaned softly as she slid into the front seat. Danbury said, "You sound a little gassy, Harry. Need some Di-Gel? Got a bottle in my purse."

Harry put the car in gear, climbed the curb, nearly clipped a phone pole, dropped down into the street. We were on our way.

"It's kind of like the Three Musketeers," Danbury said, winking. "Where's my feathered hat, guys?"

We'd estimated our arrival at eight fifteen. At nine we were raising dust across half the roads in Florida's western panhandle. It had been a quiet trip, Danbury trying to make small talk with Harry, him grunting responses. She finally said, "Is there something wrong with you, Harry Nautilus? You're treating me like my cologne is eau d'ratshit."

"How well do you remember our last encounter?"

She wrinkled her brow in thought for a few seconds. "A guy got shot over by Tillman's Corner. I said, Who was it?

You said Johnny Armstrong or whatever. I filed the story, moved on. Why?"

"I got cold feet, said drop it."

"You made nervous noises. I don't recall a hard-and-fast *don't*."

"I flat-out said not to run it."

"You told me you shouldn't have told me. That I recall. You putting the kibosh on the story, huh-unh."

"Guys," I said.

"I nearly got my ass transferred to ticket-writing limbo, Danbury."

"Yo, guys."

"Sorry about the misunderstanding, Nautilus. But not my fault."

"Not your fault? Who else would –"

"HEY, GUYS!"

Harry looked in the mirror, Danbury turned in her seat. I pointed to a hand-made sign beside the road.

"Didn't we pass a 'Prepare to Meet God' sign like that a few miles back?" I said. "Same bullet holes?"

Harry grunted. "A little help here, reporter lady."

Danbury unfolded the map. She spun it one direction, then another. "Borg always reads the maps. These things confuse me. N is north, right?"

We saw a mirror-bright dot a couple miles down the road, an object seemingly constructed of chrome. Approaching, we discovered it was a gas station – or so they're called – gleaming architectural whores screaming *Look at Me!*

"Stop for directions, Nautilus," Danbury said. "Before we drive up our own tailpipe."

"Me?"

"I'm not the one who took the wrong exit."

"There was no right exit, *Miss* Danbury. They all dump you into this endless damn nowhere."

"I'll do it," I said, hoping they didn't kill one another while I was inside.

Of all the abominations contemporaneity has visited upon the South, one of the worst is the gas-station-cum-convenience-store-cum-restaurant. The old stores-slash-fill-up stations were magic places, shady and comfortable, a good ol' boy or two hanging out, sipping a pop, stopped on the road between hither and yon. If you needed a stars'n'bars flag, a *Jesus Saves* bumper sticker, a decent machete, a box of twelve-gauge shells, there it was. There'd be a stack of melons outside, maybe some tomatoes and okra. If the pop machine stole your money, you always got it back.

They're disappearing fast, the stores near the main roads nearly extinct. It seems like a huge mother craft floats softly through the night skies, searching for the remaining ones. When it spots them, it hovers above, makes a shivering electronic sound, and drops a sparkling new BP or Exxon or Shell station over the old store and whisks away for new conquests.

In the morning no one seems to notice.

I bought root beer for Harry, a Dr Pepper for myself and a Diet RC for Danbury, asked the sullen lady at the counter for directions, then hustled outside. Harry and Danbury stared out their respective windows.

"The lady at the checkout said she thinks it's about five miles thataway," I said, pointing and climbing into the rear.

Harry said, "She wasn't sure?"

I shrugged. "Someone from the mother ship might have known, but they're long gone."

Danbury looked at Harry. "Mother ship?"

"You get used to it," Harry sighed, putting the car in gear. Asphalt turned to gravel. The double lane turned single. We pushed forward another mile or so, slowing at a railroad crossing.

I said, "The woman mentioned tracks. We're close."

We slowed to a crawl and banged over the poorest maintained crossing in the Western hemisphere as a treeful of buzzards looked on. Danbury reached into her outsized bag and produced compact binoculars. She lifted them to her eyes and studied the leering creatures as we approached their roadside haunt.

"Turkey vultures," I ventured.

"Black vultures, Ryder," Danbury corrected. "*Coragyps atratus*. Smaller and darker. White wingtips, too. A lot of people get 'em mixed up. Check the heads: red on turkeys, bald on blacks."

Harry drummed his fingers on the wheel. "Both are carrion eaters, Cars. But black vultures got a taste for live meat, too. The menu includes fresh-born calves, which doesn't make them real popular with ranchers."

Danbury turned to Harry, raised an eyebrow. She started to say something, but closed her mouth. His eyes didn't stray from the road. We continued down the gravel lane at fifteen miles an hour, piney woods on one side, fallow field on the other. We took a slight curve and I glimpsed an old house trailer tucked into a gnarl of brush a hundred feet from the road. The battered mailbox said WICKY, painted in an unsteady hand.

"Who do you think Heidi Wicky is, Danbury?" Harry said. "Why did you get the call? Why do you get any of these calls?"

She stared uncertainly at the trailer and shuddered. "I don't know, Nautilus. All I know is it's got to be eighty-five degrees in this car and I feel cold."

"Must be contagious," I said. "Pull in and let's see what there is to see."

We edged into an overgrown yard. The screen door of the trailer hung open, half off its hinges. The door behind it was ajar an inch or so. We climbed out to a welcoming committee of hungry skeeters.

"I spent all last night growing new blood," Harry said, slapping his neck. "There it goes."

I walked to the trailer carefully, peeked in the front windows. Harry headed around back. Danbury skirted past me, up the steps of the trailer. She knocked, called inside.

"Hello? Anyone home? Hello?"

"Stay back from there," I said. "Let me take a look."

Danbury called into the trailer again, then pushed open the door and stepped inward. "Damn," she said. "The place stinks like a –"

"Don't," I yelled. "Stay out until –"

Danbury screamed and exploded from the trailer backward, as if fired from a cannon. Black shapes hurtled through

184

the door behind her. She tumbled down the steps and rolled into the weeds. The shapes resolved into shrieking vultures winging furiously away. I ran to her.

"Are you all –"

"Yes, yes," she gasped, jabbing a finger toward the trailer. "Inside, Ryder. Jesus! Look inside."

She was shaken but unharmed. I climbed the steps, knowing too well the stench issuing from the door. Holding my breath, I stepped inside.

CHAPTER 24

Lieutenant Dorrel Ames of the Florida State Police looked up from his notepad. He'd removed his sunglasses to speak with us, a professional courtesy. The hat stayed on. Sweat beaded his frown-creased forehead and fell to his barrel chest.

"And you say you were here to . . ."

I said, "An interview, that's all. Questions about a thirty-year-old case."

He paused, lifted a sun-bleached eyebrow. "Still open?"

"Closed. We're not sure what we're looking for. One of those name-came-up sort of things."

I didn't mention our tip had come from the woman beside me. I didn't see how that would add anything but obfuscation. Maybe Ames would step into this hall of mirrors, see something we hadn't, more power to him.

Ames shot the cop eye at Danbury. "You say you're a TV reporter over in Mobile, ma'am?"

Danbury shined the pearly whites. "Channel 14."

Ames looked between me and Harry, his eyes splitting the difference between confusion and suspicion. "You fellas always travel with reporters?"

"It's temporary," Harry said. "Like a hurricane."

We turned to watch grim-faced local boys haul the body bag out the door and toward the ambulance, its lights pulsing red and white against the blue sky. They didn't have a hard time with the bag; there wasn't much left to carry. Ames pushed a pinch of snuff under his lip and shook his head.

"Doggone, that body got tore up good."

"The back door was open," Harry said. "Must have been how the *Coragyps atratus* got to her."

Ames said, "Beg pardon?"

"Black vultures," Danbury interjected.

Ames looked confused, so I offered him familiar cop words. "Did you know the deceased, Lieutenant? Is there anything in her past to suggest foul play here?"

Ames shook his head, tipped back his hat. "She wasn't open to getting known. Not nasty about it, just kept to herself. Never any kind of trouble here. I stopped by a time or two to see if she needed anything . . ."

"Hey, Lute," an evidence tech with a camera yelled from the door of the trailer. "Got something strange here." The guy stared at an object in his hand. "Taped to the ceiling right above where her body was, like she was looking at it when she died."

His gloved fingers displayed a small snippet of art, a few inches square. Heavy glazing, rich color, dense texture. Little wriggles of gold spun from what might have been the eyeholes of a crushed skull, or maybe it was just the effect of the shadowing.

"Is that some kind of worm?" the tech said, pointing beside an eyehole. "Or just a weird shape?"

"I don't know what the hell any of it is," Ames said softly. "But damn, I can't keep my eyes off it."

"We've got to get to Hutchins," I whispered to Harry. "Fast."

We turned onto Hutchins's road after only two white-knuckle hours of Harry with his foot deep into the floor. There was a line of dust in the air from a postal carrier chugging down the road, the snubnosed white van stopping beside the sparse mailboxes. Harry bleated the horn and shot past the van. We pulled into Carla Hutchins's front yard and Harry drove to the front porch, almost up the steps.

"Carla," Harry bayed, thundering up the steps. "Miz Hutchins! It's Detective Nautilus. You inside?"

The screen door slapped open and Hutchins stepped onto the porch, her eyes quizzical. She was in a white tee and jeans, a blue bandana holding back her long hair.

"Are you all right?" Harry asked. "Everything fine here? We've been trying to call, but couldn't get through."

"Internet. I leave it on, no one calls but people selling things." Hutchins's eyes found Danbury. "She's that reporter. Why's she here?"

Harry said, "She knows about the case, Carla. Not much, but she knows. But Ms Danbury pledges not to use your name in anything without your written approval or she goes right back to the car and stays there until we're done. Right, Ms Danbury?"

Danbury wasn't happy with Harry's ad hoc rules. But she nodded and said, "Right."

Hutchins said, "What's going on?"

"It's about a woman named Wicky. Heidi Wicky. Ever hear that name?"

Hutchins's eyes stared into Harry's for several seconds. "I knew a Heidi once. Back in the you-know-when."

"I thought you didn't go by regular names, you made up –"

"Demeter. That's what most people knew her as. But she spoke French and English. Some German too, I think. I asked her about it once. She said she was Swiss. The only Swiss name I could think of was from a movie I saw when I was a kid, *Heidi*. I joked about it, asked if her name had been Heidi. She said yes, thought it was funny. She never mentioned her last name. I guess by that time it didn't mean anything anymore."

"By that time?"

"She'd been with . . . him from the start, from the Paris days."

I shot Harry a look; Marie Gilbeaux had also been with Hexcamp's original contingent.

"Who else was in from the start?"

"Persephone – Marie. Calypso, of course; she may have been the first to attach to him. Heidi. There were a couple of others, but I think they just drifted away. Why do you want to know?"

Harry took a deep breath. "We're just back from Ms Wicky's place over in the Panhandle. She's been living in Elrain, just a few miles above –"

The postman rolled up, honked, waved a few pieces of mail. "Be right back," Hutchins said, striding the hundred feet to the roadside. She took the mail from the carrier, made a few seconds of small talk.

"How much you want to tell Carla?" I said to Harry, keeping my voice low as Hutchins started toward us, shuffling through the letters.

"At this point? Whatever keeps her safe."

"But from what?" Danbury said.

We heard a piercing wail. Carla Hutchins stood a dozen steps away, pointing at the ground and making nonsense noises. Harry got there first, me on his heels. Hutchins held an opened brown envelope. I recognized the block lettering. My eyes followed her hand to the ground. There, in the grass, lay a strip of art on canvas, so deliciously bright it looked wet. Harry pulled her away from the scrap.

"Easy, Carla. We don't even know what it is."

"*I* know what it is," she keened. "And I know who made it. Something horrible's happening, isn't it? He, they, *something's* found me?"

"It's all right, Carla," Harry said gently, keeping her hand in his. "You'll be fine."

"I'm out here in the middle of *nowhere*," she wailed.

Danbury stepped up and took Hutchins's arm, moved her gently from Harry and toward the porch.

"No you're not, Carla. As of this afternoon you're staying

in Mobile in a big secure house. Mine. I got enough alarm systems to call J. Edgar Hoover out of his grave."

"It's not your place to . . . I can't let you do –"

"You can and will. Let's go get you packed." Danbury steered Hutchins toward the door. "Besides, Ms Hutchins, it won't be for long. You've got the pogobo twins on your side, the golden hounds of the PSIT, and they got their picture in the paper to prove it. They'll clean up this little matter in a day or two." Danbury shot a worried look over her shoulder at Harry and me. "Right, boys?"

CHAPTER 25

Harry and I waited while Danbury helped Hutchins get packed. Hutchins was too shaken to drive, so Danbury handled the chore. We escorted them to Mobile, then broke off and headed for Forensics. Hembree was pouring a cup of tea from a beaker. I handed him the bagged piece of art and gave him a quick synopsis of our day.

"You get anything back from the Bureau on that piece of art from the convent?" I asked.

He reluctantly set the swatch of bright and swirling color on the lab table. "I know a few folks at the Bureau, managed to get it front-burnered."

Hembree's technical and intuitive abilities had, over the years, dramatically heightened his stature in Bureau eyes. They even brought him to Quantico to lecture once in a while, the result being a few important strings he could pull when the occasion warranted it.

"Timeline?" I asked.

"They're making some progress, and hoping to overnight what they have so far."

Harry said, "What sort of work would they do on art?"

"You want the ten-dollar answer?"

Harry put his hand in his pocket, jingled his coins. Hembree looked disappointed. "OK then, the quarter-nickel-dime version is laser-directed spectrographic analysis plus a carbon-fourteen . . ."

Harry held up his hand. "Already more than I need to know."

Hembree sighed. "They check the age, check to see if it's layered – anything underneath – test pigment composition and so forth. That's the medium, the paint and ink. Then they'll check the canvas, basically for the same qualities. They were also having one of their art types study the composition itself, brush strokes, pigment mixture, and so forth."

"We blissfully ignorant types thank you. That'll give us all there is to know about this swatch?"

Hembree grinned. "Hardly. That's a prelim. We're talking complex analyses here. It could be weeks before anything else comes through."

"So we probably won't have anything to help us find this stuff that's floating around?"

"Not unless the Bureau can make the scrap of painting talk: 'Hi, I was torn from a larger canvas currently at 15 Maple Lane, Atlanta, Georgia.'"

Harry frowned. "They can't do that? Well, shit, Bree, what the hell good are they?"

We gave Danbury a couple hours to get Carla squared away, then headed over. She was in the front yard filling feeders with birdseed.

"How's Carla?" Harry asked.

"In the guest room. Snoring. I don't think she's slept since you guys first showed up last Saturday; it brought back too much of the past. Today she went into stress overload and I think her mind felt like shutting down for a while. She relaxed a bit after I showed her my fondness for locks and alarms."

Danbury set one bag of seed to the ground, picked up another. "Driving down here with Carla I got an idea of what you're looking into. She told me the highlights about crazy Marsden and his down-on-the-farm circus."

I said, "She mention Marie Gilbeaux?"

"What little she knew. Poor Marie. I got the impression there were just a few bloodthirsty types on this tour from hell, the rest were pathetic little followers. The savagery seemed to come from Hexcamp, channeled through some wacko Nazi bitch . . ."

"Calypso."

"Jesus, yes. Just saying her name made Carla start shaking. Marsden and Calypso were like, 'Hey, kids, let's put on a show,' and little Buffy and Timmy and Marie and Carla and Heidi and Johnny – or whatever their Marsden names were – all these ragtag castoffs lined up for instructions, thinking they were part of some great experiment in artistic expression." Danbury's eyes flicked to the house. "Over thirty years later and that woman in there still basically thinks of herself as a piece of walking filth."

"Did talking with Carla give you any insights into what might be going on? Or spark questions we might not have considered?"

Danbury poured black seeds into a long tube, re-hung it in the magnolia. "One thing stood out. Doesn't it seem little Marsden bloomed in a hurry? One day he's a hotshot student at a hoity-toity Parisian art academy, the next he's leading a tribe of nutcases through south Alabama, killing people and behaving in a woefully inappropriate manner. I'd like to know if Marsden left anything behind him on the fields of France."

Harry snorted. "It's hard enough to find out anything that happened in Mobile thirty years ago. Tracking events ten thousand miles away'd be almost impossible."

"More like five thousand miles," Danbury said.

Harry shut his eyes and shook his head. "What's it matter? It's still a major hassle; in case you ain't heard, Danbury, they speak French in France."

Danbury looked surprised. "Really? Where do they speak Italian?"

Harry glared at her. She said, "Don't shoot those eyes at me, Nautilus. If you'd like a look at the French connection, pass the hassle my way."

"What are you talking about?"

She said, "You've got other things to do, right? Let me do what I do damned good – research."

"You'd do it anyway, wouldn't you?"

"Of course. But I'd prefer to do it for us and not me."

Harry went to the car, got copies of a few files we'd gathered on Hexcamp, enough to get her started. He said, "Count us, Danbury."

"What?"

"How many people in the yard?"

"Three."

"Which is exactly how far this information goes, got it?"

He handed her the files. She looked at him, cocked an ear toward his belly.

"You're getting that gassy sound again, Nautilus. You sure you don't want a Di-Gel?"

CHAPTER 26

Harry and I went to HQ to fill out paperwork. It was closing in on nine p.m. in a day that started before four a.m., taking us to Florida, Chunchula, and back to Mobile. We were too beat to speak, communicating via grunt. He grunted he was getting coffee, I grunted I didn't want any. My phone rang and I grunted at it. It kept ringing so I picked it up.

"Hunh?"

"That you, Carson? This is Taylor Maybry."

Maybry was CAP, Crimes Against Property, theft mainly, an empty-the-ocean-with-a-spoon kind of job, given there were people who considered theft a legitimate job category.

I staunched a yawn. "Hey, Taylor. What can I do for you?"

"I been away a few days, fishing up in Tennessee. Striped bass. I was up three days and we nailed over a dozen stripers.

You been fishing lately? Last I heard you'd been out in that kayak, but I think that was last year . . ."

With Maybry you waited for a split-second hesitation, jumped in. "Something get stolen, Taylor?"

He paused, trying to remember why he'd called. "Oh yeah. Got back yesterday and heard about the woman in the motel, the candles and all, y'know? Freaky piece of action. Good thing you and Harry are on it . . ."

Mabry hesitated a millisecond. I said, "Candles?"

"Last Tuesday I got a call to a boutiquey place in the Azalea Center, little strip mall. Store called Karmic Revolution. Like where hippies go when they get old."

"Candles, Taylor. Candles."

"A woman, fifty-four, calls herself Freedom Sunshine, real name's Esther Gargletta, was closing up. She steps outside to haul in a display of books and CDs – whales yodeling, that kind of thing – when bam! someone knocks her cold. Call came in at nine oh-six. I rolled up, paramedics are there. She's woozy, but wants to check things out. Nothing seems missing. Cash in the drawer, plain sight, untouched. We figured maybe someone's got a grudge against Lady Sunshine. She'd run some skateboard punks off the lot the day before, maybe they wanted revenge, bonked her with a board, y'know . . ."

"Candles, Tay?"

"She got around to taking inventory today, Carson. What's missing? Two cases of candles from the FlameBrite Waxworks in Lexington, Kentucky. An assortment – different colors and smells and sizes, but more of what they call their Jumbo Brites than anything. Can you believe they make a cantaloupe-

198

scented candle, Carson? What you think they do, chop cantaloupe into the wax?"

"Not a clue who did it, Taylor. Am I right?" I was beginning to associate this perp with extreme caution.

"Bonk, y'know? Miz Sunshine goes lights out with not a witness around. Or how about a celery-scented candle? Can you believe that? Who'd want their whole house smelling like celery? It's a strange world out there, Carson. Scary, you think about it, celery candles . . ."

The night was sliding from dark blue to black when we turned onto the street holding the Karmic Revolution. It was in a small strip mall holding a dry cleaners, an H&R Block outlet and a defunct pizzeria. Everything around it was dark.

Harry pointed to the store-wide front window of Karmic Revolution, a good twenty feet of glass. Painted across the window in foot-wide brush strokes was CANDLE SALE – *50% OFF!* The red words were backlit by the light in the store.

"Letters big enough a bat could see them from Birmingham," Harry said. "That's kind of interesting."

A bell tinkled as we walked into a cloud of sandalwood incense. The store was half devoted to contemporary versions of bell, book and candle, the other to clothing. I had thought tie-dye dead. A heavyset woman with a haystack of frizzy gray hair studied us from behind a counter, probably guessing we wouldn't buy a lot of celery candles. Harry buzzed the woman with his badge. Madam Freedom Sunshine herself.

"I knew you'd find them," she said. "The cards told me."

"Cards, ma'am?" Harry said.

I looked at the counter and saw an array of Tarot cards. She tapped one with a blue fingernail. "Justice. That's you. You've found who knocked me out, stole the candles."

"Sorry, ma'am," Harry said. "The candles might be evidence in another crime. We just need you to run through it again, if you'd be so kind."

She frowned at the cards, then pushed them into a drawer like they were being punished for lying. "I was closing up Tuesday night, bringing in the outside sales racks. I bent to pick up a crate of CDs when everything went black. I woke up a few minutes later and called 911. Then I made a headache tea of betony, marjoram and cloves."

"You'd been in an altercation with some skateboarders recently?" I asked.

"A couple days before. They're always racing through here, jumping from the steps or hopping up on the railings. I went out and chased them off. They were shooting the finger, laughing."

"Did you feel threatened?" Harry asked.

"No. It's almost like a ritual, been going on for months. They sweep in, do their hops and whatever, until me or Ben from H&R Block run them off. But I can't think of anyone else angry at me. And to steal some candles seems so juvenile . . ."

While Harry re-interviewed Sunshine, I inspected the latest in healing crystals, moon-print gowns, scented balms, and body adornments. I was in an aisle of Close-Out Specials when I froze at the sight of a basketful of rings, a sign above them proclaiming ALL RINGS $5.99.

I ran my hand through the basket and plucked out models worn by Marie Gilbeaux. I yelled "Heads-up" and tossed a startled Harry a Celtic cross ring followed by a pentacle ring.

He stared at them. "Someone did a lot of last-minute shopping here, Cars."

"Were any of these taken the night you were assaulted?" I asked Sunshine.

"They're just cheapies. Someone could have grabbed half of them and I wouldn't have noticed. Did you hear that a dress was wadded by the back door? Like the kid grabbed it, decided at the last minute he didn't want it."

"Dress?" Harry said. "It still around?"

"It was filthy and torn. I threw it away."

Harry studied where the dress had lain, then walked quickly to the front of the store, checking displays. He walked to the basket of rings, then looked at the rear door.

"Come on, Cars. Let's take a ride."

Harry fired up the engine and we screeched from the lot. He blew through a red light, setting off a blare of horns, then drove a block north on Highway 31. He swung into a restaurant lot and 360'd back to the street, heading back toward Karmic Revolution.

"Harry? There lyrics to this tune?"

"Pretend it's last Tuesday night," Harry said. "I'm the perp. I'm heading into town from somewhere north. There's a body in my trunk or wherever. For some reason I just dug her up. For some reason I'm taking her to the Cozy Cabins."

I started to twit him, but held my tongue when I realized he was riding an intuition rush, something singing from his gut. He said, "It's like now, dark. This street shoots me straight across town to Cozy Cabins. I'm driving along . . . then BANG!" He slammed on the brakes and squealed to the curb. I jammed my hand against the dashboard.

"Jesus, Harry – what?"

"I look over there and see . . ." he aimed his finger and my eyes followed: CANDLE SALE – *50% OFF!*

Harry motored into the strip mall's lot and slid behind the building, stopping in back of Karmic Revolution. We got out. He checked the steel rear door of the store; locked. Harry did stealthy, flattening himself against the side of the building, peering around the corner.

"OK, our perp sees Freeshine Sundown outside, taking the items inside, her back to him."

Harry three-stepped to the door, made a swinging motion. "The killer slips around the corner, coldcocks Miz Sunfree, drags her inside. Five seconds total, it's a slam-dunk. C'mon."

He thundered into the store. Ms Sunshine looked up, surprised. "Won't be but a moment, ma'am," Harry said, striding to a rebuilt display of candles. "The candles were out here in front or in the stockroom?"

"In front. I used full cases to build up the display."

Harry jogged to the stockroom, looked inside, nodded at the back door.

"Was the back-door alarm armed, ma'am?"

"I'd taken out the trash and hadn't reset the alarm."

Harry pushed the door open. A large trash bin was in back. Harry rooted through it until he found a torn yellow drapery, probably from the dry cleaners.

"What the hell's that?" I asked.

"A dress," he said over his shoulder, running back inside. Ms Sunshine shot me an *is-he-sane?* glance.

"Method detecting," I whispered. "Stanislavsky."

We followed Harry to the display of candles in the front. "Begging your pardon, ma'am, but you're now unconscious on the floor. I see the display of candles, maybe look in back, find the location of the door. I want a couple boxes of candles for later. They're heavy. So I . . ." He reached to the nearby dress rack, mimed pulling a dress from a hanger. "So I grab a dress and lay it on the floor."

Harry laid the drapery down and put two crates of candles on it. He picked up the edge of the fabric and backed toward the storeroom, the candles following easily on the waxed floor. He passed the basket of rings.

"I'm pulling the candles out when I see the basket of rings. So I pick up a handful."

We followed back into the storeroom as he bumped open the back door, laid the boxes in the alley, kicked the drapery to the side.

"That about where you found the dress, Ms Sunshine?"

"Exactly."

It all fit. It may have been wrong, but in theory it was elegant. "That's incredible, Harry."

"This trip's not done yet."

We bade farewell to a bemused Sunshine and rejoined the Crown Vic, roaring back onto 31.

"What else was in the room, Cars?"

"Flowers. Some OK, some worn and wilted."

Harry drove for six more blocks, looking side to side. He pointed and grinned and pulled into a small cemetery. Graves surrounded us, many decorated with flowers. Harry leaned against the fender, gestured at the graves, some with bright bouquets, others topped with faded flowers.

"Folks set out fresh posies on weekends, Sunday, mainly. The killer could grab up a few sprays easy. Fresh ones, old ones. Toss 'em in the vehicle with the candles and cheesy rings."

He smiled and crossed his arms, his foot tapping like there was music in his head.

"It's possible our perp was making up a lot of stuff as he went along, Carson. I think that's real interesting. How 'bout you?"

CHAPTER 27

"Carrol Ransburg."

I recited my alter ego's name to the face in the mirror while pasting down my hair with goo. It was Friday, and I had an eight a.m. date with Marcella Baines. I studied my face: suntanned from fishing, the beard line no razor could completely erase, brown eyes that occasionally scared me with their intensity, as when captured on film by the *Mobile Register*'s photographer.

What had compelled Trey Forrier to see kindness in such a face?

It didn't matter; he was mad down to his marrow. Probably saw the world in reverse. The man had a harsh and ugly face, made hideous masks before killing people.

"Carrol Ransburg."

Yet Ava had found something in my face, or seemed to. Her fingers often trailed delicate patterns across my brow and cheek as we made slow and gentle love in my box in the air above an island, the surf rolling against the sand a hundred yards away.

I'd thought those moments but a foretaste of the magic to come, making our way into and through one another's lives. Jeremy was right in one respect: I believed the feeling to be Love, as I had never known such a potent feeling before. Women had come and gone in my life, delights laid easy and often into my memory, but I had never lost my breath when any other woman walked through the door, had never stared at the phone waiting for a call, had never felt myself one of the *chosen*.

And then – just like that – she was gone.

"Carrol Ransburg."

I called out my false name one more time, tightened my tie, and turned from the mirror. I slipped on my suit coat, and headed for Pensacola and my encore visit to Mme Baines's chamber of horrors.

"I could have been Marsden's queen, you know," Marcella Baines whispered. "The Queen of the Final Moment . . ."

This time Marcella had opened her door not in a pantsuit but a high-slit sheath of white silk, the décolletage cut to her sternum, her low, hard-tipped breasts shivering against the fabric.

". . . one of the great tragedies of my life . . . had I known Marsden was thirty miles north in his studio, I would have been with him . . ."

There had been no caviar and talk of the weather. She led me straight to the "gallery", leaning against me on a love seat beneath the twisted photographs. I had maneuvered her into talking about Hexcamp, and she seemed almost hypnotized by her own words.

"I would have been a few years older than the others, but it would have given me an advantage. I would have been his inspiration, his triumph, his glory."

"I'm sure you would have, Ms Baines."

Her perfume filled the air. It wasn't the cloying floral scent of older women, but something tart, youthful. She'd added crimson highlights to her hair, now lacquered in unruly spikes. Iridescent green shadow pushed the boundaries of her eyes. Her lips were the purpled red of venous blood, her teeth wet and somehow obscene.

"He would have died for me, and I for him. That's what love is, Mr Ransburg." Her eyes were distant, her words spoken from afar. I wondered if she was using a drug.

"You would have been perfect, Ms Baines."

When she crossed her legs I noted how high the slit in her dress was cut. One long leg floated before me, blue-green veins visible beneath white hose garter-belted in place. She leaned harder against me, and I felt her hand rest on my thigh.

"Marsden worked only by candlelight, did you know that? He said when you work by fire, the fire reaches inside your work, illuminates it from within. That was Marsden, Mr Ransburg, lit from within, drawing so many beautiful wings to his light."

"Moths die in pursuit of fire," I said.

Her hand began crawling upward, her nails red flames on my black suit. "Butterflies, Mr Ransburg. They exalt in the sun." Her mouth was inches from mine, her eyes glazed. "Where was I at the time? Married to a succession of fools and eunuchs. Hiding in my room with my collections of coins, using them to discover who I was, to make sense of life, find its fire. All the time Marsden Hexcamp was a few miles north, seething with magic, burning with genius."

"Miss Baines, Marcella –"

Her nails scratched at the top of my thighs. "He had to see them die, you know, see the whole of the final moment. It's all there if the moment is done correctly, everything is revealed. My fellas, my beautiful boys, they knew that. But they could only enjoy, not create."

Her hand reached my crotch, began kneading. Her breath was shallow, her face flushed. Her eyes looked through me. "He's coming back, Mr Ransburg," she purred. "Marsden's coming back."

"What do you mean?"

"Someone's been found."

"Who?" I gasped, closing my legs tight.

"Someone with the voice to say, 'Yes, Marsden Hexcamp created this work . . . it can finally come alive!'"

"Who? Who is this person?"

Her bright nails hissed across the fabric of my pants, burrowed beneath my testicles, squeezed. "It doesn't matter, Mr Ransburg, it only matters that Marsden will be alive again! Oh my god, I'm about to . . ."

208

She grabbed my hand and jammed it under her dress. "I'm flowing like a river," she choked. "Like a fucking goddamn river." She clamped her thighs around my hand while hers clawed at my zipper.

"When will . . . the work . . . be reviewed?" I gasped. She dropped her huge mouth into my lap and began gnawing and licking. I felt saliva falling from her mouth.

"Ms Baines, I can't . . ."

"Don't fail me, Ransburg," she grunted, her breath hot against my groin. "I *own* you."

I pushed away. Standing on shaking legs, I jammed my shirt back into my pants, retreated to the door. She wobbled erect. Her hair had fallen to one side, her dress clung between her thighs. Her lipstick had smeared to a crimson slash. The glassiness in her eyes was replaced by hatred. Her lips were drawn back and I saw the full fury of her teeth.

I spun wordlessly and escaped from the penthouse, feeling the room about to burst into a black fire kindled long ago.

CHAPTER 28

"She was howling and growling in your lap?" Harry stared from his desk across from mine. It was ten a.m., my visit to Marcella Baines accomplished in two and a half hours, travel included. If nothing else, I was efficient.

"I don't want to talk about it." I was working on my written postmortem of the visit to Ms Baines. They'd be strange notes.

"Carson?"

"What?"

"You said she ran her hand up the inside of your –"

"Briefly."

"She had on hose and garters? Without any, uh –"

"Not a stitch."

Harry twirled a pencil in his fingers for a few seconds, then tapped a nervous rhythm on the desk. "Um, was there any point in the process, Carson, where you felt, uh, the least bit . . . ?"

"Never."

The eraser tapped for another minute. "Cars . . . ?"

"*What?*"

"When she jammed your hand up her dress, talking about rivers and suchnot, an old lady like that, was she, was it . . . ?"

I closed my eyes. Did a half-millimeter nod.

"Lawd," Harry whispered, then retreated across the room to seek the solace of a donut. Bertie Wagnall's voice wheezed from my speakerphone.

"Ryder, there's a Lydia Barstool for you, line five."

The name threw me until I remembered she was the AWOL Coyle's paralegal.

"Barstow, Bertie."

"Close enough. Hey, what happened with that Danbury broad? She ain't leaving call slips down here. You guys have a tiff, or what? You did, you can send her my way. I'd sure like to –"

"Hello, Ms Barstow. How can I help you?"

"I'm – I'm not sure if you can. I was going through Rubin's raincoat in the closet this morning. I found some kind of tape."

"Recording tape, like a cassette?"

"From one of those pocket recorders. He doesn't sound right. Like he's nervous or something."

"What's the tape about?"

"That's another thing. I can't tell. Usually I know the

211

project, it's immediately evident. Not this time. Maybe it's nothing, but . . ."

I looked at the paperwork on my desk, sighed. "We'll be right there, Ms Barstow."

"I'd like to meet somewhere other than the office, if that's all right. There's a coffee shop two blocks to the west?"

"Give us twenty minutes."

The coffee shop was a multinational corporation masquerading as a neighborhood establishment. The paralegal was at a table hidden behind a potted plant with fronds the size of canoe paddles. Above her was a huge painting that looked as if a chimpanzee had dipped its ass in paint and scootched across the canvas. I peeked through fronds. "Dr Livingstone, I presume?" The table held a cup of coffee and a silver microcassette recorder.

Lydia managed a half-smile. Harry pushed past me and sat, meaning I was supposed to fetch the brews. I jogged to the service counter, considering getting him a Caramelized Frappacilious Macarena or whatever, then, sane again, asked for two regulars. I went back to the table, set a cup in front of Harry and sat across from Miss Lydia. Harry was saying, "And the tape you found this morning was where?"

Lydia was muted for business – beige skirt, jacket, shoes. The past few days seemed to have aged her, or maybe the sun from the window laid harder shadows into the corners of her eyes.

"The recorder was in his raincoat, Detective Nautilus. In the office closet. It's not unusual, he was always dropping things like his good pens and his cellphone and whatnot in his raincoat. It's one of those coats with all the pockets. We laughed about it, called it his 'second office'."

"Anything else in there – his raincoat?"

"No, just the recorder. Oh, and a map, sorry."

She reached to her purse and produced a folding map of the Mobile area. Harry took the map and set it aside, picked up the recorder.

"Why didn't you take the tape to the head of the firm, this Mr Hamerle?"

Her eyes skittered from the floor to the wall to the fronds to the door.

"Miz Barstow," Harry said. "You all right?"

"I don't know quite how to say this. I'm . . . frightened of him."

"Mr Hamerle?" I said.

She nodded, two small twitches. "Since Rubin's disappearance, Mr Hamerle's become very demanding and quick to anger. He's also been very interested in Mr Coyle's office, sometimes going in and closing the door. I hear things. He's searching. When I found the tape, I wondered if . . ."

"The tape was the object of his search."

"I'm just a paralegal, part-time at that. There might be legal ramifications, confidentiality. It's beyond me. That's when I thought I'd kind of . . ." she pushed on the half-smile again, "pass the buck to you people."

Harry patted Lydia's hand without making it an invasion of space, something I had yet to learn. "You did good, Miz Barstow."

I said, "What made you think the tape was important?"

"There's an edge to his voice, an intensity I've never heard before. Usually, even on a major project, he's almost chatty when recording, like talking to a friend. But this sounds like he was scared, like he didn't want anyone to hear. Plus I can't tell what client he's working for."

"Let's take a listen," I said.

The cassette hadn't progressed much from start point. Harry rewound it, pressed Play. A voice came from the silver box.

"That's Mr Coyle," Lydia said. "He always started with the client name and project number. He doesn't mention either here."

"Off the books? Or a personal project?" Harry mused.

Coyle had a reedy but well-modulated voice with a soft whisper of southern accent, the aristocratic version, or what passes for it. Even if Lydia hadn't clued us in to the tension she'd found in Coyle's voice, I'd have picked up on it. He spoke in the *sotto voce* of a person carrying on a clandestine conversation. There were pauses between his sentences as he formed thoughts.

". . . negotiations must be conducted in utmost secrecy and will involve moving quickly between parties. It should be considered that the object of the bidding may frequently wish to be viewed by the involved parties while bidding is under way. This is not a negative in this situation, the nature of the object will, by its viewing, spur additional bids . . ."

I heard him writing in the background, then a sheet torn from a notepad, crumpled.

"Object?" Harry said.

". . . consider a resort setting. Or a motel where the units are individualized. Bidders may not wish to see one another. Secure one unit per party to allow bidders privacy. There are several almost unwholesome places which actually might be better suited than more expensive venues . . ."

"Individualized unwholesomeness," Harry said. "Is that the Fodor's listing for Cozy Cabins?"

". . . I anticipate bidding to become very intense near the end . . ."

"Whatever it is, it sounds big," Harry said.

". . . at a set time the final bids will be reviewed. Care must be taken that the departing participants have no contact with one another, again respecting their privacy."

The tape hissed for several more seconds, then the sound of unrecorded tape. "That's all," Lydia said. "On the whole thing."

Lydia looked between us, perplexed. Harry snapped open the map found in Coyle's pocket. He studied for several long seconds.

"My, my," he mumbled.

"What?"

He pushed aside his coffee and set the map on the table, tapping it with his finger. "A half-dozen locations circled in red. It looks like one of them is our old friend, the Cozy Cabins."

I felt a buzz of excitement, a sense that we were finally touching something that might lead us forward. Harry called them the invisible lines. We rarely saw them until closing in on a case, when it was revealed that we had been tripping over them all the time.

"Privacy's real big," Harry said, more to himself. "Doesn't want whoever to bump into one another."

"And you have no idea if this is a project for the firm, Ms Barstow?" I asked.

"It's nothing I ever worked on," she said, fear in her voice. "Though he had been giving some thought to upcoming negotiations for Lewis Aragorn. That's nothing specific, it's kind of like an on-going project."

"Lewis Aragorn?" I said. "*The* Lewis Aragorn?"

"A genius, he's a fucking genius. When you guys called and told me he was missing, I felt so sick I nearly ralphed, the Big Gorgonzola all across my desk, y'know?"

Lewis Aragorn slapped the top of the desk he'd nearly done the Big Gorgonzola on, then stood and walked to a window overlooking the Mobile River, a vista of cranes and containers and ship superstructures.

Aragorn was the approximate size of a channel buoy, and when he stood in front of the window, the room darkened. It wasn't that bright to begin with – a single bank of fluorescents above mason-block walls with faded blue paint, brown industrial linoleum on the floor. The desk's warpage suggested Cuban refugees had sailed it to Miami by way of Juneau. Aragorn jammed his hands into the pockets of unpressed khakis and made a guttural sound I took as a sigh. His thick-furred forearms jutted from rolled-up white sleeves and resembled phone poles with a slight taper at the wrists. Aragorn's hard-worn face looked like his parents were Charles Bronson and Keith Richards, and there was genuine sadness between the crags and wrinkles.

"The man was a fucking genius, a born negotiator. He saved our ass a couple times; everybody's ass."

Aragorn headed the dockworkers' local, a hard and hard-core occupation. He'd held it for fourteen years, after spending almost twenty as a dockworker himself. He looked down as if studying his loosened blue tie, maybe wondering how'd he ever come to wear such a useless item. When Harry leaned forward, the folding chair squeaked beneath him; Aragorn wasn't big on office furniture.

"And you'd meet him in motels to hammer out these nego-tiations or whatnot, Mr Aragorn?" Harry asked.

"Hell-fucking-yes, we'd meet in motels for planning sessions. I'm not high on trusting my opponents. No big deal; they don't trust me. You never know who can get into a fancy office and lay out some electronic shit, pick up on your pos-itions, what's real, what's fallback. Shit, I'd do it to them if I could."

"You had no quarrel with Rubin Coyle?"

Aragorn's eyes widened. "Quarrel? He fucking kept us out of nasty strikes, wildcats. There are new things going on in the industry, new loading, unloading facilities. Container-ization's getting sophisticated, computers doing more. We got to balance getting our honest cut with keeping the work flowing. That's what Rubin did. He'd take their position, ours, then diddle a line here, a benefit there, keep us moving together. It's hard to find someone both sides trust, but everybody trusted Rubin Coyle. Damn, if he's gone . . ." Aragorn shook his head and upended palms the size and texture of baseball mitts. He looked like tears were about to flashflood the gulleys of his face. "What it is, I think, he knows people. You can't learn that shit in school, you just know it."

I fired a shot in the dark. "What about the Cozy Cabins? They ever enter the negotiations?"

"Hunh? The what cabins?"

"Nothing. Just a part of the investigation."

"You ever hear him talk about art, Mr Aragorn?" Harry asked. "Or maybe a portfolio, a collection of art?"

The cragged face showed confusion. "Rubin? I know shit about art, buddy. That means Rubin probably knew like minus shit. He never cared about fancy stuff like that. But I'll tell you what, you got some kind of negotiation has to do with art – or fuckin' anything – Rubin Coyle would be your go-to guy."

CHAPTER 29

We figured it was time to talk to the senior partner at the law firm, Warren Hamerle. Since it appeared he wasn't going to come to us – convalescing from what Lydia Barstow referred to as an attack of angina – we went to him. We had to play it light, no inference that we'd talked to Miss Lydia, sensing Hamerle would take it as betrayal and boot her out on the street.

The lot of Hamerle's large, two-story Spring Hill home was canopied with live oaks and sunlight broke through the leaves and spangled the ground with gold. Harry and I wound back the long drive to a parking area beside a three-bay garage. The house was so white it looked painted yesterday, the windows framed with blue shutters, the front door an imposing wall of dark and heavily shellacked wood.

When the door opened, I recognized Warren Hamerle from his participation in several of the photos on Rubin Coyle's wall. He was over six feet tall, wide-shouldered, the shoulders sloped by six-plus decades of fighting gravity. Like hurricanes and earthquakes, gravity always wins. In contrast, his white hair was victoriously full, and made his water-blue eyes seem bluer than genetics built. The effect was enhanced by a white Oxford-cloth shirt above cream twill pants, beige bucks on his feet. He shook our hands in introductions made somber by our mission, and led us to a glassed-in sun porch at the rear of a home furnished with wood and leather and brassy accessories. It was a masculine home without trace of a woman's input.

"You'll have to bear with me at times, gentlemen," he said, tapping an ear. "My hearing's deteriorating, comes and goes. Getting old holds its own set of trials."

We sat in slat-back chairs surrounding a circular glass table thick as your average novel. An insulated urn, cups, and attendant necessaries centered the glass. Without urging, Harry and I poured coffee. It was the good stuff, plucked by Sherpas from the cliffs of Shangri-La, or whatnot. We asked about Rubin Coyle's potential enemies, and heard of accomplishments stacked against awards, of recognitions buttressed by achievements. Hamerle claimed little knowledge of his employee's personal life, seemingly unaware Coyle was occasionally negotiating Miss Lydia. I poured another cup of the fragrant coffee and shifted to Coyle's business life.

I said, "I hear Mr Coyle's hell on a biscuit with contracts and negotiations, Mr Hamerle."

"The best. Phenomenal."

"Something he learned from you?"

Hamerle blew on his coffee, took a sip, seemed satisfied. "I specialize in wills and estates."

A squabbling pair of gray squirrels scampered past the porch and we all turned to watch the display. They disappeared up a tree.

"Does Rubin confide everything to you? Every aspect of his work, his negotiations?"

I saw a wariness come to his eyes, a crinkling of the brow. "One doesn't inspect every thread in a garment to be secure in its quality, Detective. Rubin relates major points, keeps me informed of progress."

Reading between the lines, I pretty much took that Hamerle was hands-off. Until it was time to add up the hours and mail the invoice.

"He keeps you informed of every negotiation?"

"I review each and every one. The basic points, of course. A negotiation is a fluid endeavor."

"What fluids had he been working on recently?"

Hamerle started to shoot me the irritated eye, thought again. "Arbitration between a highway contractor and the state regarding a cost overrun. Trying to work out common ground between a developer and an environmental group. There's also the upcoming work on the contract for the dockworkers local. It's a couple months off, but pre-planning is essential."

That would be Aragorn's ongoing work. I shifted gears.

"Did he ever work on projects that maybe you weren't informed about? Like freelance."

221

"No." Almost too fast.

"Did any of them have to do with artwork, his clients?"

For the briefest moment I thought I saw a wisp of consternation quiver through one white eyebrow. He paused and stared at me. After a couple beats, he frowned and said, "Dartboards?"

"*Artwork*, sir. Did Rubin ever mention anything about art in connection with a contract or negotiation?"

He cupped a hand behind his ear and raised an eyebrow. "Art," I enunciated loudly. "Did any contracts have to do with art?"

He shook his head. "Not at all. Never came across anything like that. What's the reason for this line of questioning, if I may ask?"

"Are you sure? Maybe he . . ."

Warren Hamerle made a point of studying his platinum Rolex. He stood suddenly. "I'm afraid I just recalled an important appointment, gentlemen. Memory is another victim of age. Please excuse my manners, but could you find your own way to the door?"

We followed our path back through the Hemingway Collection. I paused at the door, turned back, yelled, "Thanks for your time, Mr Hamerle."

"You're welcome," he called back, sounding distracted. "Please keep me apprised of your investigation."

"Hearing's back," Harry whispered.

I smiled. "But no mention of getting together soon to finish up."

Harry put the car in gear and started down the drive. We

paused at the street as a line of traffic passed. I twisted for a final look at the white house tucked deep in the trees.

"You think maybe the art question threw him? He did the bad-hearing bit to cover for a second, collect his thoughts? Harry? Harry?"

I turned to my partner. He cupped his hand behind his ear and stared goggle-eyed at me. "Dartboard?"

"Not real convincing, was it?" I said.

"I expected a lot better from a lawyer. Think we can get Lydia to let us in Coyle's place? I got to use the john."

Lydia pulled into Coyle's circular drive and stepped slowly from a well-traveled Accord. She paused to straighten her skirt and jacket, smooth back her hair, paste a flat smile to her face. As she walked toward Harry and me, it hit me that despite her Walgreen's exterior, there were moments of Saks in her bearing. It was there, not there; the kind of woman you'd pass by on the street, then turn to look at, not knowing exactly why.

"Thank you for coming, Ms Barstow," I said. "It makes it better if someone has a key."

"I've never used it," she said. "Rubin has one to my place, and I pestered him to return the favor. It wasn't a matter of being able to get in . . ." she paused, as if unsure of the next words.

"But a symbol of closeness," Harry said. "Sharing."

"Yes," Lydia said. "Like that."

Her keys were on a loop of braided wire, no plastic flower or smiley face or other embellishment; sensible, functional.

She flicked through the dozen or so keys, found a shiny brass one, inserted it in the lock.

"Nice lockset," Harry said. "Got the heavy deadbolt. Mr Coyle didn't skimp."

Lydia fiddled the key left and right. Slid it in and out, tried again.

"It's not working."

"Let me give it a shot," I said.

Didn't work for me either. I passed the key to Harry. He'd spent two years in Crimes Against Property before jumping to Homicide, learned a lot about how locks work. Harry moved the key gingerly, as if feeling for something. He studied its teeth, tried again.

"It's almost right," he said. "But not perfect. Either the maker of the key was inept . . ."

"Or Rubin had it made wrong," Lydia said. She turned abruptly and stared down the street, hiding tears. I took the key and stepped into the sunlight. The ground surfaces of the key seemed slightly different in places.

"Do you have reading glasses, Ms Barstow?" I asked.

They were perhaps the 2.50 magnification, medium strength. I studied the key through a lens. "The grooves from grinding all run at right angles, except on one tooth. The filing is coarser and a different angle."

Harry took a look. "Hembree'd know better, but it looks like someone filed off half of a tooth, all it'd take to kill the key."

Having discovered the problem, getting in turned out to be no more than a fifteen-minute round trip to a hardware store.

"You need what?" the clerk had asked.

"A duplicate key," Harry said. "Except where this tooth is flat, I want you to fix it so it pokes to a point."

"Never done that before," the clerk said, holding the key to the light and squinting. "Shouldn't be hard."

The cool air in Coyle's home smelled unoccupied. Lived-in homes smell differently than those without passengers. Maybe it's cooking smells, or exudations of the human body, or some form of psychic aroma, but I always seemed able to determine when a dwelling had been unoccupied for even a few days.

We walked into a great room with vaulted ceilings, floor of polished wood. The furniture was primarily a gray leather grouping arranged around a low table of green marble. There were accent rugs and lamps. A credenza. Corporate-type art on the walls. Harry slid a finger across the table.

"He pay his housekeeper a lot?" he asked Lydia.

"He didn't have one."

"Good, 'cause she ain't dusted in a couple weeks."

Our heels ticked across the wood as Harry and I progressed from room to room. There was no spontaneity to the dwelling, everything in order, nothing in transition. The magazines were racked, the remotes side by side, the chairs perfect beneath the dining-room table. The throw pillows had never been thrown.

"This place is more anal than a proctologist convention," Harry whispered. Lydia followed several feet behind us, jumpy, eyes darting, as if expecting Coyle to pop from a closet.

We came to an upstairs room, tried the knob. Locked. "What's in here?"

"His office. That's what he calls it."

"You've never been in here?"

Her embarrassment was painful. "I've only been in this house a few times. He liked to come to my place. He said it seemed dead here, but my house was alive and exciting . . ." She paused, spoke in a monotone. "Like me."

"I'm sure that's how he feels, Miz Barstow," Harry offered. "A guy gets tired of staring at walls. Especially his. A different place and person make life worth looking forward to."

Lydia smiled *Thanks for the try*. I shook the knob a couple more times. "I'd really like to look in here," I said. "If it's his office it might hold something that tells us where he is."

Harry knelt beside the mechanism. "It's not like the front door, but it's more lock than people usually keep on an interior door. Opens inward; that's good."

He stood, pointed out the window at the end of the hallway. "Hey, is that a turkey buzzard?" Lydia and I turned to look, saw blue sky and tree limbs outside. An explosion spun our heads back to Harry. The door was wide open.

"Whoops," Harry said. "Guess it was just a robin."

The room was dark, the window at the far end shrouded in drapes. Harry stepped inside. I followed, Lydia at my back. Harry fumbled at the wall inside the door. "Got to be a switch somewhere . . . there."

The room brightened, not from floor or ceiling lamps, but from lighting within a dozen display cases hung on the walls. The boxes held cords, blooded wads of cloth, a railroad spike, a pair of broken eyeglasses, a chunk of something resembling beef jerky. All mounted like art at a museum.

"Lawd," Harry said as the scene registered. "Carnival time."

"What is this stuff?" Lydia whispered from behind me.

"A collection of shadows," I said, easing her from the room.

CHAPTER 30

Coyle's fingerprint at a murder scene and subsequent disappearance – combined with his newly revealed fondness for serial-killer memorabilia – allowed a search warrant. We sent a pale and frightened Lydia Barstow home. Harry and I started back into the house. He stopped, a stricken look on his face.

"I hate to say this, but given the burr under the chief's britches, you think we should call –"

"Yep," I said, less irritated than I should have been.

Ten minutes later Danbury was in the driveway in an unmarked van, savvy enough to forgo the logo-screaming newswagon. Given the trees and the curve of the street, few would notice our discreet little group. She'd brought Zipinski. The diminutive cameraman gave Harry and me a wide berth, tripoding his camera at the far end of the drive, framing the house in the background.

"So we file this footage away?" Zipinski asked Danbury.

"For now," she said. "It's for a possible story. Just get the house. Anything comes out, we'll get that too."

"This has something to do with the crazy you told me about?" Zipinski asked. "The artsy crazy?"

"That's what the guys will tell us. Right, gents?"

Harry sighed. "Is Carla all right?"

"Secure in the fortress and didn't want babysitting."

Zipinski shot footage of Harry and me standing outside. It was illegal for a news crew to accompany us inside, so we went in alone. Danbury wasn't happy, but knew the law. "I want a full report," she called out as we entered.

Harry and I split up inside Coyle's office, Harry taking the desk area. I checked a closet, files in a credenza, a stack of papers in a chair. Everything seemed related to cases and negotiations and I couldn't look without violating lawyer-client privilege. When my eyes lingered benignly on the pages, I saw nothing allied with art.

"Carson," Harry said quietly, "I've got something."

He was behind Coyle's desk. I set aside a file and walked over. Harry lifted a foot-square Plexiglas box from the top drawer, a small white envelope taped to the box.

He held up the box with gloved fingers. Inside was a painting of a skull, dark with browns and umbers. The skull had been overpainted with glazes and highlighting and tiny flecks of red, giving it a trompe-l'oeil sense of depth and dimension. There were more of the squiggly wormlike shapes.

The image was so hyper-real it seemed possible to pick up the skull, give a soliloquy on slings and arrows. Harry set it carefully on the desktop and opened the white envelope. He removed a card, four by six inches or so, holding three paragraphs of typewritten text.

"Well ain't this interesting," he said, passing me the card.

Marsden Hexcamp, reportedly a study for "The Art of the Final Moment". Painted July 1970(?). One of seventeen studies for a final canvas measuring 367 (h) x 212 (w) centimeters. The studies are explorations of subject matter within the final work. Fourteen are of high-quality, two have moderate environmental damage (water, probably), one heavy damage, probably due to haphazard last-minute packing.

Several small canvases Hexcamp employed as "test" versions also are extant, two having been scavenged and cut into smaller pieces for the market. Nine of these "works" are also currently available, five of high quality, three rather heavily damaged by exposure to the elements.

Note: *The accompanying piece has been cataloged as MH – AFM, stud. 012.*

I digested the information. Brief as it was, it provided a treasure trove of insights. "It's a catalog entry, bro, or similar: Marsden Hexcamp, 'Art of the Final Moment', study number twelve."

Harry, reading over my shoulder, caught it. "Seventeen studies, one major work, 'The Art of the Final Moment'. What size is it, Cars? Outside of buying scotch by the liter, I never made the jump to metric."

"About twelve feet high by seven feet wide."

"Damn," he said. "Almost a mural."

"And now we know why the pieces we're seeing are snippets," I said. "Someone's cut a couple of studies up, selling them piecemeal, literally. Maybe they were part of the damaged canvases."

"Maybe they're worth more that way, Carson. People aren't looking for art, specifically."

"Right. They just want something pretty touched by Marsden's hot little fingers."

Harry thought a moment. "The mailing to Coyle might have been a purchase. This is his. Maybe permanently, or maybe he's bringing the whole collection together for the big show."

I mulled the possibilities. "Or whoever's selling the collection sent this to Coyle as good faith, Coyle's payment, a sample of how they're displayed. Who knows."

Harry said, "Could Coyle be the guy who's verifying this stuff?"

"I'd bet against it; but this about clinches his role as salesman, or facilitator. It's almost a given he knows who's doing the verifying. Maybe even hired our authenticator. Who else could write the catalog information?"

The painting was all we took from Coyle's office, its technique and composition a match with the art found in

Marie's room and Heidi's trailer. The narrow search warrant didn't allow removal of Coyle's "art" from the walls, it lacking direct connection to our cases. I looked at it again and suppressed a shudder; between Forrier's mask and Hexcamp's skull, I was getting an unsettling glimpse into the dark underbelly of creation.

Harry bagged the painting. We went outside and walked to the edge of the lawn, where Danbury and Zipinski waited in the dense shade of a magnolia tree. Danbury rushed up. Borg stayed beside his tripod-mounted camera, probably not wanting to get caught between Harry and me.

"What'd you find?" Danbury asked.

Harry held up the boxed artwork. "My God," she said. "It's a photograph from the dark side."

Zipinski took a look, frowned. "I can almost smell rotting meat. How about a shot of it?"

Harry started to say no, caught himself. Zipinski shooting the painting was no different than when the newsies videotaped cops carrying potential evidence from any legal search.

"Yeah, fire away," he muttered.

"Stand there and hold it," Zipinski said. "Let me get the light right. He started fiddling with a reflector. There was wind today, but it was hot, and the windblown reflector kept zapping Harry's eyes as he waited for Zipinski to get set. Harry squinted, growled, shoved the painting at me.

"You do this, Cars. I just made you official poster boy of the PSIT."

The reflector flashed in my eyes until Zipinski got it clamped down. I let him run footage, a red light flickering on the camera. After a few seconds he said, "OK." I returned the painting to Harry and he walked it to the car.

Danbury's phone rang. She began talking to someone about a motorcycle crash on I-95 and how she'd had two crashes already this week and *someone else can by God do this one*. She walked toward the street, still arguing into the phone. *How about one of the freakin' anchors does it, if they still remember how . . .*

It sounded like she was winning.

"Damn, it's gotta be ninety-five degrees," Zipinski said. He yanked out his shirttail and wiped his sweating face. His stomach was as furred as an orang-utan's. He set his ballcap atop the camera, blotted his balding head. It gleamed in the sunlight. He looked at me, started to speak, looked away.

"What is it?" I said.

"I screwed up the other day. We do some investigative work. Ambush interviews. Y'know . . . pop out of a car in front of some sticky-fingered bureaucrat. She asks, 'Just how much money did you take from the Orphaned Children's Fund?' or whatnot. I make sure his face gets on tape – that first guilty expression, just before the denials kick in. I was still in that mode when I fucked with you in the parking lot. I apologize."

He offered his hand. I made it a brief handshake. I didn't much care for Borgurt Zipinski, but no longer wanted to make him walk bowlegged around his own camera. He started to break down the video equipment, paused, a confused look on his face.

"Let me ask you a question, Detective Ryder. That painting

was pretty and freaky at the same time. You really think this crazy guy – Hexcamp? – painted it? And a whole bunch of stuff like it?"

I nodded yes and glanced at Danbury in the distance. She shook her head, dropped the phone in her purse. She looked weary, almost deflated. It hit me that cranking together the news might not be as easy as I thought, asking questions, jamming a microphone in people's faces, running down tips, most probably going nowhere. I guess you had to do a lot of planning, meet a lot of people you didn't want to meet, see a hell of a lot of vehicle crashes, shootings, drownings. Kind of like me.

I watched her walk my way, then stop. She closed her eyes and took a few deep breaths. When her eyes opened, the game face was back. She moved our way, fumbling in her purse. She looked up, grinned, shot a thumbs-up, her face alight with mischief. I waved back, admiring the strength it took to keep kicking when you were drained almost dry.

"Detective Ryder?" Zipinski repeated, and I realized I'd zoned out on DeeDee Danbury. "How could a crazy guy make something like that?"

I'd been wondering that myself. "Maybe the genius was fighting the sociopath, Zipinski. Some days the genius won out."

Zipinski shook his head, put his cap back on his sun-reddening pate, and continued packing equipment. Danbury walked up.

"You're not going to keep anything from me, are you? We're the Three Musketeers, remember? Pogie, Nautie and DeeDee."

Danbury climbed in the van, wind puffing at her skirt. She let it fly, unconcerned. Her legs were long and smooth and her panties were a flash of scarlet. The door closed and she winked. "Hey, stop by later you get a chance. Maybe I'll have some results on that research. It's your turn to buy the wine. Hint: Don't buy anything with cartoons on the label."

They drove away, Danbury waving with her fingers, Zipinski at the wheel. I joined Harry in the car, trying hard to recall the rich and magical colors in the painting from Coyle's desk, but all I could see were flashes of scarlet.

We headed back to the department with fresh wind in our sails. We'd pulled covers from a guy who appeared to be a major player in the Hexcamp drama. I'm not sure how much progress it marked, but at least I didn't feel I was practicing astronomy by jamming my head into the dirt and asking when the stars came out.

"Think we should fill Willow in on Coyle's private gallery?" Harry said.

Keeping Willow in the loop sounded like the right thing to do. We made it a conference call, sitting in the small meeting room off the detectives' room and talking at a device in the middle of the table. It looked like a spaceship from a fifties movie.

"We found another stash of memorabilia," Harry yelled at the spaceship.

"No need to scream," Willow said. "I hear you fine. Where?"

"Our missing lawyer boy, Rubin Coyle. He's a collector, got a house full of nightmares. I thought he was a nobody at first.

Now he's looking like the belle of the ball. Naturally, he's got the usual credentials – fine upstanding citizen, blah, blah, a credit to his community, blah, blah . . . the standard shit-warble. He's also an expert in negotiations. And guess what? It looks like something big's coming to market, and needs someone to negotiate the sale or whatever."

"The collection," Willow said. "It has to be."

"We're pretty sure Coyle knows who has it," I said. "But it tells us nothing about why we have two dead women and a third who's been threatened."

"All this sicko lawyer boy does is negotiate?" Willow asked.

"He's the hard-dealing hotshot of Hamerle, Melbine and Raus."

Willow's end seemed to go dead. I looked at the space-craft; the connection light was lit. "Mr Willow?" I said.

"The law firm. You never told me that before."

"About Coyle, the lost lawyer?" Harry said. "Sure we did. Left a print at the Cozy Cabins five days before Marie Gilbeaux was found, one of a hundred thousand other prints."

"You never mentioned Coyle worked for Warren Hamerle."

"What's Hamerle to you?" I asked.

Willow laughed, dry and humorless. "It's who he was, Detective Ryder. The last time I saw Warren Hamerle he was a scared, skinny little court-appointed attorney . . ."

I dropped my head forward until it bumped the table. "Don't tell me," I said. "He was representing Marsden Hexcamp. Am I right here?"

CHAPTER 31

"I received nothing from Marsden Hexcamp. And I know nothing about Rubin's art proclivities."

This time Hamerle hadn't offered coffee, instead directing us to chairs nearest the door. Not a subtle man.

"He didn't want to compensate you for your fine defense?" I said.

Hamerle paced in front of us, a glass of scotch in his hand; he didn't offer us any of that, either.

"I was young, had never tried a capital case. That's why I was selected. The political types wanted a fast trial, not some sharpie wasting the state's money filing motions, parading experts. They wanted a slam-dunk."

"They got it," I said.

"Hexcamp wanted it, too. He contributed nothing to his

defense. I'd ask him about times, dates, possible alibis. You know what he talked about? Art history. 'Who do you think history will treat most fondly, Warren?' he'd say to me, smiling that fucking lunatic smile, 'Monet or Cezanne?' Shit, half the time I didn't know who the hell he was talking about."

"Tight race," I said, "but my money's on Monet."

Hamerle grunted. "He liked to give speeches, too. Big dramatic pronouncements, like he'd just come up with them. I once heard him quote Blackstone as if the words were his own. A reverend in the courtroom that final day recognized Hexcamp's tabletop rant as a paraphrase from Jonathan Edwards, an eighteenth-century Puritan minister."

"Fits the mindset," I said. "He wouldn't have seen it as plagiarizing, but as using words and ideas someone had simply thought of before he did; he understood them, therefore they were as much his as the originator's. That make sense?"

"No," Harry said. "Which is why it probably fits."

Hamerle scowled, shook his white-maned head. "Once or twice a year, I get calls asking if I know anything about Hexcamp's art. From different people. They're always cagey, always talking around the subject."

"Explain," Harry said.

"'Do you know if Mr Hexcamp left anything of interest, Mr Hamerle?' 'Are you sitting on anything that might make you a lot of money, Mr Hamerle?' They're creepy, oily. I hang up the phone and wash my hands. They're mostly men. Two or three times it was women – they were the worst."

I said, "You were Hexcamp's lawyer. Yet one of your top

partners collects souvenirs from serial killers – including a piece that looks a lot like it was done by Hexcamp – and you know nothing about it. That's your story?"

Hamerle's jaw clenched. "It's the truth. I had no idea Rubin was . . . of that mindset."

We stood to leave. Hamerle followed us to the door. I stopped just outside, looked him in his cold blue eyes. "What if Coyle walked through this door right now, Mr Hamerle? What would you say to him?"

Hamerle took a big suck of his drink, thought a second.

"You're two weeks behind on billing, Rubin. Where are your time sheets?"

The door closed.

It was twilight when we left Hamerle's. Harry cut over to Cottage Hill Road, a section where live oaks canopied the street. An elderly black man pushed a three-wheeled shopping buggy down the sidewalk. The buggy held a solitary lamp, its shade askew. The man looked deliriously happy with his life. I waved at the guy as we went by. He shot a manic toothless grin, and pointed excitedly into the buggy like he was pushing God's lamp. Harry said, "If someone's written the definitive catalog of the Hexcamp collection, maybe the same person who's going to verify the authenticity . . ."

I nodded. "Whatever's going down must be coming up."

"You think Coyle's even alive?"

"If we're right, he's got to be alive. He's the contact man, the auction impresario or whatever. I'm seeing three participants so far: Coyle, the authenticator, and the owner of the collection."

Harry's finger tapped rhythm on the steering wheel. "If the painting in Coyle's desk is a Hexcamp, it's worth tens of thousands of dollars. At least by Willow's estimate. Why'd Coyle leave the Hexcamp in his desk?"

"He didn't expect we'd be inside, thought it was safe. Maybe he expected to be back sooner. Maybe authenticating this crap has him traveling. Maybe he's already sold the collection."

"A lot of maybes, Carson. Like maybe Marie Gilbeaux's motel scene was an on-the-run job."

"Seems right. Everything about this case has been mirrors and maybes."

Harry decided the stop sign in front of us wasn't going to disappear, so he jammed on the brakes. I steadied myself with a hand on the dash. "At least we know Coyle's a collector. That's his tie to Hexcamp. Now we got to figure out how Coyle connects to Marie Gilbeaux and Heidi Wicky."

Harry yawned. It sounded like a foghorn. "That's tomorrow's gig, Cars. Right now my head feels like it's filled with wet sand."

He punched the accelerator and off we flew toward downtown. I checked my watch and noted the date. Ava had bailed out eight days ago. It seemed like a month. Harry hadn't once mentioned her departure, save for fast and indirect references, the *You doing all right, Carson?* and *How you holding up?* type of thing.

Over the six years of our friendship, we'd evolved a methodology for personal information: neither walked into the other's head without an invitation. I'm not sure how we got to this protocol, it just seemed to be on the table when we arrived.

"Harry?"

He stifled a yawn. "What?"

"What do you think about Ava leaving?"

Nothing from Harry for three blocks. On the fourth, he wheeled to the curb and parked under a tree. It was turning into night and passing headlights filled our car with shadows. Harry squeezed the wheel for a few seconds, turned to me.

"Carson, I think Ava's one of the sweetest women I ever met. One of the prettiest. Maybe one of the smartest too. That's what I think."

"There's a *but* in there, Harry."

He turned away and watched the traffic sizzle past.

"Harry? But what?"

"I also think she's one of the troubled-est. Is that a word? It doesn't matter. She's been through a helluva lot of nastiness. Most came from outside, bad forces. But she's got things to find out about herself. It's kind of like what you went through a few years back, Cars. You finally stood still and let your past run up and bump you in the ass. Then you turned around and dealt with it. I think Ava will come through in the end, but right now she's . . ." His words trailed off. His fingers drummed the steering wheel.

"Harry?" I prompted.

"She's on a journey, maybe it's hers alone right now. What I think is, she's got to do a bunch of traveling before she knows what home really means."

He put the car back in gear, aimed for the department. I started to ask what he meant, but it was a Harry-ism.

241

Harry-isms were similar to Zen: if I had to ask his meaning, I wouldn't understand his answer.

We hit the station, spent fifteen minutes on paperwork, then took off. A day trapped in air conditioning made me feel disconnected from honest air, so I rolled down the windows and aimed the headlights for home. It had rained recently, in this stretch at least, and the air was thick with the scent of wet grass. I recalled that Danbury lived nearby and wondered if rain had come to her yard, if it was suffused with heat and the perfume of drenched grass.

There was a liquor store down the block and I stopped. Wine has never been a study of mine, but the proprietor assured me the California chardonnay earned every penny of the fifteen-buck price tag. It didn't have a cartoon on the label, so I said sure, put a bag around it.

The porch light was off at Danbury's, but there were lights in the downstairs windows. I parked and walked to the door, but for some reason stopped short and sat on the porch. The wine felt heavy in my hand and I set it beside me. Rain had fallen and the air was steamy. The flowers in her yard smelled bright, the scent pouring colors into my mind, purple, lavender, pink, scarlet. The colors made me lightheaded and I lay back on the wood slats of the porch and flung my arms to my sides, like holding on. I closed my eyes and breathed the floral colors from the air, amazed as the air turned to water, blue and shimmering . . .

Hold on . . .
To the blue water
And kick breathe kick

242

Something clicked far away. A door latch. It must have clicked underwater; I was swimming, wasn't I?

"Pogie?"

Exploding through surface sparkles . . .

I opened my eyes. Danbury was backlit by a globe of light on the ceiling of the porch. I sat up abruptly, my arm sending the wine bottle clinking down the steps. I stumbled after it.

She said, "You've been asleep on my porch?"

My mind was still in water somewhere. I tried to make it swim toward my tongue. "Oh, I was just . . . I mean I thought . . ."

She laughed. "How long have you been out here?'

"I, uh –" I squinted at my watch. "A half-hour or so. I'm sorry."

"Sorry for what?"

My senses started lining up again. "I'm not sure."

"Come in. Or I'll come out. You're obviously comfortable here."

I handed her the chardonnay. "I've got to be going. I just came by to deliver a bottle of wine. Payback."

"It only counts as payback if you have some with me."

"I have to go. It's getting . . .'

"It's just us. Carla's upstairs reading. Or asleep. She keeps country hours." Danbury reached out, took my sleeve, pulled gently. "Come on."

I stood motionless. Light poured from her open front door. It seemed inviting. I said, "I really can't."

Her face was in shadow. The scent of the wet flowers was overwhelming. She opened my hand and returned the wine.

243

"Bring it back when you have more time. I'll polish up a couple glasses, keep them out and waiting, right?"

She leaned to me, stood on tiptoe, kissed my forehead.

And then I was alone in her front yard.

CHAPTER 32

I got a call from Danbury at five-forty-nine a.m.

"Good morning, merry sunshine," she said. "I put a pillow and a couple blankets on my porch last night in case you came back, maybe were in some sort of nesting phase."

"Do you know what time it is?" I said.

"Here or there?"

"What?"

"It's noon in Français. I've been on the phone for three hours. You and the Nautster should come over to the house and pow-wow with moi."

I unwrapped the sheet from my legs. If I slept without covers, I felt strangely vulnerable; with them, I tried to mummify myself.

"Is this pow-wow necessary?"

"I have an update on the amazing Mr Hexcamp. Or maybe not so amazing. It depends on your point of view."

"An hour," I said. "Or less."

I hung up and called Harry, said I'd grab him at the station, head to Danbury's. He made unhappy noises, but relented. I nuked some leftover cheese grits, rolled them up in a flour tortilla, and took my invention, the grittito, out to the deck with a high-performance cup of chicory coffee. The water was almost still, six-inch waves washing the shoreline. I looked east. The Blovines had been in full throat when I'd come home last night, but the place was now quiet. The house to the west was the same. The car had moved a bit, and the back porch now boasted a beach ball, but the occupants were nowhere to be seen. I wondered if they only came out at night.

We got to Danbury's at seven. She led us to the kitchen, large and high-ceilinged, a fan whisking slowly above our heads. Copper pots hung above a restaurant-quality range. Morning sun tinted the windows orange. Carla Hutchins sat at the table having coffee.

"You all right, Miz Hutchins?" Harry said.

She lifted her mug in salute. "I feel safe here. But I feel like I'm taking advantage of DeeDee by –"

Danbury cut in. "Crapola. Carla's cleaned the place from top to bottom. It had gotten bad; I was using one of the cobwebs as a hammock."

"You're going to talk about . . . him?" Carla asked. Danbury nodded. Carla took her coffee and retreated upstairs. Harry and I sat at a kitchen table made of maple, a bowl of fruit in the center. Danbury poured coffees, set down some sugar and cream.

"You gents eat yet? I've got some granola, yogurt, bananas, apples . . . How about you, Harry? You look like a guy eats a big breakfast. Want me to open a canned ham or something?"

Harry growled; he was big enough to carry a lot of weight, but was storing about twenty surplus pounds at the beltline and didn't like being reminded of it. "How about we get on with this?" he said. "Jeez, what time you get up this morning?"

Danbury said, "Three."

"When did you go to bed, eight?"

"Eleven on the nose. I was going to stay up and have a glass of wine, but it left early."

She shot me a wink. Harry caught it and narrowed an eye my direction; I studied a napkin rack, fascinated by the many wonders of plastic. Harry gave me another eyeball shot, then fixed it on Danbury.

"You had something to tell us?"

She leaned against the counter, a sheaf of notes at her elbow.

"I've been researching Monsieur Hexcamp the past couple nights. I finished up this morning about four."

"And?"

She held up a blank piece of paper.

"This is the page I'd planned for Hexcamp's French transgressions. He's clean. Never arrested for beating someone to death with a baguette or parking his Citroën on a tourist."

Danbury set the page down, picked up another blank sheet, held it above her head, grinned.

Harry rolled his eyes at the theatrics. "And what the hell's that?"

She gave it three beats of dramatic pause. "Little Marsden's attendance record at L'Institut des Beaux-Arts."

Harry's eyes went wide. "What?"

"He arrived in France in July of '66, departed in May of '70. Never during that time did he attend a class there."

I said, "He's a fake?"

Danbury set several pages on the table, all filled with precise writing broken up with lines and arrows and question marks. "Not completely. He went to another school – l'Académie d'Art Graphique, no longer in business. It wasn't world-class, but not gumball tech either. Fairly small, maybe three hundred students back then, just starting up. The joint was run by Henri Badentier, an eccentric but well-regarded prof trying to jump-start the school's reputation in the art world."

I considered Hexcamp's ruse. "The deception makes sense. Typical self-aggrandizement of an egocentric sociopath. He couldn't stand attending any school other than the best, adding a scholarship for dressing."

Harry studied the pages of notes. "How'd you dig all this up, Danbury?"

She took a two-handed sip of coffee from a mug with Channel 14's logo on it. "Talking to people. Asking about travel records, visas, foreign-student stipends. Plus France has an excellent bureaucracy, and you know how bureaucrats like to save stuff. I picture the basement of France as being filled with boxes of index cards."

Harry said, "This Baw-dent-yay . . . he's dead, right?"

"Badentier. I talked to his sister. An unhappy woman, nasty. I told Madame I was researching influential persons in zee art-academy world. The French pride themselves on being artistic, and I used it shamelessly, lots of *ooh*-ing and *ah*-ing and *ooh-la-la*-ing. It finally broke her ice. Well, chipped it for a few minutes."

"Whatever works," Harry grunted, trying to hide being impressed; given nothing more than a phone and her instincts, Danbury had returned with loaves and fishes.

"Anything else?" he said.

"One thing did catch my attention. When I talked to Madame, I heard Badentier himself in the background. When I made up a story about a native Alabaman who'd made a name in the art world, a Marsden Hexcamp, I heard her relay this information to her brother."

"And?" I asked.

"He started laughing."

"That's it?"

Danbury said, "It wasn't that he laughed, it was *how* he laughed. You should have heard him. It's like the old boy was going to hack up a lung."

"Why didn't you talk to him?" Harry said, caught himself. "Oh, he didn't speak English."

"He could have spoken thirty languages, but he wouldn't have come to the phone."

"How so?"

"His sister volunteered the information that Monsieur Badentier considered only two forms of communication valid: via handwritten letter or face to face over a glass of red wine."

"Why would she tell you that?"

"I think it was her way of signaling my contact with the great man was *fini*; especially when she alluded to screening his mail. Like I said, not an upbeat woman."

"Nice job of digging up Hexcamp's past, Danbury," Harry conceded. "But it doesn't exactly put us anywhere new."

"It's a fresh starting point," she said. "Admit it, Harry."

"He died three decades ago and we've got two women dead in the last two weeks."

"The more we know about his past the more we can . . ."

Danbury and Harry devolved into argumentation. I stared out the window and sipped at my coffee. Sunlight reflected from the leaves of a sycamore. Birds flitted to Danbury's feeders, pecked at seeds, flicked away again. A gray squirrel ran the top of a fence.

"What the hell was Badentier laughing so hard about?" I wondered aloud.

CHAPTER 33

I pondered Badentier's response for several minutes, Harry and Danbury pecking at one another in the background. My cell rang and I saw the caller was from the Alabama Forensics Bureau.

"Carson," Wayne Hembree said, "I need to see you and Harry."

"On Saturday, Bree?"

Harry set aside his coffee mug and looked at me curiously. Hembree said, "Now'd be good. Five minutes ago would be better."

"We're about ten minutes away. See you."

I dropped the phone in my pocket and looked at Harry. "Bree's got something hot in his skinny little paws."

"I'll grab my bag," Danbury said. "And tell Carla to lock tight."

"Whoa," Harry said. "Case you didn't notice, Miz Danbury, that call wasn't to you."

She picked up her car keys from the counter, dropped them in her purse. "We're on the same team, Nautilus. Who just spent most of the night digging?"

"If it's something important about the Hexcamp stuff, we'll let you know in a few . . ."

Danbury pulled a cellphone from her purse, dialed furiously.

"Who you calling? Harry said.

"Chief Plackett. I need a second opinion on being cut out of the loop. Think he's out of bed yet?"

Hembree nodded when he saw Harry and me. His eyes were huge behind the black frames, excited. Danbury shuffled in behind us.

"Uh, is that . . . ?" Bree angled his head at Danbury.

"Treat it like a mirage," Harry said. "What you got?"

Hembree led us to the meeting room, long table, outsized TV monitor, corkboard walls for pinning up photos and notes. He spun a wheeled chair from beneath the table, pushed it my way.

"What's going on?" I asked.

"It's a chair. Sit."

I grabbed the chair and spun it beneath my butt. Harry and Danbury took their own seats. "Bree?" I asked. "What's happening?"

Hembree ignored me, flicked off the overhead lights. He touched another switch and a viewing screen whirred from the ceiling. Hembree took a deep breath, let it out slowly.

"I've got preliminary results on the art from the Sister's room. I pulled some strings, got it jumped ahead in line. I want to stress it's *preliminary*, first-glance kind of thing. The FBI shot slides in several ASA ratings and film types, assuring the full range of definition and color density, not to mention . . ."

"Bree," Harry cautioned.

Hembree stopped talking. He thumbed a button and the screen filled with a close-up of the art mailed to Marie Gilbeaux.

"This is what we all saw, the surface coat of paint – a glaze, actually – over a thicker underlayment of pigment . . ."

Hembree shifted to another view, an extreme close-up of the edge. The paint had been applied in an impasto, thick and textured.

"Analysis of paint layers and the dating of the canvas indicates an older composition, between twenty-five and forty years old."

"Hexcamp's time," Danbury said.

Hembree nodded. "Strangely enough, the Bureau discovered this piece of artwork had a second image on it. Invisible. Something perhaps sketched on, the erased. A ghost image."

Harry's head spun to Hembree. "Say again?"

"An image in the canvas that may have come from a drawing done on the canvas. When hasn't been determined. The image appeared in the more esoteric tests, when spectrographic data was augmented via . . ."

Harry said, "What's our bottom line here?"

"I've racked a photo of the isolated image, the ghost image."

"Pop it up, Bree," I said. "I haven't seen a ghost in a while."

Hembree shot me a strange glance, then flicked the control button. A photo appeared, blurred. Then slipped into focus. A line drawing appeared on the screen.

"Jesus," Harry said.

"Unreal," Danbury whispered.

I couldn't say a word because I couldn't breathe. It was a picture of me. A drawing; nothing more than a few dark lines. Simple, direct, fluid. I stood, drawn to the projection as if by gravity. My finger traced my eyes, my hair. Lines radiating from my illustrated shoulder indicated a tree. At my waist seemed to be a fence, deft embellishments indicating scroll-work, like an iron fence. There was another image in the background. My fingers traced its sparse lines, a structure in the sky behind my shoulder.

"Is that what I think it is?" Harry whispered.

"*Oui*," Danbury replied. "It's the Eiffel Tower."

CHAPTER 34

Chief Plackett sighed. He glanced toward his office window, as if hoping he might escape out it. Or toss me through it into the Monday-morning traffic.

"You want to go to France, Ryder? Is that what I'm getting? Because of a homicidal artist who died thirty-odd years ago?"

"There are contacts Hexcamp may have made in France. Or murders committed there. We opened doors, but can't step through them from here. Add to that –"

"I know. I saw the picture," Plackett said. "I stopped by Forensics an hour ago. Freakish stuff."

He looked at me as if I was supposed to explain it. I shrugged. "It's a total enigma. There's no way it could be me, not if it was created years ago. The face is mine today, or at least recently."

"It sure looked like you. Even as simple as it was."

The drawing was simple, but so skillfully executed that the economy of line added to the resemblance, my face and stance reduced to an essence, every line mine alone. Plackett walked to his window, hands clasped behind his back. The sky was darkening, thunder tumbling nearer. It was getting ready to rain on my parade.

"We're operating on bare bones now," the chief said, his pat speech whenever a department tried for a few extra bucks. "Cutbacks in equipment, community programs, vehicle maintenance. There's absolutely no way I can send you gallivanting off to Paris when I can't even –"

"*Us* to Paris," I said. "Harry and me."

"We can't possibly find the funds necessary to –"

"Excuse me, Chief," Gloria Besherle, the chief's administrative assistant, said from outside the door. "I couldn't help hearing. May I come in?"

Plackett nodded. Gloria was a large woman and seemed to be wearing a tent decorated by Jackson Pollack. She winked as she brushed by me, pulled a spiral-bound folder from the shelf beside Plackett's desk, and flipped through it. "This trip you're considering, Carson. Will you talk to any French law-enforcement types while you're there?"

"Why's that, Gloria?" the chief asked.

She tapped a page with a two-inch red fingernail. "There's a special grant, Federal monies earmarked for continuing international education in law-enforcement. Mobile's a world port, and the grant supposes we might need continuing education on international legal issues with shipping and

256

smuggling and whatnot, such as extra-departmental inter-facing with Interpol."

"Interpol?" I said. Our usual extra-departmental interface was with the county mounties.

Gloria looked up. "It's worded vaguely enough that contact with French law-enforcement administration would just about satisfy the grant requirements."

"We could stop by a cop house over there," I said. "Ask what wine goes best with handcuffs."

Plackett took the book from Gloria, moved his finger across the passages in time with his lips. "It's not much of a grant, under three grand. I guess I could squeak Ryder *or* Nautilus into Paris for a couple days, but one's the limit. Detective Nautilus, you're the senior man. The trip is yours to refuse."

Harry wanted to take a two-day tour of France as much as I wanted to fly-fish the Gobi Desert.

"Much as I'd love the opportunity to *interface* with our French counterparts, it's not my face on the art. I think Detective Ryder is the right choice, Chief." Harry looked at me and winked. "*Bon voyage*, Carson."

"If you're going, Ryder, I'm going," Danbury said. "It's part of the story and part of the deal."

I paced her porch. Thunder rumbled in the distance, purple clouds skirting the western skyline. "You've got to watch Hutchins. You volunteered, she's yours."

"I told you, my house is like Fort Knox. I sneeze too loud and cops come." She tried the bright-smile gambit. "Harry'll keep an eye on Hutchins, won't you, Harry? Maybe fill my birdfeeders so Carla stays inside? I'll leave instructions."

"Harry can't do that," I announced. "He's putting the full-court press to finding Coyle, right, bro?"

Harry leaned against a porch column with his arms crossed. He looked dispassionately at me, then at Danbury. It was an unsettling look; he appeared to be measuring something, like a carny trying to guess a person's weight.

"I guess pouring some seeds down a tube ain't too difficult. How many these feeders you got, Danbury?"

Danbury clapped her hands. "Atta boy, Nautilus."

I gawked at Harry. What the hell was he doing?

"You can't go," I repeated to Danbury. "One person moves faster than two."

She jammed her hands against her hips. "Answer me three questions, pogobo. One: Who made the contacts? Two: Who already has a working relationship with Madame le sister? And three: What will you say if someone asks you the meaning of life?"

I shook my head; talking to Danbury was like talking in a blender. "I don't expect I'll be asked –"

"*Je ne comprends pas le sens actuel de la vie,*" she said, "*mais asseyez-vous et servez-vous du fromage et du vin et nous nous en disputerons pendant six heures.*"

I stared at her. I think my mouth was open.

She winked, gave me a *gotcha* grin. "Translation: 'I don't know the current meaning of life, but sit and have some cheese and wine and we'll argue about it for six hours.' It's a Frenchie-type answer."

258

I continued to stare.

"I grew up speaking Français with my maternal grand-mother; it's all she spoke. I ever tell you what DeeDee stands for? Danielle Desiree." She put her chin on her uplifted index finger, batted her eyelids. "You like zee pretty name, no?"

"I 'spect that clinches things," Harry said, not hiding the smile at all.

CHAPTER 35

"Back in a few, pogie. Don't try to change seats. I'll find you."

Danbury excused her way to the aisle, walked toward the head. The coastline had disappeared hours back. I felt the jet shudder through a pocket, wings quivering outside the window. Miles ahead I saw a blinking light approaching at what appeared to be our altitude. Another jet, perhaps launched from Orly at the same moment we departed Atlanta, mirror planes trading places in the sky. I hoped our pilot or some form of instrumentation – radar? – noted the approaching aircraft.

What if our radar was broken?

The other plane's radar would surely handle things; that's the way it worked.

What if the radar was broken on both planes?

My palms started sweating and I recalled the James Dickey poem titled "Falling", about a stewardess tumbling from the heart of the sky. Beautiful and horrifying, the poem mythologizes the sometimes plunging, sometimes flying woman until she unites mystically with the earth. I rarely think of that poem until I'm trapped inside a plane, when the myth and metaphor strip away and all I see is a woman spinning from a broken plane to the ground, "Oh God" her last words before she becomes red mush.

Danbury returned, settled into her seat, gave me a quizzical look. "Don't look so anxious, Ryder. They'll break out the peanuts soon enough."

Another shudder; a creaking sound from somewhere in the guts of the plane. The wingtip fluttered. Did they always flex like that? What if they didn't?

Oh God.

She glanced down, saw my fingers clutching my knee. "How can you be afraid of flying? You drive around with Nautilus."

"Small aircraft don't bother me," I confessed. "Cessnas, Beeches. With a pilot I know." The plane quivered through turbulence. My stomach followed.

Danbury nodded toward the cockpit. "But now you're at the mercy of a pilot you hope isn't having a suicidal meltdown and a crew of mechanics you hope haven't been on a cocaine binge for eight days running. I'm not even going to mention terrorists."

"Thanks for the encouragement."

"I hear that even with all the factors thrown in, it's safer than crossing the street."

261

"The difference is, crossing the street I choose where and when to cross. Or if."

She smiled. "It's control. Up here you have to rely on people you don't know."

I grunted a non-response. Her eyes scanned my face. She said, "You don't trust many people, do you, Ryder?"

"Sure I do. Lots."

"Who?"

"Harry Nautilus."

"That's one. Care to try for two?"

The lights of the approaching plane crossed by, miles away; we weren't going to crash, at least not yet. I hid my exhalation of relief and turned to watch an infant squirming in its mother's arms three rows up.

"Ryder?"

I signaled for a headset. "I'm going to watch the movie, maybe get some sleep. Talk to you later."

The weariness from days of racing down blind alleys overcame my tension and I fell into a rich and soothing sleep, awakening over green French fields. Perhaps it was the sleep or simply knowing there was land beneath me – even if miles down – but I felt solid and refreshed. Danbury had herself succumbed to sleep and was snoring lightly. The attendant walked past.

"We're beginning the approach, sir. Perhaps you wish to awaken your companion."

"I would, but she specifically asked to sleep until the very last possible moment."

"I heard that, Ryder," Danbury muttered, pushing up from

dreamland. She scrabbled through her purse for a breath mint and popped it in her mouth, then finger-combed strands of hair from her face. "I'd kill for a cup of coffee."

"They're not serving anymore."

"My head's numb. I need coffee."

"Maybe when we set down."

The attendant passed by again, solicitous eyes over the passengers. Danbury grabbed at her throat, made a dry coughing sound. The attendant turned.

"Are you all right, miss?"

Danbury's chest heaved. She made a raspy sound. "Just a dry throat, a tickle. Can't breathe."

The attendant patted Danbury's shoulder. "I'll get you a bottle of water."

"Coffee . . . would be . . . even better," she hacked.

The attendant retreated to the galley for the coffee. Danbury winked. The plane tipped forward and I closed my eyes and tried not to think of Dickey's plunging stewardess, but it didn't work.

We touched Orly's runway at noon local time. I'd bumped the chore of hotel selection to Danbury, and she'd found an old and elegant establishment near the Seine, the rooms small but well appointed. The furniture was honest wood, the ceilings high. The lamps were brass as bright as new trumpets. There were flowers and bottles of water. She went to unpack and shower, and I did the same. The soap was translucent and smelled like fresh-cut wood.

My sense of living was returning when a light knock came at the door. I finished dressing and answered it. Danbury rushed in, holding a copy of *Le Monde* she'd picked up at the front desk. She'd changed into a dark suit with a white silk blouse. Her skirt broke at her knees, and she wore black hose and black semi-heeled pumps. Her outfit was attractive, professional with artsy overtones. She sat on the bed, bounced, kicked off her shoes.

"We're in. I just spoke to the nasty Miss Mimi and she says Monsieur Badentier will see us at three. It's when he rises from his afternoon snooze."

Danbury scooted to the top of the bed, yanked a pillow from beneath the covers and cushioned her back against the headboard. She sat cross-legged with little sense of modesty. I worked hard to keep my eyes on her face.

She said, "We've got to get him talking about Hexcamp. What if all he wants to talk about is art? I can't keep saying, 'Ah, Picasso.'"

"You speak French, I speak pidgin art, mainly Post-Impressionism through Moderne."

It stopped her. "I'm impressed, Ryder. No, speechless would be a better term. You've been hiding your light under a barrel. Someone told me you got a degree in psychology."

"Somehow and barely. But the early days of psychological analysis, Freud mainly, had a major impact on the art of the day. Since my scholastic career generally involved studying anything but my major, I started reading about Dada, sur-realism, and suchnot. For a month I even wore a Salvador Dali mustache . . ."

I shot my index fingers straight up, one on either side of my nose, not mentioning that while I've never been

264

considered particularly bright-looking, it was the stupidest look I'd ever achieved.

"Dali? I remember him. He painted that thing with melting clocks."

"Watches. *The Persistence of Memory*," I said.

"I knew there was a reason I brought you along." She leaned back on my bed, snapped *Le Monde* open and started reading. I couldn't prevent my eyes from flicking to the generous stretch of thigh gliding into the shadows beneath her dark skirt.

I told her I needed a walk to get my head straight.

The door of our hotel closed behind me and I walked up the street to a small outdoor café. For a moment I felt overwhelmed by French voices and wished I'd invited Danbury along. After a few minutes and a cup of coffee – a word understood most places, I suspect – a sense of comfort set in, though this was easily the most distance ever put between me and Mobile. This was also the farthest I'd ever been from Jeremy, who would, in the remaining thirty-five or so years still Biblically allotted him, travel no farther than the confines of a maximum-security hospital-cum-prison not far from Montgomery.

For a moment, I fantasized sending my brother mind flashes: *Look, Jeremy*: the woman dropping the cube of sugar into her espresso, lifting the demitasse as though it were made of ice, her pinkie aloft and delicate; *Over there, Jeremy*: the matron wrapped in fur, cording round her feet two yapping dogs, performing le wee-wee against a lamppost. *Across the street, Jeremy*: the florist in the sun outside his shop, sitting at a small table and paring thorns from rose stems.

My brother murdered our father when I was nine and Jeremy was fifteen. He did it – as he claimed and I believed – to save me from my father's blind rages, until then directed at Jeremy. A few years later, Jeremy directed his anger at our mother for never protecting him from our mad father. But to kill her was to consign me to an orphanage or foster home, so, as Marcella Baines noted, my brother sought surrogates.

He wasn't a stalker but bait. Jeremy positioned himself in a park, or the lobby of a hotel, looking dejected, his frail and sensitive features eliciting pity, drawing concerned, motherly women like ants to sugar.

"Can I help you, son? You look so sad . . ."

Though Jeremy's hatred of our mother was a constant in his various denunciations, she was blameless, a woman of childlike naïveté unable to fathom the world into which she had been plunged. She could not shield herself from either my father or cancer, and when the final days of shrieking pain arrived, refused any medication, hoping agony would scour away her sins and allow entrance to heaven. I was the only one in our family spared, "neuroticized without having my soul burned away," as my brother once framed it.

A soft voice at my shoulder. "Monsieur looks sad. I hope it will pass."

My waitress, a woman in her forties with concern in her eyes. I pushed a smile to my lips. "I was thinking of a distant friend and how sad it is he can't be here," I said. "I myself am fine, thank you."

She studied me for a moment. "*Bien, monsieur.* Life is too short for sorrow. I wish your friend all the best."

She returned to the kitchen. It suddenly struck me that this was how it had worked for Jeremy – a sad face, a concerned woman, the eruption of his madness.

I finished my coffee and stood to leave. The waitress waved farewell like I was an old friend. I stopped at the florist across the way and had him deliver her two dozen roses.

CHAPTER 36

Nearby churches took several minutes to disagree on the meaning of three p.m. as we crossed the road to the address Danbury had received. The buildings lining the wide avenue were brick, long and slender and between four and six stories tall. Some windows held flowerboxes, flat smiles of red and yellow and white. We turned up a short flight of concrete stairs from the sidewalk to a large wooden door. Danbury pressed a buzzer, announcing us into an electronic box. The lock on a glass door buzzed and we pushed through. There was a small elevator to the right and I entered, jumping in fright when a voice at my waist asked, "Are you going up or going down?"

I looked down and saw a dwarf. He was the elevator operator, something I thought existed only in black-and-white movies. He wore a well-appointed dark beard, round brass-framed glasses, and a uniform similar to a bellhop's. Oblivious to my stare, he closed the grated door as Danbury stepped aboard.

"Though I offered the choice of up or down," he continued, "I admit there is no down, at least not so far as this floor is concerned. Your choices are between floor one and floor five. I can stop in between floors, if you wish. I must advise that it makes exiting the elevator difficult."

"You speak English," I said, ridiculously. He spun a small wheel and we rose, wheels squealing beside us and cables rattling above.

"No, I'm speaking Chinese. You're only hearing it in English. Floor?"

"We're going to five," Danbury said.

"To see Monsieur Badentier or Madame? If it is the latter you may prefer I stop between floors."

Danbury looked down. "I've spoken with Mme Badentier a time or two, monsieur. She seems rather difficult."

Our operator considered for a moment. "Having sex with a taxicab is difficult. Mme Badentier is impossible."

"We are actually here to see Monsieur Badentier," I said.

"No matter. You will see her. She is inescapable."

The floors passed by. The elevator trembled. "What is he like?" I asked. "Monsieur Badentier."

"He picks times and places that make him happy. He will want to play. I advise you to play. I offer one thought: the commonplace will never win."

We reached the top and stopped abruptly. The operator

retracted the grates. We stepped into a narrow hall with a door at the end. The dwarf engaged the Down mechanism.

"In an elevator traveling near the speed of light," he said, disappearing into the floor, "we would all be much shorter. Even me."

Danbury pulled me from staring at the departed elevator and led the way down the hall. The door swung open with my knuckles poised to strike. Behind it stood a sixtyish woman who redefined "severe". Critical, perhaps.

Her face was white and heart-shaped, chin tapered to a point, an improbably long neck. Jet-black hair was pulled straight back and anchored. Her lips were thin and reddened. She flared her nostrils, as if gauging us by scent, then pulled the door open, a flick of her head bidding us enter.

Mimi Badentier wore a full-length dress as black as her hair and embellished at the swooping décolletage with small opaline stones reminiscent of eyes. Around her long neck hung a pendant, the eye motif again. I was reminded of Cerberus, and hoped she was less diligent in her guardian-ship of Le Monsieur.

Danbury said a few words. When she pointed to me and said, "Monsieur Carson Ryder," I held out my hand. Madame studied it like a curiosity until it returned to my care. Mimi pointed a long finger at a pair of chairs against the wall and we sat. She spoke a few words and disappeared behind the brown door. Danbury said, "She's going to announce us to *L'Homme Grand*. Sit tight."

Danbury pulled *Le Monde* from her outsized purse and read as I scanned the room. There was a small, neatly kept desk in the corner, a rack of books, a grandfather clock against the wall. When Mimi left, the clock seemed to tick louder.

When I was young, five perhaps, and we'd moved to a temporary setting while my father worked some engineering miracle, our furnished rental house had a grandfather clock. I recall how it focused attention on the silence of our home by cutting loudly across it, like a lighthouse calls attention to the dark. My child's mind had invented two-beat phrases to accompany the tick-tock swings of the pendulum, filling the darkness with imagined sounds.

Tick-tock
Don't walk
Tick-tock
Old sock
Tick-tock
Hard knock. Door lock, don't talk . . .

I wanted to cross the room, open the case, grab grandfather by the pendulum and throttle him into silence. When I didn't, he mocked me for another five minutes, until the door opened and deposited Mimi in the room.

"Monsieur Badentier will see you now."

"*Merci*," Danbury said, returning the paper to her purse. "Come on, Ryder. Let's meet the great man."

We started toward the room. The woman stopped Danbury, spoke in a whisper for a minute. The woman tapped her watch. Danbury looked at me, raised an eyebrow.

I said, "We're on a time budget?"

"She's leaving for the market after our introduction. When she returns our time is up. She figures twenty minutes. But that's not the big story. Seems Mr Badentier takes little fits from time to time, imagines he's famous French painters. I guess today we're talking to a guy named Marcel Duchamp. You familiar with that one, Ryder? He someone famous?"

"*Sacré bleu,*" I said.

We followed Mimi through the door. The room was perhaps fifty feet in length, a quarter that in width. Add the twelve-foot ceiling and you had the proportions of shoebox. Paintings were stacked against the walls, some boxed, some loose. In the far corner several canvases were covered with an old dropcloth. The only light came from a large window at the far end, opening across the vista of Paris. The room was thick with the scent of linseed oil and pipe tobacco.

My eyes took several seconds to adjust to the dim light. I saw a bed at the far end, backlit by the window. In the bed a small man lay propped up on pillows, motionless. We approached. At first it seemed the only living portion of the old man was his eyes, black and bright and riveted on our passage across the room. His mouth resurrected, stretching from flat line to wide arch of smile. His voice box kicked in with a hoarse rasp of what I took to be pleasure. Thin arms lifted from the bedclothes and waved us closer. I looked at Mimi Badentier. She did not appear pleased.

A black marble-topped table perhaps a meter square stood between us and the old man. He suddenly sat fully erect and spun to face us. He wore a heavy woolen robe, purple, and his bare legs dangled over the side.

"*Les oreillers,*" he said, his eyes never leaving Danbury and me. His sister moved to him and adjusted the pillows to prop him in our direction.

"*Pantoufles*," he directed, and she knelt and tucked his white feet into brown leather slippers.

"*Vin*," he said next. Sister Mimi reached behind one of the canvases and produced an almost-full bottle of red wine, and a wineglass.

"*Trois verres*," he snapped. Mimi reddened and produced two more glasses. As she filled the glasses I studied the table. It seemed a repository of detritus: a wine cork, salt cellar, bottle cap, several colored buttons of mother-of-pearl, a thimble, white feather, earring, and so forth. All items were approximately equidistant, as if an attempt at order was under way. At the edge of the table was a ceramic ash tray, its pipe rest cupping a well-worn briar.

The man pointed to the pipe and made some command to his sister. She twitched at his words, then set down the glasses and lifted the pipe to her lips. She struck a kitchen match and fired up the dottle, clouds of gray smoke pouring forth. After several seconds of puffing, she held the pipe low. Badentier leaned his face into the rolling plume of smoke, breathed deeply.

"*Ah, l'odeur du ciel.*"

She set the pipe in its holder, shot us a hot eye, spun, and retreated silently from the room, her turbulence roiling the smoke in the air. I saw the man staring at the table and followed his eyes to a small spider crossing the table slowly, seemingly numbed by smoke. It crawled to the edge and retreated to the underside.

I smiled at the old guy. "Howdy, Marcel."

He stared at me without expression, then shivered a finger at the black tabletop and said several words.

Danbury looked at me. "He says he wants to play."

I studied the pile of refuse on the table, tried to make sense of it. Marcel took a sip of vino and seemed to enjoy my confusion.

"Pardon me?" I said.

He raised a puckish eyebrow. I looked at the objects on the table and searched my memory. "He wants to play chess," I said finally. "Marcel Duchamps quit his art career at its height and studied chess, claiming it was the only true art."

Danbury stared at the junk-filled table. "You're saying this stuff, this table . . . is his chessboard?"

The old man nodded at the bits of detritus, waved his hand like a benediction. "*Echecs*," he said. "Shess."

"It appears that way."

He spoke again, followed by a wink at Danbury. She gave me a grim smile. "He says if you win, he'll talk with us. If you lose he'll take a nap."

I looked at Marcel. He had turned away, an enigmatic smile on his lips. I reached to the table and pushed a thimble two inches ahead. The old man shot his arm to the table, set a finger atop a button and slid it to my left. I countered by moving my coiled pipecleaner to face his feather. He shifted a matchstick. I retreated the salt cellar. He moved a paperclip, I advanced an earring. His pen-cap fled. I chased it with a nutshell. He studied, looked perplexed, then quickly switched positions of a bolt and eraser.

274

"I think he castled," I said.

"Do something."

I advanced my button to his penknife. The old man raised his face and smiled wickedly. Danbury whispered, "I think you're tanking." The old man brought his nail into play and in three swift moves took my nutshell. He emitted a short bark of laughter and set a cork beside my earring.

"Shaques," he announced.

"I think he's saying *Check*, pogie."

I studied the table, sweat gathering beneath my arms. Marcel watched me carefully, his dark eyes unblinking. My heart was the loudest sound in the room. A motion caught my eye: the spider that had previously crossed the table reappeared on my side. I watched its halting progress, an idea forming. I set my finger in the path of the spider and it crawled aboard. I set the smoke-woozy arachnid in front of the cork. Badentier leaned forward, transfixed. The spider hesitated, scuttled right, corrected left, then climbed atop Badentier's piece and stopped. The old man's eyes widened.

"*Dada shah-mat*," I said, recalling shah-mat was the original word for checkmate, Persian. The spider had created a random occurrence, a dadaist checkmate. Only a Marcel Duchamp could appreciate the beauty of the moment.

"*Alors*," he said, shaking his head. He tipped his cork in surrender. The spider staggered away. The old man looked at me and raised a gray eyebrow, inviting questions.

"Marsden Hexcamp?" I said.

He started laughing.

CHAPTER 37

"Ex-comp? Marss-den Excomp?" He slapped his bony thigh and continued to laugh, a high reedy quiver broken by gasps. I moved back a step to let Danbury ask questions or administer CPR. She said a few words, then handed Marcel a photo of Hexcamp taken at the trial. The old man nodded.

"Oui, 'excomp."

"Ask him about Hexcamp's art, Danbury."

She spoke a sentence or two. Marcel held a bone-white thumb and forefinger a half-inch apart and replied. Danbury asked a couple more questions and the old man repeated a briefer version of the cackle and the fingerspace gesture. This was followed by pinching his thumb and forefinger over his open mouth, as if dropping something in.

"Danbury?"

"Mr Duchamp remembers our Mr Hexcamp quite well, instructing him in figure drawing and perspective in particular, as well as painting."

"And?"

"What he recalls most about Marss-den Ex-comp is his talent was about this much –" Danbury repeated the old man's gesture, thumb and finger a half-inch apart. "He also referred to Marsden as a charming young man who firmly thought himself a misunderstood genius. And who probably went home at night and ate bugs."

"Not a candidate for the well-adjusted club? See what you can get on Hexcamp's mental state."

Danbury fired strands of French at the old man. In Mobile I would have watched the interviewee's eyes and body for reactions to words and phrases. Lacking that ability, I studied Danbury's voice, her French an aural version of a mountain stream gliding over rounded stones.

"*Ceci est fini!*" a woman's voice cawed.

The door behind us opened and Mme Badentier strode in, her high heels gunshots on the wooden floor. "*Fini!*" She clapped her hands, spoke rapidly to Danbury.

"We're getting the bum's rush," Danbury said to me. "She thinks we're tiring Marcel."

I held two fingers up. "Two minutes," I pleaded to Mimi. "Please."

The woman crossed her arms and glared. "*Non.*"

Non I understood. Not knowing this, she repeated it.

I looked at the old man. "Another game?" I said, pointing at the board. "Chess, Monsieur Duchamp?"

The old man's eyes lit with delight.

"*Non, non, non,*" the woman said, taking me under the arm and trying to pull me from the room.

"Mimi," the old man said softly. She froze, turned to him. He looked at the door. "*Quittez la chambre.*"

Her eyes blazed at me and she spat a few words in French, not water over stones, but rocks against my head.

"She's coming back in ten minutes," Danbury said. "Hurry."

Marcel reset the table, this time adding a corkscrew and empty snailshell to the mix. He checked beneath the table for another spider. Finding none, he advanced a white feather. I greeted it with my thumbtack. He grunted.

"Don't piss him off. Lose, just take a few minutes to do it."

"Ask him questions, Danbury. And hit him again with the vino."

"*Vin?*" The old man's eyes sparkled as Danbury poured a healthy shot into his glass. He tapped the glass with his finger, grinned at Danbury, said a few words.

"Oh shit," Danbury said.

"What."

"He wants me to smoke the damned pipe."

"Fire it up. Bet they didn't teach that in J-school."

Danbury made a face and lit the pipe. She puffed and hacked and gagged, tears welling in her eyes. "Scent of heaven, my ass," she gasped. "It tastes like fried lint." When it was burning strong, she lowered it to his face. He wafted smoke to his nose with his hand.

"*Ah, l'odeur du ciel.*"

Marcel and I moved and countermoved, tacks and feathers and shells shifting on the surface of the table. While we dueled in the smoke-filled air, Danbury kept up a running conversation with the old man, translating without missing a beat. She didn't ask questions while Marcel pondered a move but after it, saving the most involved questions until he took one of my pieces, which made him more garrulous. It was the perfect response to the situation, probably as useful to a reporter as a cop.

I listened and fired questions back, simultaneously trying to ascertain the rankings of the items on the table, hoping to stay in the game long enough for Danbury to ask all the questions. It became rhythmic, dance-like. Danbury and I were almost in the zone Harry and I sometimes reached, knowing in advance how the other will act, even in a completely fluid situation.

I advanced a pen nib, and Danbury kept up her dual conversation. "He says Hexcamp had a crude vitality to his work. But he wasn't masterful, more an illustrator than an artist. Hexcamp never realized his limitations, calling his critics liars and jealous of his talents."

My nib fell to the salt cellar. Danbury kept translating.

"Hexcamp fancied himself a roué, a playboy. But again he deluded himself. He was a . . . a . . ."

The old man cackled at Danbury and made a circle with his left thumb and forefinger, thrusting his right forefinger through it. After several repetitions, he clamped down with his left hand, trapping his finger. He giggled, that high keening sound, followed by a few more words.

"Translation, Danbury."

"Hexcamp was a slave to, uh, pussy. Evidently he needed to dominate women in public, be dominated by them in private."

I answered a paperclip thrust with my button parry. "How does Marcel know this?"

Danbury spoke. Marcel replied briefly, aiming his hands at one another, opening and closing them quickly. I heard the sound *pa-ree*.

"It's Paris, everyone gossips," I ventured.

Danbury grinned. "Damn. You're learning the language."

Marcel spun a matchbook in a circle. I jumped it with an eyedropper. He whispered *merde*, bumped the eyedropper with his cork and spoke several more sentences.

"He says Hexcamp's charm, his words, his lovely face, drew women like moths. But the women were always burned."

Badentier's snailshell took my candle nub. "By Hexcamp?" I asked.

"*Vin*," the old man bayed.

Danbury jumped for the bottle and refilled his glass while translating. "By another woman; she'd let the new women stay for a few days – fresh toys for Marsden – then send them packing. It was the woman who herself drew Hexcamp like a moth. He loved her fire and sought it. She held his heart in her hands, alternately kissing and biting it. It drove him insane with need."

I took his eraser with my button. Danbury froze, cocked her head. "I hear the elevator. It's not been ten minutes."

"Maybe metric minutes are shorter. Ask about the woman. Who was she?"

He set a thimble behind my bobbin, flicked the bobbin from the table. My pieces were disappearing. He traded sentences with Danbury.

"One of a circle of friends of Hexcamp's. Some students, some the usual crowd of Paris drifters. They blew in like gypsies, stole what they could, then scattered like leaves."

"What was her name, Danbury?"

I met his breadcrust with my watch crystal. He snorted, then zoomed in a bottlecap from the far edge of the board and dropped it over my watch crystal. He started laughing, wiggled a gnarled forefinger at me.

"*Echec*," he said. Check.

"The damned cap," I said. "I never saw it coming."

Danbury turned an ear toward the door. "Footsteps outside. Madame is closing in."

"Did the woman have a name, Danbury? Ask him."

As Danbury leaned in with her question, the door opened and Mimi strode across the floor like a bee-stung Amazon. She grabbed us by our arms and pulled us toward the door with surprising strength. The table tipped, wine slashed across the floor. Danbury yelled, "What was the name of the woman? Hexcamp's woman?"

But Marcel was studying the wet floor, perhaps planning his next game. Mimi hustled us into the anteroom. The door to Marcel slammed with the concussion of a shotgun blast. Her long finger twitched at the front door. "Out."

"Please," I begged the statue of her face. "One more question, *une question*."

She walked to the door to the hall, opened it. "*Non*."

"You were *there*, weren't you?" I said. "At the academy? You've always cared for your brother in one way or another?" We were in the hall. Danbury spun my words into French. The woman stared at me. I saw fear in her eyes.

I said, "You were there, Mimi. I see it in your face. Tell her the truth, Danbury. We've come five thousand miles because people are dying and I don't know why."

Danbury spoke as the door squeezed shut. The building went quiet as stone. "I think we've worn out our welcome," she said quietly.

We shuffled down the hall to the elevator. Our diminutive operator was nowhere in attendance, a rolled-shut paper bag left in his place. I opened it to discover a croissant and a single white ballet slipper. After several halting attempts – and one terrifyingly fast two-floor descent – I deposited us on the first floor.

"Watch your step. Where to now, Danbury?"

"You have to meet with some local cops to make the nut on the grant, right?"

We headed out the door. I shrugged. "It would make the chief happy. The accountants, too. Might as well do something."

She pulled out her notes, flicked her hand in the air, and had a cab in front of us in seconds.

CHAPTER 38

Security at the police substation was rigorous. While our papers were scrutinized, we were led to a small bench in a corridor and told to sit and not move. We did just that. I scanned the bustle of activity, finding patterns recognizable from home. My gaze brought me to a square-built man with ruffled gray hair. He leaned against a pillar two dozen feet away and studied us from beneath a frown. I looked away, locked my fingers behind my head and enjoyed the show until a beefy French cop told Danbury whoever she'd spoken to from Mobile wasn't in and we'd have to say *au revoir*.

He escorted us toward the door as Danbury argued the point with little success. Just when it seemed the street was inevitable – how many places could we be booted from in one day? – a gruff voice behind us made our escort disappear without a word.

I turned to see the man who had been studying me from across the room. He gestured us back into the station and led us to a small, glassed-in office awash with files and papers. He sat, nodded toward two chairs. He looked at me.

"You are a gend—, a policeman."

I was surprised. "How do you know?"

"I watched you walk in the door. You studied the room and relaxed. There are few people who relax while in a department of police: hardened criminals, and, of course, other police."

"What makes you think we're not hardened criminals; jewel thieves or the like?"

He paused a moment, as if finding the precise English before he spoke.

"I saw you smile before; it was real, a smile using both eyes and mouth. Criminals can't smile: the eyes never perfectly synchronize with the mouth. The smile is the first item a life of dishonesty steals." He nodded toward Danbury. "Plus, criminals do not generally travel in such lovely company."

"Who are you, sir?" I asked.

It turned out that we were in the presence of Deputy Inspector Bernard Latrelle, which explained our sudden acceptance into the heart of the department. We introduced ourselves and I handled the major business first.

"We have a strange story, Inspector Latrelle," I said. "But first I have to say, 'smuggling.'"

A raised eyebrow. "Your strange story is about smuggling, Detective Ryder?"

"No. But now that we've discussed smuggling, the government will pay for my trip."

Latrelle had a rich laugh, and it punctuated my explanation of the payment plan for my journey. As a cop, he'd seen it before, bureaucracy having no borders. I shifted subjects. Latrelle was fascinated by my story of Marsden Hexcamp. "The art of the final moment?" he asked at one point.

"Yes," I said.

Latrelle shook his head and kept writing. My telling took ten minutes and he reviewed the notes carefully.

"I will look back through the records for any crimes corresponding to yours. Are there any other questions before you leave?"

On a whim, I handed him a copy of the art with the Eiffel Tower in the background. He studied it, looking between my face and the drawing. "And?"

I said, "Is there a location from which such a drawing could be made?"

He looked at me. "You don't know?"

"It's a puzzle, sort of."

He looked around the file-blanketed office. "You have paperwork, do you not? At your police department in Mobile."

I held my palm a meter off the floor.

"As you've noticed, so do I," he said. "You've given me a reason to escape it for a few moments."

We followed him to a large black Renault parked outside by a hydrant. I gestured for Danbury to take the front and I sat in back. We whisked through the streets of Paris, me studying everything from the corner of my eye, trying to seem jaded, *just another day in the City of Light.* Not Danbury. She pointed at everything, asking rapid-fire questions in two languages. Latrelle enjoyed her enthusiasm.

I had but one question: Would Monsieur Latrelle be so kind as to engage the siren for a moment? He did, and it performed a satisfying wah-hunh, wah-hunh.

Ten minutes later, Latrelle parked on a narrow boulevard studded with trees. He pointed to a cluster of rectangular brick buildings with gray mantels beneath the windows. A small courtyard separated the buildings and young men and women sat on benches or sprawled on the green lawn. Most were conversing, others drawing in tablets. A young man sat against a tree and strummed a water-blue guitar.

"Formerly l'Académie d'Art Graphique," Latrelle said, "now l'École d'Art et de Conception – the School of Art and Design. Paris is always changing, never changed."

We walked past the buildings and up a rise to a small park overlooking the city. There were a dozen empty benches and the requisite bronze statue. Several large and stately trees were in attendance, a species of oak, it appeared, ringed at their bases with yellow flowers. A sense of tranquility suffused the place.

Latrelle led us to a small brick circle at the edge of the overlook. An iron fence denoted the perimeter. A spreading tree stood twenty yards beyond, down the incline. In the distance, over rooftops and between buildings, was the Eiffel Tower. Latrelle bade me lean against the fence.

"Here is where you stood," the old gendarme said, tapping the photo with his finger. "Now do you remember?"

"I've never been here. There's speculation the drawing might have been made thirty-five years ago."

"A relative?" he asked, glancing between me and the picture.

"No one in my family has ever been to France."

He studied the picture again, then raised a world-weary eyebrow.

"Someone is lying," he said. "You or time."

Latrelle dropped us on the opposite side of the wide boulevard from the hotel. We crossed it in a scattering of pigeons, our steps quiet in the grass. A trio of young mothers sat on a bench and watched toddlers play with an orange ball. For a moment I recalled the shotgunned woman in the Mobile alley, her body in the street and the orange in the nearby grass. I wondered if Roy Trent had nailed it shut.

Surely, I thought; it's been two weeks.

"Over there," Danbury said, touching my arm and pointing. On a park bench opposite the entrance to our hotel sat the lone figure of Mimi Badentier. She looked frightened, her white hands clasping and releasing on her dress.

"What do you think she wants?" Danbury said.

I had thought Mimi's guardianship of her brother excessive, overwrought, like she had a personal stake in our questions.

"Maybe she needs to tell us secrets," I said.

CHAPTER 39

"Most were children with faces like poems by Verlaine," Mimi said in a hushed voice. "They were beautiful, but haunted."

We sat on facing benches pulled closer. Rather than sit across from Mimi – as I had done – Danbury sat beside the woman, a message of camaraderie over opposition.

"Marsden Hexcamp?" I said.

Mimi spoke in heavily accented English. "He was pure beauty. Like a ray of light. People only had to see him to want to be his friend, to make him happy, to make him say, 'Come with us tonight, we're going to a club.'"

I paused as a pair of taxis passed by fifty feet away, horns blaring at some slight. "What did people think of his art?" I asked.

"Most didn't understand it. My brother thought it excessively emotional and simplistic – zeal eclipsing talent."

"What was Hexcamp's reaction?"

"He declared no one had the capacity to understand his art but him and a few select comrades. He claimed a different artistic language, one not available to the bourgeois mentality instilled by the art establishment, my brother included. Marsden was adamant, almost obsessive, that art be his legacy. It seemed all he wanted from life was to be the next Picasso."

"What did people think of him?"

"Most thought him a little –" Mimi spun her finger at her temple: *crazy*. "Or maybe not so little. He didn't care. In the system of belief he cultivated, those who questioned or laughed at him were lesser beings, cattle. After a while, most people simply ignored his pronouncements. Except for a very few."

"The select few," I said. "The chosen."

"The wounded," Danbury corrected, her voice almost lost in the nearby traffic. "The tormented."

Mimi Badentier shook her head sadly. "Marsden gave off a sense not so much of personal strength, but of nurturing a grievous wound, one to his soul. He claimed he created from that suffering." Her eyes looked into mine. "Some people would rather follow a wounded man than one who is whole."

"They have a closer identity, perhaps?" Danbury said.

"The wounded man provides hope," I said. "The followers might never be whole, but could imagine their special pain provided abilities not available to others. Not to the degree of Hexcamp – someone had to be the leader, the paradigm – but they'd finally been granted worth."

"Abilities not available to others . . ." Danbury looked at me, raised an eyebrow.

I nodded. "Manna to a sociopath like Hexcamp. If the group's abilities were beyond the normal, it's axiomatic that the standard laws of society no longer applied."

Danbury said, "Insanity. But they lined up to follow."

Mimi's eyes stared into the past. I felt waving a blazing torch in front of her face wouldn't draw a flinch. "Mimi?" I said. She didn't hear.

"Mimi?" I repeated. "Hello?"

Her eyes came back. I put on my gentlest voice, one I'd learned from Harry. "These children, the lonely and special children, Mimi – were you one of them?"

She closed her eyes and turned her head away. When she turned back, her eyes were wet and her voice was a whisper.

"I wasn't yet thirty. I had never been to college; my only study was the typewriter, the stenography pad, the Dictaphone. My brother employed me as an assistant as a favor to our parents. All the while, swirling about me, were lovely young men and women with talent and sophistication. Or so it seemed to someone like me."

Danbury took Mimi's hand, held it. A shudder went through her body, passed into the ground at her feet like electricity. She took a deep breath.

"One day after work I walked into a café. Marsden was there. I knew who he was, of course. He knew me only as a lowly clerk, wandering the halls with papers and files and

290

mail. Yet he waved those around him into silence, and walked – no, glided – across the floor to me. His smile was a beacon, his eyes blue as the Mediterranean. He took my hand in his, said, 'Mimi Badentier, it is so nice to see you out on this beautiful evening. Please join us.' I was amazed he knew my name."

"He stole your heart," Danbury said.

"For several months I was one of them. Not openly; I didn't want to incur the laughter of others or the irritation of Henri, who considered Marsden a scandalous poseur. I met them outside Paris, in the countryside. Or at the parties in the garrets and basements. There was talk of art and music and . . . the physical pleasures."

"Was there talk of death?" I asked.

"Marsden loved to speak of it. The Holy Moment, he called death. Or the 'sugared edge of the razor'. He loved to invent phrases like that. But it was all just talk until . . ."

Another tremor passed through her. Danbury clasped the woman's hand tighter. Mimi whispered, "Until *she* came."

"She?"

Anger cut through the pain in Mimi's eyes. "*La femme de l'Enfer*. The woman from Hell. She wasn't a student, but we'd seen her before. She was attractive, aloof, always at the edge of our conversations, always listening, ears keen as a bat. I caught Marsden's glances at her. She always looked away, as if he was too insignificant for her eyes."

"Sounds like a tease to me," Danbury said.

"Several of us went to a bistro. It was late, but time meant nothing to Marsden. *She* was there. But different; she had colored her hair as red as fire, and wore a black dress. Someone whispered her dress was so tight you could count the hairs on her sex. Her lips were rouged dark, like a mix of blood and soot. When she walked, it was like an eel, everything flowing. I'd never seen anyone move like that. Her shoes were spiked like icepicks.

"She sat two tables away drinking something with fruit. She sucked the cherries, ran her tongue around slices of lime. Marsden was hypnotized. The talk at our table grew strident as we tried to distract Marsden from the woman. But he saw only her."

"Did she come over to your group?" Danbury asked, transfixed by the image.

"No, that's not how it worked," I said, seeing the moment full in my mind. "The woman didn't go to Marsden, did she, Mimi? She made Marsden come to her."

Mimi stared in amazement, as though I'd performed a psychic feat. Her voice went low.

"The woman crooked her finger and Marsden ran to her table like a dog in heat. They talked in candlelight and shadows. I watched her fill her mouth with ice, take his ear in her teeth, bite hard. His eyes glittered like stars. She led him out the door and we didn't see him for a week. He returned exhausted, as if he'd run around the world."

"After that?" I asked.

Mimi shook her head. "It was never the same. All his energies focused on her. His finest words went into her ears, his passionate glances were hers alone. Most left. The few who stayed were too needing of anything he could give them to leave. The separation would have been unbearable."

"Did you stay?" I asked.

Her eyes flashed. "You're strong by yourself. I feel strength pouring off both of you. I'm weak; I needed him like a drug; anything he could give." She lowered her head. "But they disappeared, Marsden and *her* and the rest of them. To America. It was the land of excess, the perfect place for them."

"This woman," I said. "What was her name?"

Mimi closed her eyes. Her lips pursed as if to spit. "The woman had no regular name. All anyone ever called her was Calypso."

Calypso.

I heard my heart pounding in my ears. If she'd called herself Calypso before coming to the US, it suggested Hexcamp might not have created the naming system. At first I'd thought the naming an affectation, artsy-cutesy. But it further removed the acolytes from their former lives, making them more dependent on Hexcamp. It also provided anonymity within the group once it fired up in the United States, making it difficult to penetrate.

It had proven to be a very effective system.

"Did you know a young woman named Marie?" I asked.

Mimi's eyes widened. "Marie Gilbeaux. Of course. Sweet little Marie. We sometimes called her Ma-*riche* because she received a parental stipend, a large one. She was generous with it. All she had to do to keep the money flowing was never go home. She joked about it, but there was deep suffering beneath the laughter. It was her special pain, I suppose."

I wanted to tell Mimi that Marie had spent over a quarter

century in peace. But she would have asked where Marie was today, and I didn't want to speak those words.

Perhaps sensing my thoughts, Danbury took a turn at the questions.

"Why did they all leave, Mimi? Marsden, Calypso, the group – you make it sound sudden."

Marie looked away. "They beat a man to death."

"Who?"

"I didn't know him. A strange man with a garret in the neighborhood. It was rumored he created wild art, amazing. But he let no one near, a hermit in the center of Paris. He didn't attend school, or join the café scene; all he did was work. Marsden had heard of the man, of his fantastic creations, and was always after the man to show him the work. Marsden was at his most charming, most deferential. One day the man took Marsden into his garret. When he returned he spoke to no one, and spent a week alone in the studio with Calypso."

A long pause. Mimi Badentier's hands started to shake. "Not long afterward I read the man had been found in his garret, robbed, beaten horribly. His studio had been savaged, his paintings set ablaze. He wasn't expected to live."

"You suspected it had been Marsden who attacked the artist?"

"The group. Some of them."

"Why?" Danbury said.

"Perhaps the artist slighted Marsden in some way, insulted him. The man had poor manners. If he'd belittled Marsden, I can see how his anger might . . ." her voice trailed off into silence.

"What did you do?" Danbury coaxed.

"I became terrified the police would question Marsden and

294

I'd be found out, my allegiance revealed. It would have angered Henri. I feigned illness and went home for two weeks. When I returned, the group had fled. I heard little more about the incident, and don't think it was ever connected to the group."

Was that their first taste of blood? I wondered. Finding they'd easily escaped detection in Paris, did they bring that mindset to America? Commence the bloody banquet across lower Alabama?

"Who followed Marsden, Mimi?" Danbury asked. "Who besides Calypso disappeared?"

Mme Badentier palmed tears from her cheeks. "A young Swiss girl, Heidi. A whiny young man named Ramone. I later saw him back in Paris. He'd been spurned by the group for turning to drugs, was a junkie when I saw him. I imagine he's dead now. There was a woman called Julia. There was Bonita, a Spaniard, Terri, an American girl. And, of course, Marie Gilbeaux, who would have done anything for Marsden, even after he was entranced by Calypso. But they all would have."

"That's the group?" I asked. "The only ones?"

Mimi thought. "Oh, and a woman named Nancy, a French girl. She was strange, a hippie type – flowing hair, bells, beads. She had a pretty voice and sang a lot." Mimi paused, said, "Oranges."

"What?"

"Nancy was the first vegetarian I ever knew. Fruits and vegetables only. She loved oranges. Twice a day she ate an orange. It was like a ritual."

"Will you excuse me while I make a phone call?" I stood, dizzied by the roaring in my ears.

CHAPTER 40

No one I needed was at the station, so I left a brief message
for Harry regarding the Orange Lady and her connection to
Hexcamp. It wouldn't be long until we'd return to Mobile,
but the info would give Harry time to pass the word to Roy
Trent, maybe get the action moving in a more productive
direction.

Neither Danbury nor I felt up to a large dinner, so we
dined modestly but well at a quiet hole-in-the-wall restaurant. We felt overdosed on information and drama, content
to let it ferment in our heads while enjoying the remaining
few hours in Paris. Danbury translated signs in windows,
snippets of overheard conversation. We dropped our
remaining euros in the hats and instrument cases of street
performers. After a few blocks the crowd thinned and we

found ourselves on a lamp-lit street bordered by three- and four-story stone buildings. Night slipped from twilight into dark, and light brightened in the windows of pawn shops and piano stores, bakeries and florists.

Danbury stopped short, grabbed my wrist.

"Look up there –" She pointed to a line of large windows on the second story of a brick building across the street. The windows were curtained with a silky, diaphanous material, shadows flowing over the fabric. Music drifted to us, rich and symphonic.

"Spooky," I said.

Danbury took my hand. "Let's check it out."

"We've got other things to –"

But I was under her control now, tugged across the street, dodging cars, taxis, a man on a bicycle. "There," she said, pointing to a sign above the door, L'ACADÉMIE DE DANSE CLASSIQUE. "It's a dance academy. Classical."

"I got that impression."

She pulled me toward a flight of stairs. Music poured down them like water in waltz time. "Come on, pogie. You're balking."

"Danbury? Have you gone –"

She had one hand on my sleeve, the other on the banister as we ascended the marble steps. There was a door at the top and she pushed it open.

Dancers. Perhaps two dozen couples. Most seemed in their sixties and seventies, the men in suits, the women in flowing dresses. They stepped and spun and dipped, amazingly adept. The room was high-ceilinged, the floor white, the walls red with triangles of light shot upward from brass sconces. The dancers were followed by shadows.

"It's like a movie. It isn't real," Danbury whispered.

I looked to the side of the room. Behind an ornate wooden bar a mustachioed man in a black suit poured glasses of champagne. He was talking to a handsome woman in a black velvet gown, her dark hair in an elegant bouffant. She looked beautiful and mysterious and every inch a painting by John Singer Sargent. The woman's eyes found us, and she brightened, moving our way with athletic grace belying perhaps seventy years of age. She offered her hand and her smile. I greeted her in English, and she responded in kind.

"I am Serena Chardin. Have you come to dance? Please tell me yes."

Danbury said, "You all dance so beautifully. This is a school?"

Mme Chardin laughed, a lovely sound. "We usually teach dance, many of us. From across Paris, beyond. Tonight is not for students, it is – what would you say? – for social. It is our turn to dance."

Danbury explained our presence. Serena Chardin nodded. "Goodness, all that way for so little time in Paris. And work besides. You must stay and dance. And, of course, share some champagne."

"I, uh –"

Mme Chardin was summoned from across the room by a dapper old gent beside a phonograph. He seemed to wish to consult on selections. She excused herself and glided away.

Danbury said, "Want to give a quick twirl around the floor? Having been invited, it's the diplomatic thing to do."

I said, "I can't dance a lick. Who our age can dance like that anyway?"

"I can. Can you believe it?"

"Your grandmother again?"

"Grand-mère thought the waltz de rigueur for all young ladies of breeding. I had no one to dance with. In my neighborhood clogging was all the rage. Grand-mère believed clogging more seizure than dancing."

I felt my face redden with embarrassment. "I don't know the slightest thing about dancing of any kind."

"Then you'll have to let me lead. Can you handle that, mon pogibeau?" There was a shadow of challenge in her voice.

"I'll manage."

Mme Chardin made a proclamation and music commenced. The recording was on vinyl, and opened with hisses and crackles. Violins swept into the room, followed by woodwinds. The dancers around us found partners, began to move. Danbury took my hands, guiding them gently.

"This hand holds my hand, this hand goes right here."

I did as instructed; she was warm both places. "Ready?" Danbury said. "*Un, deux, trois?*"

I started haltingly, stumbling, mismatched to her rhythm and motion. My knees knocked hers, my feet kicked her toes. She held me tighter, whispered, *relax . . . un deux trois*. I searched for her rhythm and released my body to it, *un, deux, trois*, my feet finding the shape of the dance. At first she used her hands and hips to show me the way, and then all she needed was her eyes. We spun, sashayed, dipped; our moves rudimentary, but fluid. We broke for champagne, returned to the floor.

Somewhere in all the *un deux trois,* an hour disappeared.

At ten p.m., the music stopped. Everyone applauded. Participants bade us farewell and drifted out the door. Mme Chardin appeared and patted our hands between hers. "You are such a handsome couple, so beautiful in one another's arms. Will you return?"

"Whenever I dream," Danbury said.

The night was soft as we walked to our hotel through cones of streetlight. We passed a wine shop. I reached out and took DeeDee Danbury's hand, my turn to lead. "I owe you a bottle of wine," I said. "Would you prefer red or white?"

"Silly you," she said. "It's a night for champagne."

CHAPTER 41

Danbury snapped the airphone back in the holder. "I can't figure out where Borg is. This is the first time in two years I haven't been able to track him down."

"What do you need him for?"

"He could videotape us coming off the plane, walking through the terminal. If this project comes together, it'll be a nice shot: intrepid PSIT hotshot Carson Ryder returns to Mobile with fresh evidence, assisted by his trusted sidekick, *la femme* Danielle."

"Two minutes after the chief saw that, I'd be washing cruisers."

"Not if the story has a happy ending, pogie. Hey, can I call you Carson now and then? I remember calling it out a time or two last night." She smiled. "You didn't seem to mind."

I tried to smile back, but it curdled and I looked away. Her fingers touched my arm, slid to my hand.

I eased it away. "I've got to call Harry."

She studied my eyes, then sat back as I made the call, hearing otherworldly sounds as the signal bounced off satellites or the moon or whatever. "Hey, bro," I said above the twitters and boinks. "It's your long-lost partner. The Orange Lady, Nancy, what'd you find out?"

"Nancy Chastain. She was with them, Cars. Hexcamp's crew. Didn't draw any incarceration, probably because she was such a sad case, and never directly participated in the killings. Later she became more disassociative. But a gentle kind of crazy; lived in the home, fed the neighborhood cats, made her citrus runs. Harmless."

"And she's killed Monday, one to two days after Marie Gilbeaux. Was there any art in Nancy's life?"

"None found; we're still looking. Anything else?"

"Lots to tell, Harry, but nothing pressing. You gonna pick us up at the airport?"

"Lawdy yessir, massa Ryder. I'se living for it." He paused. "Cars?"

"What, bro?"

"You and Danbury work out fine together?"

I started to answer, but something jammed in my throat. "I can't hear you, Harry," I rasped. "We're going through sunspots or something." I jammed the device back in the holder.

The attendant wheeled the cart down the aisle. I got a ginger ale, Danbury a coffee. She blew across its surface, turned to me.

"Are you OK about last night, Carson? You seem different this morning. Like you've got a touch of the regrets." She paused. "Oh my gosh . . . are you seeing someone? Is that it? Jeez, we should have talked about that beforehand, not that there was much time. Are you involved?"

I looked out the window. The clouds were bursts of white above a sea like blue mercury. "No. That is, I was. I don't know."

"A relationship in transition."

"That's a good way to put it."

"Transition up or down?" She did the Roman emperor thumb, skyward, floorward.

"I don't have a clue."

"Which way do you want it to go?"

"I'm not sure."

"Where does she want it to go?"

"I can't tell."

"How about this one, Carson: Do you know her name?"

I couldn't help it; I laughed, full and open. The sound rushed through me, like the first breath after a long underwater swim. It occurred to me that last night had felt pretty much the same.

Her finger touched my chin, angled my face to hers. "We made love, Carson. In the City of Light. I think if you get a chance to have an intimate experience with a person you trust, go for it. That kind of trust is rare, at least in my experience, and to be savored. I thought last night was beautiful all the way through morning." She thought a moment. "And comfortable, too. Like we were still dancing."

I glanced around; all of our neighbors were either sleeping or watching a movie which, without sound, seemed a series of car chases interrupted by shootings. "Last night was very . . . I thought it was . . . I mean . . ." I stopped babbling, looked at my hands. "I'm not thinking very well here."

"Things sometimes need time to sort themselves out," she said.

I nodded. "I guess so."

"One final question, Carson, then I'll clam up." She leaned close. Perfume flooded my senses, her breath hot against my ear. "I'm going down memory lane here; last night, *après la danse*. Our moments of trust. Do you think that sort of thing should happen again?"

"It's nice to finally have a question I can answer," I said.

We landed in Atlanta and waited for a Mobile flight, arriving in late evening. I should have been ass-weary, but felt a strange buoyancy. "Looky ahead," Danbury said, pointing. "It's Harry Nautilus. He's been lonely without me, I'll bet."

Harry leaned against a column beside Baggage Claim, resplendent in a teal suit, yellow shirt, red tie. Last time I'd seen that ensemble was at a funeral. Danbury shot off for the restroom and I walked to Harry.

"We found the background for my likeness in the Wicky piece, a small park beside the academy Hexcamp attended. Still no idea who made it or why."

"Hexcamp turn out like Danbury's research predicted?"

We walked toward the luggage carousel. "Egomaniacal in galactic portions. And a masochist, hard core. Calypso used it to own him. She scoped him out, smelled his darkness, and provided what he wanted. A lot of it."

"Strip me, whip me, beat me 'til I come?"

"She sounded scary before, now she sounds pure freak. It's why he emerged from his so-called 'creative sessions' so drained. She probably took him to the edge for days at a time."

Harry wrinkled his nose. "I'll never understand this stuff. Which ain't too bad because I don't want to." He shifted gears. "Orange Lady, the case Roy Trent can't dent, his backshot victim. After I told Roy about the connection, we went to the group home where she lived. No art in her room. Her mail comes through the front desk, goes to the director of the home, gets disbursed to the residents. Only eight folks live at the home, so it's not a huge volume. All Nancy Chastain – Orange Lady – received in the previous week were a couple occupant–type fliers. She didn't get a lot of mail."

"You tossed her room?" It was a rhetorical question.

"Vents. Fixtures. Everything. We also tore apart every other room in case she'd had someone hide it for her. Nothing. The director said there'd been no change in Chastain's personality or actions before her death. She wandered in her happy fog, got her daily oranges, sang her songs, helped around the house."

I watched baggage climb from the bowels of the terminal, tumble onto the track. Harry said, "I've been giving it some thought, laying out a timeline: Heidi Wicky, Marie Gilbeaux, Nancy Chastain . . . The whole weirdness side of this, with the candles, the flowers, started at the Cozy Cabins with Marie G. The art started there, too, even if it was sent to the convent."

305

I said, "But the weirdness seems spur of the moment. If we go by your take, the perp drove by a candle sale, thought they'd be a nice touch, picked up some rings, stopped at the cemetery for flowers . . ."

Danbury reappeared, her brown bag swinging over her shoulder. "How about we head to my place? I want to check Carla."

Harry said, "I checked before coming here: she was washing clothes and getting ready for bed."

She narrowed an eye. "How about my feeders?"

"You were out of cracked corn. You owe me eight bucks."

Danbury took Harry's arm, leaned her head against his shoulder. "He fills my feeders, buys treats for my birdies. What a guy."

"Ease up, Danbury," Harry rumbled. "I had to go to the pet shop anyway."

"When'd you get a pet?" I asked.

Danbury said, "Let's grab the bags and git. We've got to tell Harry about the big chess game. The elevator operator. And waltzing the night away."

She saw her bag circling and ran for it. Harry nudged me with an elbow.

"Waltzing the night away? Ooo-la-la, Monsieur Carson."

CHAPTER 42

The next morning we regrouped on Danbury's porch and sipped coffee. Birds flitted between feeders in the trees. I heard Carla Hutchins inside watching TV. As always when we discussed Hexcamp, she wanted to be elsewhere. I couldn't blame her.

Danbury said, "The only ones to die are from Paris, the charter members of Club Hexcamp. There weren't many, because he finally drove off all but the most devoted – read dysfunctional – followers. Why?"

Harry said, "Maybe because they knew he wasn't much of an artist?"

I shook my head. "If Hexcamp had drawn piss-pictures in snow, his followers would have swooned in ecstasy. Maybe it involves the attack on the Parisian artist."

Danbury said, "They beat him to death, or so Mimi Badentier believes. Could there be a fear of prosecution after all these years?"

It didn't work for me. "These people, or this Calypso, didn't seem particularly worried about prosecution. I get the feeling she was fearless, and everyone followed her lead."

"We're talking big money for the collection," Harry said. "What if it came out, even after the fact, the deal was bogus, or tainted somehow? Buyers who can afford that much for garbage from a killer might take some action, the painful kind. Or worse."

Danbury stood, walked to the edge of the porch, her brow lined in thought. She tucked sprigs of blonde behind her ears, tapped a pink nail on the porch rail. "Does anything really have to be sold?" she asked, turning to Harry and me. "I've probably done two dozen stories where people lined up to buy things that don't exist. Shares in thoroughbred horses, beachfront lots in Cancun, a saint's bicuspid . . . How many times has the Brooklyn Bridge changed hands? Give people an offer to believe in with all their souls, and the greed kicks in. No matter how smart or common-sensical people are, push the Greed Index past that, and they'll stand naked on your porch at midnight and push hundred-dollar bills through the mail slot."

I leaned back, ran the possibilities. "What if she's right, at least hypothetically? Suppose there's no collection. Nada. Not even fake art. All that exists is the story about the collection, and the promise one fantastically lucky person will own it with the right dollar amount."

She said, "A promise of a lifetime, drawing big-money nutcases to town for Coyle's backlot Sotheby's. What you want to bet the deal is cash and carry?"

"Cash," Harry said, snapping a finger. "Wads of upfront cash. That could be the point of the whole screwy thing." He paced the porch for several minutes, his face darkening with every pass. "It's possible," he finally whispered. "Sixteen years a cop, you give me enough information and I'll smell it. Danbury's onto something. This has the stink of a scam, a rip-off."

I did rhetorical. "How many customers did Walcott say might be involved in this? A half dozen or more?"

Harry said, "And Willow guesstimated the price at a half-million? At those kind of bucks we're talking three million dollars. I saw two guys shot dead at a crap game over forty-three bucks. What'll a minimum of three million bucks do?"

"Three bodies so far," I said, showing the count on my fingers. "Wicky, Gilbeaux, Chastain."

"Would this Coyle guy do that?" Danbury asked. "Or is he just running the deal portion? The verification and whatnot."

I snapped my fingers and jumped up, suddenly too charged to stay sitting. "If the collection isn't Hexcamp's, the person verifying it is a fake. Or an expert paid to issue a false statement of authenticity. It has to be someone in on the deal," I said. "Maybe even the person behind this house of mirrors. I've got to talk to Walcott again. I'll need both of you on this one. Borg too, if you can get hold of my good buddy."

* * *

Twenty minutes later we were crossing the causeway toward Spanish Fort, everyone in on my idea for opening Walcott up. "Where the hell is Borg?" Danbury said, tapping on her cellphone as Harry blew by an ancient pickup stacked high with furniture.

"I don't need him to shoot pictures," I said to her. "But I want him to look like he is."

She laughed. "That'll be a switch. He's a master at making like the camera's off when it's sucking up every word and gesture; a natural sneak."

"Just keep him aiming the big glass eye at Walcott and his house, that's all I need."

"Maybe he's with a woman friend," she said, glaring at the phone in her hand. "It's rare, but when he digs up a bimbette, he goes at it like a pig in slop. I'll send someone from the station over to bang on his door."

I looked at my watch. "It's getting late. If Borg can't meet us, we'll go it alone. He's window dressing. Just having you there will mess with Walcott's head. Then, of course, there's our outsized amigo. If Walcott's not intimidated by the media . . ."

"A large and irritated-looking black cop is not something to be trifled with," Harry said. "You has my word on it."

We pulled into a supermarket lot in Spanish Fort and let Danbury try the videographer again. Nothing. We crossed Zipinski off the list and headed for Walcott's. He was standing amidst the manicured shrubs of his front yard.

"He's out, Harry; let's go for it."

The Crown Vic thumped into the driveway. Walcott's dark

suit had been traded for a gold-buttoned navy sport jacket over a white crew-neck shirt. He wore white pants and white shoes. Going casual didn't diminish the cylindrical effect of his long, shoulderless body; he looked like a cigar on a cruise.

Walcott's face angered when it saw mine. He strode toward us, jabbing his finger at the car. "That vehicle. It's so obviously police. Do you have to park in my drive? We talked about this last time. You said my business would remain . . ."

"Don't give me that pissy look, Giles. I haven't burned you. Not just yet. And as long as we keep our lines of communication open –"

"I don't have any other names for you."

"Yes you do. The thing is, I don't want them now. I want to talk more about the Hexcamp collection."

He did exasperated. "I told you –"

"It's a dream, or a gorgon or a whatever. It doesn't live in this world."

"I didn't say it didn't exist. I said there was no authoritative proof of its existence."

I said, "Jibble-jabble. They're pretty much the same."

"Not in my world."

"That world is what has us beating a path to your doorstep, Giles. Why don't we step inside and discuss it in detail?"

"I don't want to . . . who's that colored man?"

I grinned. "That's Harry Nautilus. He's joining us. Big, ain't he?"

Walcott crossed his arms defiantly. "Neither of you is joining me."

"Both of us is joining you," Harry rumbled on cue, exiting the car. "And guess what . . . ?"

Danbury had been leaning out of sight in the back seat. She popped out, hair bouncing, white teeth beaming, notepad in her hand. Giles Walcott turned as white as his pants, and I took it he was a viewer of Channel 14.

"Here's the deal, Mr Walcott," she said. "I'm just here on a small research mission, a story on people who collect serial-killer memorabilia. There are two ways you can be identified in my story. One is 'an anonymous broker who lives in the South.' The other is, of course, by name. Much of it depends on your cooperation."

I put a brotherly hand around Walcott's semi-shoulders, pulled him close.

"There a pizza joint around that delivers, Giles? It's almost lunch time, and we figure on being here a while."

CHAPTER 43

"I have never sold a piece of work represented as a Hexcamp," Walcott complained. Harry shrugged, took a bite of pizza, burped. The pizza box sat on a very shiny and probably very expensive cherry table in Walcott's expansive dining room. Harry set the remaining piece of pizza on the table. We weren't exactly doing Good Cop/Bad Cop; more like Polite Cop/Impolite Cop.

Harry said, "There's money in Hexcamp, Giles. There are also pieces floating around. What I want to know is why some of these pretty little pieces of history haven't passed through your palms."

Walcott walked to the arched window overlooking the front lawn. The idiotic dolphin sculpture spewed its stream into the air. Walcott turned to me. "Can we talk alone, Mr Ryder?"

"He ain't a mister," Harry said with his mouth full. "He's a detective. He's Detective Ryder. I'm Detective Nautilus. This here's Countess Danbury. And no, he ain't talking to you alone."

"Countess?" Danbury said.

"A field promotion," Harry said, smacking his lips. "Just for the day, though."

Walcott was confused, the desired effect. He had a penchant for evasion, but flustered easily. He disliked being flustered, thus answered more readily, hoping to rid himself of the source of confusion.

"Countess is cool, even if it's a temp position," Danbury said. She pointed to Walcott. "What's his title?"

Harry set a baleful eye on the broker. "Sicko."

"I am *not* one of those people," Walcott protested. "I explained this to Detective Ryder on his last visit." He looked to me for support; I busied myself with my napkin.

"You've sold Hexcamp pieces," Harry said. "You're not just a sicko, you're a lying sicko."

My turn to ring in. "He's got you, Giles. Please don't argue. We've looked deeper into this than you can ever imagine." I gave him the *gotcha!* eye. Pure bluff.

He looked away, guilty. "I sold a few small scraps, that's all. And I never said they were by Marsden Hexcamp, I represented them as 'In the Hexcamp tradition.'"

Harry said, "From what I heard, it's the same."

"If the buyers wanted to believe the pieces were Hexcamp's, I can't help it."

"You've moved Hexcamp pieces," Harry growled. "You're

tied in. People across the country call you for information, right?"

"Of course, they do," Walcott snapped. "I'm a well-known broker."

Harry's fist slammed the table. "THEN GODDAMN TELL US WHERE AND WHEN THE HEXCAMP COLLECTION'S BEING SOLD!"

"I don't know," Walcott rasped, eyes wide. "It's the truth."

"YOU TUBULAR SONUVABITCH! STOP LYING AND TELL ME . . ."

Harry leaped up, shoved the table aside, jumped at Walcott. I dove into Harry, holding him off. We'd practiced this ploy about six months back, Harry nearly driving me through his living-room wall until we got our act down.

"Powerful drama," Danbury said, pulling her phone from her purse. "I've got to get a video crew over here now."

Walcott said, "No, stop. I'll tell you what I know. It's not much."

I managed Harry back to his chair. Danbury sighed and dropped the phone into her purse.

Walcott kept a wary eye on Harry. "I'm speaking from rumors, you understand."

"They better be damn good rumors," Harry rumbled.

"The collection – yes, there *is* a collection – has been authenticated to the satisfaction of potential buyers. Recently, I understand. There's to be an auction, and the event is nearing."

I said, "Who authenticated it?" One name, and we could get real close.

"I don't know who he is. A person in a position to know. We've discussed this. I've heard rumors that the particulars of the event are to be handled by a lawyer, a man with impeccable credentials in, uh, involved transactions. I assume the person handling the authentication has similar credentials."

"Rubin Coyle's handling the particulars," I said. "He's a local collector. He lives ten miles away and you're telling me you don't know him?"

Walcott said, "Coyle? Never heard the name."

"COYLE'S A CUSTOMER OF YOURS, ASS-COTT!" Harry howled, pounding the table again.

"I don't know that name," Walcott pleaded, scooting back a foot. "You've got to believe me. Some people use cut-outs, intermediaries. Especially if they have a high community profile."

That was likely, I thought; score one for Giles Walcott.

"How do we find out when and where?" Harry repeated.

"You're asking me questions I can't answer. I'm trying to be helpful."

"You're trying to be on the nightly news." Harry said, looking at Danbury. She reached for the phone again. As ensemble players, we were getting good.

Walcott waved her off. "I've got an idea. Only a few collectors have the financial means for such a collection. I could call them. See what I can determine."

For the first time since we'd arrived, Harry smiled. His teeth were red with pizza sauce. "Atta boy, Giles," he said. "When can we expect to hear something?"

"Tomorrow morning. Afternoon at the latest." Walcott

looked pointedly at the front door. "The faster you leave, the faster I can get started."

We left Walcott's with the feeling that maybe, just maybe, this tunnel had a light. It was about half a watt and ten miles away, but it was something.

"Way to go, Nautilus," Danbury said, sitting next to Harry and clapping his massive shoulder. "Love the intimidation factor."

Harry looked at his watch. "We don't hear by tomorrow afternoon, I'm going back and make him ride that idiot dolphin bare-ass naked in his front yard."

Danbury's phone rang. "Probably Borg," she said. "Coming up for air."

She popped open the phone, jammed it to her ear. I watched her face go from anger to confusion to disbelief. She kept repeating, "My God." We were crossing the causeway to the western side of the Bay and Harry pulled over. He looked at me, *What now?*

Danbury closed the phone and stared at it, like she couldn't believe what it had just told her.

"What's wrong?" I asked.

"The station sent a gopher to Borg's house, an intern. When she peeked in the window, he was on the floor, blood everywhere. The police are there now."

Zipinski lived in a gray two-story bungalow just south of Jackson Heights. The yard needed mowing and the house needed paint. We arrived as Borg was leaving. The attendants rolled him to the ambulance, slid him in, drove away without

317

flashers or siren. The team catching the call was Roy Trent and Clay Bridges. There were Channel 14 station personnel at the scene and Danbury ran over to talk to them.

Harry and I walked into the house, saw Roy in the dining room talking to a tech from the ME's office. Wayne Hembree was studying the bloodstained living-room carpet. Careful where we put our feet, Harry and I walked over to Roy Trent and the tech. Zipinski kept a neat house; the place shone.

"Hey, Carson," Trent said. "Thanks for the heads-up on the Nancy Chastain case. We were looking into her past, but only about a year. Getting close on anything?" Trent's face was hopeful. I jammed my hands in my pockets, rocked on my heels.

"Ten minutes ago I thought I knew something, Roy. Now I'm back to I don't know."

Harry looked at the carpet in the living room, a rusty red Rorschach-image, four feet across. He shook his head. "What went down here, Roy?"

"Mr Borgurt F. Zipinski went down, Harry. Fast, too."

The ME's tech stepped up. "Looks like a knife from behind. Deep and through the jugular. One cut. Clean, no sawing. At least not from a fast visual exam. It looked professional grade. Grab and slit and jump away from the spray."

"But they're still alive when they go down," I said. "You get to see their eyes in that final moment."

The tech gave me an odd look. "Uh, right, I guess."

Trent walked up. "No sign of forced entry. Looks like a let-in. Someone he knew, I'd say."

Hembree stood. I said, "No art, Bree? Nothing like that around?"

318

He shook his head. "Or candles or flowers or cheap-ass jewelry. You think this has something to do with the Wicky–Gilbeaux–Chastain cases?"

"I think I should have taken up alligator wrestling."

Hembree nodded at the stained carpet. "At least I can tell you this guy wasn't buried and exhumed."

"Yo, pogo-boys."

Harry and I saw Danbury at the door, kept back by a uniformed cop. I went over and brought her inside. Harry followed Hembree to the kitchen. Danbury looked around, seemed mystified.

"It's like a show home, Carson. At least compared to the few times I was here."

"Not usually this tidy?"

She wrinkled her nose. "Clothes on the floor, dishes on the clothes, dried food on the dishes, bugs on the . . ."

"He cleaned for company," Trent said. "Special company. I'm a bachelor. I know the ritual."

Harry called me into the kitchen. He'd been studying various papers on Borg's counter. There was a grin under Harry's mustache. "What's the first thing you do if you come into a big hit of money, Carson. Like, found money?"

"Pay down the credit cards. Tuck some in the retirement fund. Put a few bucks into home maintenance . . ."

Harry stared at me.

"Buy something cool that I really don't need," I admitted.

"Like this?" he said, holding up a sales brochure for Corvettes, a business card stapled to the front page.

* * *

319

". . . convertible, Millennium yellow, magnetic selective ride control, the performance package, five-spoke aluminum wheels, satellite radio, automatic transmission . . ."

Delbert Jennings, Automotive Representative at Perform-ance Motors, recited from the printout in his hand. Harry, Danbury and I were crowded into Delbert's small office, all manner of automotive awards and recognitions on the wall. I resisted telling Delbert he was in the company of the Mayor's Officers of the Year, not wishing to upstage him.

"Automatic? On a Corvette?" I said. "Blasphemy."

"One hand on the wheel, the other honking the horn at women," Danbury said. "Borg in his glory."

"How much would this particular vehicle cost?" Harry said. "Forty grand or so?"

"Closer to fifty-five," Delbert announced. "Small price to pay for a true piece of Americana."

"I own a twelve-year-old Volvo wagon," Harry said. "Blue Book's about four grand. Small price to pay for a true piece of Scandinavia."

"Of course," Delbert said, unsure of whether to smile or not.

"He gave you a something down?" I asked.

Delbert consulted his sheet. "Two weeks back he gave us ten thousand down. The car's on the lot and prepped."

"And when is Mr Zipinski scheduled to pick up his new toy?"

"Today. I've been trying to get in touch with him . . ."

"Bringing by a check?" Harry asked.

"Cash. Just like the down payment." A look of fear crossed Delbert's eyes. "This deal's not going down, is it?"

We retreated to my place after leaving the dealership. The Blovines' Hummer was gone and they'd neglected to leave the usual TV on, cranked up to jet-engine decibels. We sat around a table on the deck and watched the sun shimmer over the water. There was a gentle breeze. I added Zipinski's actions to the timeline.

"Borg laid down the money on his pussywagon two days after Marie Gilbeaux was discovered."

"Do you have to keep calling it that?" Danbury asked.

"It's a valid automotive term," I protested.

"Any ideas on how Borg made the money?" Harry asked Danbury.

"Borg was freelance. He was good at surreptitious stuff, like for private agencies, a natural at getting shots on the sly."

"Footage of couples in flagrante delicto?" I said.

"If that's cop for sneaking around on the side, yes."

"Working for private investigators, you mean?"

"PI's, law firms, or anyone with fifty bucks an hour plus expenses."

Harry said, "Fifty grand in ten days? I don't think he put in over a thousand hours; that's lawyer-type billing."

"I think events parallel the pussywag—, uh, Corvette purchase," I ventured as a weaving strand of pelicans swooped past the deck. "Two days after Marie ended up in the Cozy Cabins, Borg got hired for something – ten grand down. Today was settle-up day. Except it was Borg who got settled."

Harry looked at Danbury. "Was Borg off station work the past couple weeks? Working some other project?"

"Except for Paris, he's been pretty much with me. We did the standard stuff, plus, of course, this project."

Harry said, "You weren't in Paris long. According to the ME, Borg spent most of it being dead. Didn't leave him much time."

"He never needed much time; Borg was great at the sly stuff. We did an exposé on a politician having an affair a couple years back – the county commissioner? Though the guy was super-discreet, it took Borg all of two afternoons to verify it, bringing in tape of the guy squiring a bimbo into a Grand Bay motel."

Something quivered in the back of my mind. *Verify?* Verification was the cornerstone of the scam. Verification of Hexcamp. Not just the art, Hexcamp. *Collectors want to believe* . . . The quiver turned to a shadow, one comprised of forms and words, a jumble of sound and shape. Standing outside Coyle's house. Danbury on the phone, arguing with the station. Me shaking hands with Borgurt Zipinski.

Zipinski patting sweat from his head.

A hat atop a camera.

I stood, began pacing the deck, trying to match my speed to my twisting memories.

"*Verification,*" I whispered.

"Carson?" Harry asked. "You OK?"

I nodded my head, kept moving; back and forth, rail to rail, trying to shake thoughts loose from the shadows in my head. Ambrose Poll's stolen items had perfect provenance,

Willow had said, verified by the MPD via evidence tags. What had Giles Walcott said? The buyers needed to believe.

A red light blinked on a camera.

Then it didn't.

The floor seemed to buckle beneath my feet. My breath disappeared, leaving only the pounding of my heart. I slapped the deck railing, swore.

"What?" Harry said.

"I know who it is," I said. "I know who verified the art." I ran to my dining room, grabbed the stack of papers on the table, threw recent issues across the floor, scrabbled through the rest.

A perplexed Harry and Danbury followed me inside. "Carson?" she said. "Who is it? Who authenticated Hexcamp's work?"

I found the paper I needed and held it aloft in shaking hands. It was the issue with the photo from the Mayor's Recognition Breakfast. I tapped the picture.

"Me," I said.

"What?" Harry roared.

CHAPTER 44

I gave my theory of events. It took two minutes.

"It fits," Harry said, rubbing his face. "The major pieces, at least."

Danbury said, "You're saying Marie Gilbeaux was dug up because her killer saw your picture in the paper?"

"Think it through: the killer's maybe spent years living off Hexcamp's supposed art, scraps of something, all the while pimping the notion that a big stash of beautiful madness is floating around. Collectors treat it like the Grail legend, but real. The killer starts thinking of the big score, killing off everyone who might get in the way – Wicky, Gilbeaux, Chastain. The Paris contingent. There's only one problem . . ."

"Getting someone to verify the art."

I read from the caption of the Mayor's Breakfast photo:

Nautilus and Ryder are members of the MPD's elite Psychopathological and Sociopathological Investigative Team, or PSIT, and are considered authorities in the area of serial killers and other psychologically deranged criminals. Having received additional training at FBI headquarters, their expertise in identification and analysis of these warped individuals puts them at the forefront of . . .

Danbury took the article, read it. "It says you're authorities, the alpha and omega of regional serial-killer knowledge. Add to that the look on your face, Carson. You look like a Fundamentalist preacher on speed. It's so righteous it's scary."

I let her photo analysis slide. "The killer sees the photo, suddenly knows what the verification mechanism will be: us, the PSIT. But how to get us on the case, weave us into the plot?"

Harry said, "Dig up Marie Gilbeaux, bring her to the Cozy Cabins. Along the way, pick up some candles, a few weirdo rings. Veer into a cemetery, pluck some posies."

"Instant bizarre," I said. "We're handed the case."

Danbury said, "What about the art at the convent?"

I ran the timeline in my head. "It fits perfectly. Remember the postmark? It was mailed the same day Marie's body was discovered."

"An afterthought?"

I felt the rush of the invisible lines becoming visible, of lamps being lit through the darkness. "The killer leaves the motel, thinks the scheme through. Art, he thinks, leave pieces

325

of Hexcamp's supposed art. He drops a swatch in the mail. It's the perfect tie-in. Rope in the PSIT with the bizarre death, tighten the knot with art."

Harry nodded. "Heidi Wicky's dead too. By a week, maybe. But that doesn't stop the perp from slipping back and taping art above her body. Nice and spooky."

"How'd your picture get on the art from the convent?"

I shook my head, waved it away. "It doesn't fit in the box yet."

"How about the art that came to Carla?"

"One more way to keep Hexcamp in our faces. Look here: Hexcamp art. Look over there: Hexcamp art. Up, down, sides and back – Hexcamp art. There was one constant suggestion: Marsden Hexcamp's art is real, and profoundly powerful."

Harry walked to the window and watched the surf. "It's like when astronomers can't see a planet, but figure it's there because it pulls on the planets around it."

"There was no planet, Harry. We were fools for gravity."

"Horseshit," Danbury said. "Don't sell yourselves short. Something's always been there: the incredible swatches of art. Without them, there was nothing to believe in. It was the art at Coyle's that got you, Carson. Right? You said something to Borg."

I thought back over the seemingly innocent exchange: his contrition, apology, handshake. His touching at the camera.

"I didn't really say it existed. But I didn't deny it. He was wiping his face, set his hat over the top of the camera."

"A red light that flashes when it's recording. He got you by covering it. I've seen him do it before."

Harry grunted. "The tape immediately went to Coyle, of course, copies to prospective buyers, the newspaper article alongside. Probably with an affidavit by lawyer-boy: 'Acclaimed serial-killer authority validates art; auction at eleven.'"

I said, "Let's see if that piece of the chain links up."

Harry and I drove to the offices of Hamerle, Melbine and Raus in separate vehicles, not sure which way we'd break after what was hopefully today's final piece of business. Danbury pulled in behind. She'd run by her station to pull a picture of Zipinski from his ID card file. I didn't want to show Lydia the final shot of Borgurt Zipinski, the one taken by the Medical Examiner's technician.

Warren Hamerle was out of the office, probably his default condition. Still, I was surprised Lydia wanted to meet at the firm, and not in the secrecy of the coffee shop. She further surprised me by wearing a mauve print dress, matching shoes, a yellow scarf around her neck. For her it seemed as colorful as an electrified rainbow.

"Sure, I remember him," Lydia said, nodding at the picture. "Mr Pizinski."

"Zipinski," I corrected. "He's worked for the firm, then?"

"Yes." I heard disfavor in her voice.

"For Mr Coyle specifically?"

"The first time was a couple of years ago. Mr Coyle was handling a negotiation for farmland sought by a developer, acreage jointly owned by a brother and sister, estranged. Mr Coyle was working to get them to agree on a selling price. He suspected the developer and the sister of conspiring against the brother to lower the price, the sister getting her cut on the side. Mr Zipinski brought us the necessary pictures. The developer and sister were having an affair. The tapes were very . . . graphic. Perhaps unnecessarily."

Harry said, "Coyle knew who would get the job done."

"That's why Zipinski provoked my little scene," I said. "After knifing the tire to keep us there."

Danbury's eyes flared and her hands balled into fists. Her voice dropped to a whisper. "I got used; I'm an idiot."

Harry said, "Relax, Danbury. Using people's what Zipinski did best, I think."

Lydia handed the photo back like she couldn't wait to get rid of it. "I never cared much for Mr Zipinski. He was somehow . . . unsavory."

"How are you holding up, Lydia?" I asked. I'd noted *Rubin* had transformed to a frost-coated *Mr Coyle* in Lydia's mouth.

"I gave my notice to Mr Hamerle three days ago. And left a letter on Mr Coyle's desk. It says, 'Go to Hell.'"

I smiled, though I figured the odds were long on Coyle's ever seeing it. "Good for you, Lydia."

She smiled tentatively; I saw resolve in her eyes. "I think so. Time to move on."

The guard in the building's lobby was a star-struck old guy who wanted Danbury's autograph. She went to do a little PR schmoozing and Harry and I walked into the sunlight. He said, "Miz Lydia confirming Coyle knew Borg pretty much ices the cake. To paraphrase Walt Kelly, 'We have met the authenticators and it is us.'"

"What's a Walt Kelly?" I asked. Harry sighed and looked at his watch. "Looks like we wait until morning, hear what Walcott gets. What are you going to do, Carson?"

"I'm going home for the night, Harry. I'm ragged." I headed toward my car.

"Carson?"

I turned. Harry walked to me. "Wanna go grab a cold one?"

"I, uh, that is . . ."

Danbury exploded through the door into the parking lot, afraid she was missing something. "Hold up, boys," she bayed.

Harry looked at her. Then at me. "Got other plans, then?"

"Hope so," I said.

Harry smiled like he'd just won a bet with himself and walked to the car whistling "What a Wonderful World".

It was almost six p.m. when Danielle Desiree Danbury and I turned into the sand-and-shell drive to the three houses on my short street. The Blovines pulled out as we entered. Mama was wearing something cut low, boobs bouncing mightily as the garish Hummer growled over the choppy drive. They made a point of not seeing me.

Loath to let absence contribute to the peace, the Blovines had left a TV on. On the other side, my quiet newcomers continued apace. The red Toyota hadn't moved. After pouring a drink, we went to the deck to let the breeze blow the day away. We spoke of Borgurt Zipinski for a few moments, Danbury saddened he'd led what seemed such a shrunken, self-centered life.

"There was nothing to him but what he could buy and who he could screw, physically and metaphorically, Carson. You know people like that?"

"From prison block to pulpit, courthouse to boardroom."

"I pray, Carson. You believe that? I'm not sure to who, or how it all works, but I do. Sometimes I give thanks I wasn't someone like that, like Borg. And probably like these . . . people you're following. The death collectors. I can't imagine the emptiness of their lives. Maybe it's a terrible thing to say, but do you think some people are born without souls?"

I started to answer, caught myself. I was tired of thinking and wanted to lose myself in something simple and honest and physical. I stood and held out my hand.

"Let's go inside," I said. "I want to learn more about dancing."

CHAPTER 45

Morning arrived clear and bright, the fresh sun pressing amber into the curtains. I fixed coffee and we drank it on the deck. It wasn't yet six thirty. I took a shower. After I dressed, I found Danbury staring at the brown box on my kitchen table.

"Carson, is this . . . ?"

"Yes," I said. "The final mask of Trey Forrier."

She thought a moment. "Can I see it?"

I removed the mask, held it to her. Sunlight glinted from the glass teeth, glistened from the black surface. The red-scribed eyes glared with menace. She accepted it hesitantly and held it at a distance, sensing its malignant potency.

I said, "It would probably make good video for your story about serial killers and collectors. A signature shot."

She shivered and handed it back. "Screw the story. Kill the damn thing; build a fire from it."

I took a final look at the hideous creation, wondering what horrors passed through Forrier's mind during the mask's construction. Did he, building it strip by strip, follow a pattern, his mind seeing the mask before his hands created it? Or was it a random creation, the shape of chance? I set the mask aside and held her, listening to the soft hiss of the low surf. I didn't think fire an appropriate manner for the mask to die. It seemed born of fire, the mask's smoke capable of tainting the air.

"Birth by fire, death by water," I decided, looking at a sun risen scant degrees above the horizon. "And isn't sunrise traditional for executions?"

Danbury ran off to check on various projects at the station. I tucked the mask into a drawstring bag and went beneath my house. I lifted my kayak to my shoulder, and walked to the water's edge. The morning was gentle, windless, the Gulf almost flat. My plans were to drop the mask into the depths past the sand bars. Dirt had not drowned its ugliness and intensity; perhaps water would.

I secured the bag to a cleat and paddled out for a quarter mile or so, small waves slapping over the bow. I snapped the paddle into the holder and removed the bag from the cleat. It hit me how little it weighed.

Idiot.

I'd brought nothing to weigh the bag down. The papier-mâché would float to shore like a jellyfish. Sighing at my stupidity, I unknotted the line to the kayak's small mush-room-shaped anchor. I removed the mask from the bag and inserted the anchor. Splashing water had soaked the mask and started to dissolve the ageing flour-and-water glue; strips of fabric and paper flapped loose on its backside, the mask beginning to die. I jammed it back into the bag, counted to three in my mind – *un, deux, trois* – and dropped it over the side.

It plummeted, a dark shape consumed by the sea, the death of the final mask of Trey Forrier.

An odd sense of relief flooded my body, relaxed my shoulders, unknotted my back. I hadn't kayaked out on the water since before Marie Gilbeaux's body was found. It felt good to be disconnected from the land again, moving any direction I wished. Setting the shore to my back, I dug the paddles deep. A pair of dolphins broke the water a hundred yards ahead, sleek and black and shining, and I chased after them. Everything clouding my mind dissolved in my wake as I followed the dolphins toward the heart of the Gulf.

I pursued them for two or three minutes, sweat pouring from my body, salt burning my eyes, muscles screaming with effort. I stroked harder, dug deeper, heard myself grunting with the strain. I shook the sweat from my hair and kept going. The dolphins breached again, farther this time. I gave up, crossing the paddle over my lap and leaning forward, sucking breath. My cupped hands reached into the water, splashing it over my face and chest.

I sighed and started paddling to land.

It appeared first as glitter on the water, an optical illusion perhaps, or errant pocket of sea vegetation colored by a climbing sun. Closing on the phenomenon, I saw rainbow patches floating on the surface, flat strips undulating like eels. And then I was in a field of raging color, reds and blues and oranges and golds. I reached down and harvested a strip of brightly painted canvas. It dripped white into the waves, dissolved flour glue.

Heart pounding, I dove overboard, kicking to the bottom through canvas patches like schooling fish. I followed them to the bag. It lay serenely on the bottom, swatches of color drifting upward from its open mouth. I snatched up the bag, drew it closed, and fought toward the surface. The twenty-pound anchor seemed to have gained another hundred pounds. My lungs screamed as I broke into sunlight, set the bag in the boat, then moved through the water, snatching every strip I could find.

I paddled home, ran to my house, called the institute. Then I phoned my brother directly and told him I needed to see Trey Forrier. I called Danbury, told her I'd fetch her at the station.

And to buckle in for a wild ride.

CHAPTER 46

I used the two-hour trip to relate how my brother and I had grown up in a situation where any word or action, no matter how innocent, might trigger my father's violent, trip-wire temper. We moved through life like blind swimmers in a cottonmouth bayou, afraid in all directions.

My father's searing, illogical anger centered on Jeremy, who, from the time he was ten, became our father's chief target. In later years I came to believe it was because Jeremy bore a close physical resemblance to my father.

"My God, Carson," Danbury whispered. "You spent every second walking on eggshells."

"It was far worse for Jeremy, every day a nightmare. I think it's why his senses are so acute, hyper-attuned. He lives in a world where everything's at maximum volume, a distorting volume. Not just sound, but all senses. Accordingly, his observations and reactions are weighted far differently than ours."

We arrived, passed through the guards and gates. Dr Prowse was away, but we were expected. We were escorted to Jeremy's room by a guard who knew me from previous visits, was aware that Dr Prowse allowed me exceptional latitude in dealing with my brother. The guard poised his fingers over the electronic lock. "The same procedure as usual, Detective Ryder, keep the door shut while you're in there?"

"Yes. Though I'll be out to retrieve this." I set a rolled-up white beach towel beside the door and stepped aside as the guard keyed in the lock code. Danbury's hand wrapped mine.

"Are you worried?" I asked.

"A little. I don't know what to expect."

"I never do either. Just don't tell him you're a reporter. He hates them."

"Why?"

"He saw his crimes as a personal mission, a holy vendetta. He's never forgiven the media for referring to him as a murderous psychopath, what he perceives as a misreading of his intentions. Like I said, his perceptions are skewed, often mirror-images of reality."

The door opened, soundless on its heavy hinges. Jeremy was framed in the doorway, five steps away, staring through cool blue eyes.

"Hello, Jeremy," I said, crossing the threshold. "I'd like you to meet a good friend of mine, DeeDee Danbury."

Jeremy grabbed my arm and pulled me across the room,

hissing in my ear. "DeeDee? What the fuck's a DeeDee? Who is this bitch? Where's AVA? Where's my sweet little nightingale?"

Though he despised her gender, my brother convinced himself of a bond with Ava based on her being a pathologist: that her hands moved inside the dead had elevated her in Jeremy's eyes.

"Ava's in Fort Wayne, Jeremy. You know that. Skip the bullshit."

He scowled and mock-whispered in my ear, loud enough for Danbury to hear. "What kind of work does Lady PeePee perform? Does it involve long hours on her knees?"

"I've got no time for games, Jeremy. Have Trey Forrier stop by for a visit."

Jeremy turned to Danbury. "He brings all his whores here, you know. He fucks them in front of me. They go at it on the floor like goats. It takes a janitor two hours to mop up all the juice."

"Can it, Jeremy. I need Forrier. Now."

Jeremy crossed his arms, tapped his toe, and regarded Danbury impatiently. "Miss Ava, my brother's former love-kettle, was a pathologist. That gave us several things in common. Are you a pathologist, Miss TeeTee? If not, may I ask how you earn your living? Assuming it's something that can be mentioned in polite company."

I said, "Ms Danbury does research for Harry and me. I don't have time for games, Jeremy. Have Trey Forrier stop by for a visit."

He raised a pale eyebrow. "What kind of research?"

"Right now that's my business."

337

"What do you want from Trey?"

"Same answer."

There was a knock and the door opened. A second guard leaned in, a younger guy I'd seen a time or two. "Excuse me, Mr Ryder? I just came on the clock. We've met, my name's Albert Jenkins; I'll be right outside if you need anything."

"Please keep the door shut, Mr Jenkins."

"Yes sir." Jenkins looked up, saw Danbury. His eyes lit with recognition. "I know you. You're on TV."

Jeremy's head snapped to Danbury. "BeeBee's on TeeVee?" He studied her with sudden interest. "What do you do, if I may ask?"

I winced. "Mr Jenkins, we're having a private conversation here."

"Sorry." He closed the door.

Jeremy let his eyes range over Danbury. "Are you an actress, Miss WeeWee? I thought all actresses today had great big titties. Are you a struggling actress, still getting small parts?"

She looked at me. I shrugged, nodded, *tell him*. He'd pick away at her until he found out the truth.

"I'm a journalist, Mr Ridgecliff."

"A journalist?" he whispered.

"Yes. A reporter for Channel 14 in Mobile."

I expected an explosive rant about television news, whores, corruption of the soul, profit-based sensationalism . . . his usual litany of invective. He surprised me, widening his eyes and crossing his hands across his chest.

"The MEDIA? Visiting little ol' me? Is this my break-through, my FIFTEEN MINUTES OF FAME? Do I need an agent? A personal stylist?" He ran to the mirror and fussed with his blond hair as if preparing for a photograph.

I said, "Get Forrier in here, Jeremy. It's important."

"One minute, Carson. I've never met a member of the FOURTH ESTATE!" He bounded across the room with puppyish enthusiasm, sat on his bed, patted beside him. "Come sit, dear, just for a minute. I have something special to confess, an exclusive."

Danbury sat beside Jeremy, playing along with him. "Anytime you're ready, I'm listening."

He mock frowned. "You're not using your microphone. How will my adoring public hear me?"

She held her hand as if grasping a microphone and aimed it toward Jeremy's lips. "The world awaits. What's your exclusive, Mr Ridgecliff?"

He waggled an admonishing finger. "You didn't announce me."

"Come on, Jeremy," I grumbled. "Stop messing around. We're in a hurry."

"Indulge me, brother. Thirty seconds, then I'll call for Trey."

Danbury looked into an invisible camera. "Today we're talking to Mr Jeremy Ridgecliff, who has a message for our viewers. Care to convey your message, Mr Ridgecliff?"

"I'd be delighted."

My brother winked into the imaginary camera, turned to Danbury and spat in her face.

Without missing a beat, she slapped him.

I pushed between them as Danbury retreated, wiping her face with her sleeve. I grabbed my brother's shoulder, turned him to face me. "Get Forrier in here, you sorry little bastard. Now."

"I'm sorry I hit you, Mr Ridgecliff," Danbury said from behind me. "It was automatic. I didn't mean to —"

"No," I said. "Don't apologize to him. It was a disgusting act. Get Forrier in here, Jeremy. I mean NOW."

He spun away from me, walked to the wall and leaned against it. He pretended to buff his nails on his shirt. "I met a reporter named BeeDee, with a pussy exceedingly seedy; it's filled with disease, and roaches and fleas, but poor Carson, alas, was unheedy."

"I can always depend on you to be adolescent," I said. "Do I have to get Forrier on my own?"

"He won't come unless I invite him," Jeremy said, looking down, continuing to buff his nails. "And that's not going to happen. Take your face-slapping whore and leave, Carson. Maybe you could peddle her at the docks."

I stared at him a moment, then yelled, "Guard! I want to report a cellphone."

My brother's eyes snapped toward me. "What are you doing?" he hissed.

"Say goodbye to the phone, Jeremy."

The door opened and the guard leaned in. "Yes, Mr Ryder?"

"Something's come to my attention and I'd like to . . ." I paused, looked at my brother.

"Request the company of our good friend, Mr Forrier," Jeremy completed, expressionless eyes moving between me and Danbury.

I nodded at the guard. "Ms Danbury and I need to speak

with Mr Forrier alone. Have my brother wait elsewhere after he invites Mr Forrier to join us."

Jeremy started to protest. I wiggled my thumb to mimic entering numbers on a cellphone, then closed my fist to crush it. He caught my meaning, glaring back but saying nothing.

"Come with me, Mr Ridgecliff," the guard said.

Jeremy started to follow, pausing beside Danbury. She stared into his eyes, holding her ground.

"I share a few traits with journalists, Ms BeeBee," Jeremy said. "For instance, I interviewed five women for the position of Mommy. Guess what?"

Danbury raised an eyebrow. "What, Mr Ridgecliff?"

He grinned. "They all got the job."

He turned and walked into the hall, then paused again, turning to smile at Danbury. "I'd dearly love to interview *you*, Miss FeeFee. In great depth. If I'm ever in your neighborhood, trust that I'll certainly drop by."

And then he was gone.

Danbury moved beside me and held my arm. "He's so volatile, Carson. Cold and hot, charming and venomous. He's terrifying. But I'm so sorry I slapped him. It was –"

"A natural reaction. It's over. Don't sweat the threat; he'll be in here forever. Now I need you to turn on the French-speak. I think we're about to open the door a little wider on Trey Forrier."

I was holding her when footsteps came to the threshold.

CHAPTER 47

Forrier entered, looked at me curiously, then walked to the corner. He studied Jeremy's wall for a moment, then began conducting his invisible orchestra.

What is he hearing? I wondered again.

Before the guard closed the door, I grabbed the beach towel from the hall. When I unrolled it across the floor, it revealed the dried strips of painting. I stood above the strange mosaic with my arms crossed. Forrier's eyes angled toward the strips, then away.

"They tried to kill your art by killing you, didn't they, Trey?" I said quietly. "Hexcamp and his followers. They left you to die. But you survived."

His hand faltered in the air.

"I know it was you in Paris, Trey," I said. "The secretive artist."

For a man who'd been in this country for over three decades, I figured Forrier knew much more English than he let on, comfortable in his native tongue, perhaps; or hiding behind it. Forrier's gestures became a rote exercise, his attention focused on my words.

"You never insulted Hexcamp personally, it was your ability that belittled him. They beat your body, crushed your temple, shattered your cheekbone, then stole your painting."

Forrier's hand drifted to his wounded face, then dropped to his sides. He closed his eyes in the throes of decision. A moment later, he walked to the injured painting, dropped to his knees.

"Put the pieces together for us, Mr Forrier," Danbury prompted. "I speak French, if you wish to talk. Please believe we are here as friends, to hear your story. *S'il vous plaît croire que nous sommes ici comme les amis, entendre votre histoire.*"

Forrier looked at Danbury and nodded. He began arranging the strips as if doing a jigsaw puzzle.

"*Marsden avait un trou chez lui . . .*"

Forrier spoke slowly, his words thick, like a man awakening from a trance. Danbury translated. "Marsden had a hole in him he thought my painting would fill."

"*Je suis arrivé aux Etats-Unis huit mois après . . .*"

"I came to America after eight months. One of his monsters was from this area. I was right; they were nearby on a farm."

"*Il aurait été impossible de tout simplement reprendre mon œuvre . . .*"

"It would have been impossible to simply take back my work; the people surrounding Marsden would have torn me apart. So I told Marsden he was a great artist and I was an ant in his shadow. I said, 'Marsden, God spared my life so I could come to America and learn from you.' I brought him flowers and kissed his feet. They smelled like rotting camembert."

Pieces aligned as Forrier worked, and I figured he had hidden a contiguous quarter of the painting's pieces in each mask.

"J'ai posé des questions sur mon art saisi: 'Qu'est-elle devenue cette toile realisée si longtemps . . . ?'"

"I asked about my captured art: 'What became of that canvas I did so long ago, Marsden? Did it find a good home? Might I see it?' He laughed and said he'd sleep on it. I learned it was a joke. He had a bedroom in the studio and had cut up my painting to fill his pillow with the scraps. Larger pieces and my studies he displayed as his own. He subjugated my work by savaging it and sleeping with it. Pillage and rape."

I raised an eyebrow at Danbury; Forrier had made an astute psychological observation. He continued adding pieces to what was now a meter-square section of painting, bringing order to the chaos. There were blank areas, pieces used for other purposes, or lost in the water.

". . . une dépendance, un édifice pourrissant . . . Marsden a appelé ces conditions mon 'stage' . . .'

"I was not there when he displayed my work as his own. I had to live far from the others in an outbuilding, a rotting structure. I was not allowed contact with anyone but Marsden and . . . a woman. Marsden called these conditions my 'internship'. Little by little I gained his confidence until allowed small use of the studio. But I could not find a way to free my painting without detection. Then, an idea: papier-mâché. I used the strips of my painting to build masks, replacing the strips from the pillow with scraps of dropcloth. I hoped to sneak my painting from the filthy life it was leading."

"*. . . J'ai rendu les masques laids et difformes . . .*"

"I made the masks ugly and misshapen. I stuck glass in them. No one wanted to touch them, much less steal them. Marsden said, 'Take those ugly things away, Forrier, keep them with you.' He was secretly delighted I made such abominations, proving I had no art." Forrier paused. "The strutting little peacock didn't realize it was my turn to joke: I shaped the masks like the souls of those who stole my work."

Deformed and hideous, I thought, astute. Forrier continued as Danbury translated, transfixed by the eerie image forming on the floor.

"Ask what he did with the masks," I said.

"*On m'a emporté aussi les masques . . .*"

"The masks, too, were taken from me. All but the one I was working on. I think they finally entranced him. Even ugly, they had strength."

"The masks showed up at death scenes over the years," I said to his face. "You were finally arrested for horrible crimes."

"*Les meurtres ont eu lieu pas loin d'où je travaillais à cette époque . . .*"

"Deaths occurred not far from where I worked, washing dishes. My lost masks were found. The police were led to me. I had a lawyer given by the court. I told my lawyer, 'It has something to do with Marsden Hexcamp.' The lawyer said if

I admitted knowing Hexcamp it would seal my tomb. The truth that should have saved me would have killed me. It was a brilliant trap."

Forrier shifted pieces until no more were left in the towel. The final result seemed the bottom quarter of the larger work, a phantasmagoria of destruction – blood, bone, body parts. Skull-heavy faces screamed beneath cascades of excrement. Tiny golden worms slithered through the carnage. It was masterfully rendered – a work of genius from a technical standpoint – but a demented nightmare nonetheless. What had inspired such hellish pictures?

Forrier stood, walked to the wall, and again conducted his silent music. He seemed to have lost all interest in the art. I recalled his final pronouncement before completing the puzzle, that he had been trapped.

"Who trapped you?" I asked. He stared at me a moment, then waved his hands as if to outline smoke. "*Fantômes*," he whispered.

"Ghosts," Danbury translated.

Fantômes seemed to have been the final word in Trey Forrier's daily verbal allotment. He fell silent and ignored all further questions. He simply stared at the wall, a beatific smile on his face.

"That's the weirdest SOB I've ever seen, Carson," Danbury whispered.

CHAPTER 48

Danbury received a dozen calls from the station during our high-speed return, something to do with a special she was producing on weight-loss clinics, not a favored assignment. I got one call from Jacob Willow, wondering what was happening. I told him I'd call back.

We blew into Mobile, headed for Channel 14. Danbury said, "I need to handle a few things. No more than a hundred. I can jump out if Walcott calls."

She ran to the door, her hair trying to catch up. I burned tires to my place, wanting to grab a shower and put the art away. Then wait for a call from Walcott.

I was stepping from the shower when the phone rang. Walcott sounded stressed. "I don't know where it's happening, but I think it's today or tomorrow. I called two clients with

Hexcamp-sized money and inclinations. Their services say they're out of town, won't be back until tomorrow or the next day."

"How conclusive is that? Regular business maybe."

"They're retired, have little to do but collect. They always answer my calls. Another client said to call back in a couple of days. She said if things went her way, she might be needing the name of a good restoration expert. In oil painting."

"Keep going."

"The last person had the most to say, though still not much. I suggested I had something he might like to see, an early Ramirez. He said I was in luck, he'd come by to see it tomorrow."

"And?"

"He owns a couple of smaller casinos in Las Vegas. But he said he had business in this area today and tomorrow. He asked how much the Ramirez was, uncertain how much he had to spend. He'd let me know in a day or two."

Depending on how much he spent on the Hexcamp collection? I wondered, though "business in the area" might refer to nearby Biloxi and Pascagoula, where casinos were located. Walcott said, "I don't have anything like that by Ramirez, what am I going to do when he –"

"You're sure you don't know a location?"

"I've told you everything. I swear."

"But you're sure the auction is today or tomorrow?"

"Something big's happening; I feel it."

"What are the names of these people?" Thinking I could run a check of local lodgings, hoping they registered under their own names. There was no reason not to.

"I can't tell you that, Detective Ryder. I've done as asked. Now you do as promised: leave me alone."

He hung up. I cursed, nearly threw the phone into the wall in lieu of Giles Walcott's head, but dialed Harry instead.

"Harry? The auction's today or tomorrow Walcott knows some of the buyers, but he locked down on me. How about you go unlock him? I'll hang here, wait for your word."

The house seemed tight, suffocating, too much tension in a small space. I went to the deck to let my eyes roam the shining water. My phone rang again. I looked at the number: Willow. I thumbed it on.

"I can't talk right now; things are breaking."

"What is it?" Willow said.

"Looks like the buyers are somewhere in the area; north, south, I don't have a clue. Harry's trying to pry more from Walcott. I'm at home, about to jump out of my skin. I need the phone."

"I've got over three decades in on this. Call when you hear anything."

I paced the deck and tried to anticipate the action when – if – we found the auction site. We had to keep the players in place, concentrating on Coyle and anyone else working his side of the table.

The nearby slamming of a car door intruded on my thoughts. A woman's voice yelled, "Rubin!"

Rubin?

The voice was next door. I peered around the side of my house. Lydia Barstow stood one driveway over, wailing up at the Martins' house.

"Rubin, come out! I'm scared. Please, Rubin."

I sprinted through my house, ran down the steps, crossed the dunes between the houses. Lydia stood in front of a blue Explorer, a brown duffel bag at her feet.

"Lydia, what's wrong. What are you doing here?"

She jumped in fright, spun to me. "Detective Ryder? What . . . I mean . . . how did you get here?"

"I live here, Lydia. The house right there. What are you doing?"

She looked between the two houses, confused. "Rubin called an hour ago. He wanted his bag. Sometimes he was yelling, then he'd be begging me to do this. I asked what was going on, he said to shut up and grab the bag and . . ."

"Whoa, Lydia. He wanted you to bring his bag here?"

She waved a pink call slip. "He said to write down this address, not to tell anyone he was here or he'd be in terrible danger."

I took the slip: the Martins' address stared back. I looked down at the duffle. Bulging.

"What's in the bag?"

"He sent me to one of those storage places. The key was in his desk." Her face reddened. "I had to do it, Detective Ryder. I tried to leave him, but . . . I have feelings there. I still . . ."

She broke down and buried her face in shaking hands. The red car was gone, the place looked deserted. I crouched beside the duffle, a big duck-cloth job with its heavy-duty zipper ending at a lock. I felt the shapes inside. Flexible bricks the size of bundled money. Lots of bricks.

Lydia pounded on the railing at the base of the stairs. "Rubin? Come out, Rubin!" She was edging toward hysteria.

"I don't think he's there, Lydia. The car's gone. He was supposed to meet you here?"

"In an hour. I got scared and came early. What's going *on*?"

I looked at the Martins' single-story stilted house. Had Rubin Coyle been hiding next door all this time? It seemed bizarre. But the whole case had been bizarre from the moment I stepped into the Cozy Cabins.

"Rubin," Lydia cried. "I'm here. Talk to me, please."

I sat her in the Explorer, said I'd be right back. I eased up the steps, stood to the side of the stoop and knocked.

"Coyle? This is Detective Carson Ryder. I need to talk to you."

I tried the knob. The door was unlocked. Chilled air rushed out as I opened the door, nothing behind it but silence. I startled to a clicking sound, then recognized it as the compressor on the Martins' deep-freezer.

"Coyle?" I repeated, stumbling over three suitcases just inside the door. There was a large main living area, the floor polished hardwood. On a coffee table lay a roll of duct tape and a sheet of paper, the standard realtor map of rental properties. A half-dozen of the properties were circled in red. All were within a quarter mile.

In the four-second space between waves falling in the distance, I moved from ignorance to enlightenment: Coyle had quartered the bidders in rental houses on Dauphin Island. It was the perfect solution to anonymity, new faces the rule this time of year. I looked closer at the map. The Amberlys' house was circled in red. The Blovines were collectors.

351

It figured.

"Detective?" a woman whispered.

I turned. Lydia stood in the doorway framed by light. Something dark was in her hand. For some reason, my chest exploded.

Waves rose from afar to float me away.

CHAPTER 49

The woman's cheery voice seemed filtered through distance.

"Hello, Mr Kern? This is Miss Barstow again. Are you comfortable? Yes, it's a lovely place. I'm calling about our little proceedings? Your special viewing of the materials will be in just a few minutes . . ."

The voice got louder. Whatever had taken me down, I was coming out fast; not a gunshot or head trauma. A white ceiling resolved into view. My chest burned, and I looked down at red pinholes in my shirt.

Stun-gun pricks.

I'd been zapped senseless with one of the new major-voltage weapons, like mainlining 50,000 volts. A few inches down and to my sides were my hands, a dozen inches apart, multiple strands of heavy gauge picture-hanging wire between them, strands looping both wrists. I wiggled my fingers, but my elbows had been drawn behind my back and locked in concrete. My back and shoulders ached.

I looked to my side and saw the business end of a broom, handle on my other side. Why was I lying on a broom?

I tried to roll to sitting position, but couldn't, something held my back flat on the floor. I blinked at the broom until things made sense. The handle had been placed in the crooks of my arms before my hands were secured, drawing the damned thing tight against my back.

I grunted my feet up a few inches, saw my ankles secured with more wire. Though my bindings had taken minimum effort, they yielded almost total immobilization. The woman's chipper voice continued.

"I'll drop by in a few minutes, take you to the viewing site. I agree, Mr Kern, an exciting day. Rubin will provide instructions on auction procedures, he's looking forward to meeting you . . ."

Lydia sat at the counter dividing the kitchen from a small dining alcove. She'd changed into a white silken blouse, pressed denim jeans and running shoes, perfect for blending into the upscale beach scene. Her shape was far more impressive than the sack-shaped work dresses had revealed. She spoke in a distinctly un-Lydia voice, charming and musical and oh-so-southern, holding just a smidgeon of command – a business belle.

"Casual dress is just fine, Mr Kern. Rubin's wearing shorts. But he's been out in the heat today, making sure everyone's prepared for the event. See you soon."

Lydia hung up the wall-mounted phone. Seeing my open eyes, she smiled like we were old friends. "You believe that idiot, Ryder? He wanted to know if the auction was formal." She smiled mischievously. "Should I call him back, tell him to wear a tux?"

"It's all fake," I said. "Everything."

"The money is as real as real gets. And speaking of money, it's time to make a withdrawal." Lydia stood. She'd lost the slouch, the frumpiness, the aura of dejection. This version moved like a leopard. She stripped duct tape from the roll, covered my mouth, then disappeared out the door. My scream produced a muffled hum that wouldn't carry to the deck.

I tried to roll and discovered the broom prevented it. I threw my heels a few inches to the side and pulled, but that only pivoted me around the axis of my pinioned back. I gave up after a few minutes of spinning like a faulty compass, finding no direction save lost.

Lydia returned in twenty minutes by the wall clock, another suitcase in her hand. "Thanks for lending me your truck," she said, shaking my keys at me. "Sorry I left it a couple streets away."

I shut my eyes; anyone coming to my house would think I was gone. Lydia's foot gave me a nudge. "Behave and I'll pull the tape back."

I nodded and she peeled tape from my lips. I looked at the most-recent suitcase. "What was the take, Lydia?"

She pushed the suitcase to its side, opened it, tilted it my way. I saw ranks of banded bills. "Mr Kern brought one point one million. Mrs Birchman a flat mill. Mr Carothers brought nine hundred thousand. Mr and Mrs Dalesandro brought seven hundred grand in bills, another hundred in Kruggerands." Lydia winked. "Two more bidders to visit and my retirement fund will be fully vested."

"Five or six million for you and Coyle. Speaking of our mystery man, when will he be here?"

A sly smile came to Lydia's face. She walked into the kitchen and out of sight. I heard knocking. Was Coyle in the Martins' laundry closet?

"Rubin? Honey? It's OK to come out now. Detective Ryder's in the living room. He'd like to meet you."

I saw her from profile as she rounded the corner. I couldn't understand why she'd donned Dorie Martin's oven mitts to carry a gray cooking crock. Lydia turned to me. Not a cooking crock: between the mitts was a frozen head.

Rubin Coyle stared at me.

"Say hello to Rubin, Detective Ryder." She dropped Coyle's head to the floor, set her foot on his face and pushed. The frozen head slid like a curling stone and stopped against my leg. I jerked away from its icy touch. Lydia returned to the kitchen, stripped off the mitts. She picked up the wall phone, dialed.

"Hello, Mr Barncamp? This is Miss Barstow. Ready for today's activities? Wonderful! Your special viewing of the art will be in two hours. You've seen the authentication materials – the articles from the press, the videotape of the detective specialist? Expert testimony, Mr Barncamp, like we promised . . ."

She looked at me and winked, then returned to her phone

duties. I studied the ceiling and listened to Lydia manipulate her quarry with assured, perfect lies, the kind of manipulation that had drawn Harry and me into the case, set us on the trail of Rubin Coyle. Employing little more than drab clothes and demeanor, worried eyes, and a weary, vulnerable posture, Lydia Barstow had moved us like chess pawns.

I glanced at the frozen visage of Rubin Coyle, eyes wide at what must have been the terror of his final moment. Had she struck from behind, as with Borg? Or smiled into his eyes as the death-blow arrived? From the front with Coyle, I suspected. Borg was an employee, Coyle a player. The entrance with the head told me Lydia had the horrific, gleeful sort of sociopathy that needed to let Coyle know he was about to die; to see it in his eyes.

I considered how she must have studied the structure of the Mobile Police Department, discovered how and when the PSIT was activated. She manipulated it with dexterity, gamed the rules.

Played the system.

She'd claimed to be in her late forties, but cosmetic surgery is almost a drive-through-window commodity today. I now figured her for the mid fifties. She was a superb actress. She seemed fearless. She manipulated people through an uncanny instinct about their needs and desires. I could smell a hunger rising from her – for money, for power, for the *game.*

Invisible lines grew bright in the dark, and I started to put it together. By any rational notion, the thought forming in my brain was an impossibility, but my gut had the edge, and I knew what it told me was true.

Lydia Barstow was, or had been, Calypso.

CHAPTER 50

The deckhand of the Fort Morgan–Dauphin Island ferry uncoiled a hawser and set it on the white-painted deck. He tapped a cigarette from a pack and leaned against the side rail to study the passengers. Vacationers, mostly: mini-vans with Midwestern tags, kids pointing at gulls hovering above the foaming stern, parents shooting pictures of the approach to Dauphin Island like it was a big deal. The ferry was about half-full, fifteen or so vehicles, a couple of them pulling boats. There were a few bicyclists. All seemed to be tourists, not unusual this time of year.

No, the deckhand thought, noticing the older guy standing on the foredeck, staring intently across the blue water; no tourist there. Tanned deep, like it went to his bones. Faded blue work shirt, worn khaki pants, scuffed

Wellingtons. Ex-construction guy, maybe; but not a laborer – a surveyor, something like that.

The deckhand lit his cigarette, set his elbows on the railing and stared across the mouth of Mobile Bay, waiting as the pilot spun toward the ramp. The red-and-white craft shuddered as the engine dropped RPMs.

"Give you a buck for one of those smokes," said a voice from the deckhand's shoulder. He spun, saw the old man two steps away.

"Sure, mister."

The deckhand shook a cigarette from the pack, waved off payment. He flicked his lighter for the older guy, who leaned in and cupped the flame. He took a drag and coughed heavily.

"You OK?" the deckhand asked.

The older guy gave a half smile, looked at the cigarette. "Not used to smoking. It's been a while."

"How long?"

"I quit January 1, 1980. A resolution. Couldn't manage it on just a year changing, had to make it a decade."

The deckhand raised an eyebrow. "Why start again now?"

The older guy took a lungful of smoke, held it a few seconds, let it drift from his lips and nostrils. He stared at Dauphin Island. "Helps me wait."

"What you waiting for?"

"Answers," the older man said, taking another pull on the cigarette. "Thirty-five years' worth."

Lydia hung up the phone and walked to the deck doors. She opened the curtains and stared over the Gulf, swaying slightly, as if dancing to music in her head. A flock of gulls tumbled by, white splashes on blue sky.

I lifted my head, called to her back. "How did you convince someone to take your place in the courtroom? To become the Crying Woman?"

She stopped swaying. I was at enough of an angle to see her face go oddly slack, followed a few seconds later by a smile rising to her lips. Lydia turned to me, neck flushed, her breathing fast and shallow, as though aroused.

She crossed the room in four fast steps and jumped on my chest. Air exploded from my lungs. She smiled down as I struggled to breathe.

"I didn't have to convince the pathetic little loony, Ryder. She begged me to hand her the veil. I kept saying, 'No, Cheyenne, it's a holy moment.' She wept and wailed. Finally I sighed and said, "All right, Cheyenne; don't breathe a word to anyone, and you can go to heaven with Marsden instead of me. I'll show up in a couple weeks.' She took instructions to the letter, blew her little head into soup. The cops rounded up a few space cadets who confirmed the woman called Calypso was the Crying Woman . . . ergo Calypso was dead. No one knew enough to put it all together, so no hounds on my trail."

She stepped off my chest and I gasped for breath. Lydia fell to the couch beside me, poked my ribs with her toe.

"Marsden's ego laid the groundwork, Ryder. Rumors handled the rest. Along with selected pieces of art fed into the system."

"The stolen work of Trey Forrier."

361

For a brief and strange moment, Lydia's eyes glazed over, her jaw slackened. It took another second for her face to re-engage.

She said, "You found out about Forrier? And doped out who I was? You're worth the pittance they pay you. Truth be told, a major reason I selected Dauphin Island was to keep an eye on you. I like to keep the major players close, make sure they're performing correctly. And, of course . . ." She raised an eyebrow, waiting for me to finish the sentence.

"To end our participation when it's no longer needed."

"You were good, Ryder. But since I gave you nothing but disconnected moments of art and weirdness, there was no way you'd catch on. Not in time."

"Weirdness like the Cozy Cabins? Candles and flowers and rinky-dink jewelry?"

"Pulled you into the case, didn't it?"

"All the way through verification," I admitted.

She jumped from the couch and went from window to window, checking outside, talking over her shoulder. "Verification was the big problem. I sold snippets for years, swatches. Major brokers like Walcott would quasi-verify petty mementos, of course, part of the game: '*Well, it does seem in the reputed Hexcamp style* . . .' But provenance for an entire collection? For that I needed a potent authority figure to say, 'Yes, I believe Marsden Hexcamp created this art.'"

"Nothing less than a member of the Psychopathological and Sociopathological Investigative Team."

She turned and winked. "I'd buried Marie two nights before, planning on creating someone to be my expert. But that meant cutting in a confederate, very costly and dangerous. Then I saw your picture with that ridiculous award, read the story. *Here* was my authority figure – steeled jaw, eyes ablaze with righteousness, a touch of pompous ass. I dug Marie up, washed her off, and built my little motel scene. I put out bait and my expert came sniffing."

"And finding Coyle's prints. Imagine that."

"I made Rubin take me there last month. *'I wanna fuck somewhere sleazy, Rubin, like where whores fuck . . .'* He had his own special needs, loved the idea. I figured his finger-prints were still on something in that crummy joint, so it fit perfectly into the plan. By the way, the tape you heard was from a deal a couple years back, Florida politicians and devel-opers divvying up a major construction project." She looked at Coyle's head with amusement. "And Rubin always talked like that, nervous, like every project was a state secret."

"You must have had fun with Harry and me, making up the swatch that came to Coyle, gave you nightmares."

"That's the trick to a good lie, Ryder, detail and images. When I left the motel, it hit me I should have left art with the body . . . to give you your first Marsden moment."

"So you mailed one to the convent the next day."

She poked her toe into my ribs again. "It hooked you, right?"

"Close," I admitted.

"I snuck back and stuck the art above Wicky's rotting head, called that idiot reporter again: *'Heidi Wicky in Elrain . . .'*"

"Why did you have to kill them?"

"I was in Orange Beach a couple months back, a restaur-ant, and Wicky walked in. Figure the odds. Her eyes about popped out. I'm not sure if she believed what she saw, but I couldn't take the chance. They might have started talking among themselves; word might have gotten to an old ex-cop named Jacob Willow. He put an end to our arty little experiments years ago, still gets a wild hair up his moldy ass every now and then, pokes around. I should have added him to my collection of final moments decades ago."

"What about Nancy Chastain?"

"I gave her a chance. I pulled up beside the moron, said hi. Unfortunately for her –"

"She recognized you. Turned and ran."

Lydia winked. "Not far."

"And Coyle? He wasn't a collector, right?"

She grinned. "That shit framed on his wall? Came from a trip to the hardware store and butcher shop: nails, cords. A couple shirts I rubbed with a pork roast. A chunk of dried cow tongue. Took me under a day to set up."

"Hamerle didn't think Coyle was a collector, but I didn't buy it. Hamerle had nothing to do with this either, I take it?"

"Warren couldn't jack off without an instructional video. But he had been Marsden's lawyer way back when." She jabbed me with the foot again. Hard. "But you know that, don't you, Mister Bright Boy?"

I nodded.

"You're so sharp, Ryder. Let's play Match Wits with Lady Calypso: What was my main reason for working at Hamerle, Melbine and Raus? Hint: It wasn't Rubin's negotiating expertise, though his reputation added another wonderful layer of validity."

The foot in my side again, toying with me, a cat with a trapped mouse. "Come on, Ryder. Think it through, if you can."

I thought of friends who seriously collected baseball cards, firearms, antique clothing – all shared one commonality: they knew the arcana of their field. The answer dawned on me. It was brilliant.

I said, "You communicated with potential bidders on office stationery. Major collectors recognized Hamerle's name as the lawyer who'd defended Marsden Hexcamp. Hamerle told us he got calls from collectors trying to coax information from him. You created a golden connection."

She mimed applause. "No one knew where the art went after Marsden's death, but everyone had a theory. Most speculated his lawyer ended up with it, or knew where it was. The letterhead confirmed their suspicions."

She stood and looked down on me, triumph in her eyes.

"They wanted to believe, I handed them art. They wanted a connection, I handed them Hamerle. They wanted verification, I handed them you."

CHAPTER 51

"Hello, Mrs Blovine? This is Miss Barstow again. How are you today? I know, and I apologize. It's kind of a fact of life here. Perhaps if you took a hose and sprayed it away? No, I'm not telling you to do it. Is your husband there? I'll wait, thank you."

Lydia covered the phone's mouthpiece with her palm and turned to me. "That Blovine cunt does nothing but whine – the water tastes funny, the beds are too hard, there's birdshit on the deck . . . I'd like to take a can opener and rip out her eyes."

"If they've seen the verification video, the newspaper article, they know who I am."

"They didn't see it until arriving, after your little contretemps. My bidders were advised you lived in the area;

they're smart enough to realize your validation was real, but you weren't a sympathizer. It made you even more believable, by the way."

She pulled her hand from the phone, the trill back in her voice. "Hello, Mr Blovine, Ms Barstow here. I wanted to advise you I'll be by shortly to . . ."

Lydia strung her web, checked her watch, re-taped my mouth, and went on a collection run. I fought my bonds for several minutes, fruitless. Harry was in Baldwin County, Danbury at the station. When I didn't call, they'd come looking. But I'd be gone, my truck gone. They'd never look next door – there was no reason.

Twenty efficient minutes later, Lydia lugged a high-end leather suitcase through the door. I craned my head to her. "You're killing them, right?"

She set the case beside the others, looked at it fondly for a moment. "You see the tits on that Blovine bitch, Ryder, the big fake hooters?"

"Hard to miss."

"It was all I could do to keep from taking a knife to those porkers, check out the technology. Unfortunately, it'd fuck my plans."

"They're still alive?"

Her grin was vulpine. "I tell my tightly tied and very frightened bidders a dead cop will be found in the neighborhood. Then I make them eat a couple pills, a date-rape drug. They hit dreamland, I loosen the bonds a bit. They'll awaken in six to ten hours with two choices. Slip back beneath their rocks and nothing ever comes of this. Or they can go to the authorities, whereupon all hell breaks loose. Investigations, lawyers, publicity . . ."

The Lydia/Calypso entity had again read people perfectly – collectors of serial-killer leavings would be sad and insecure people, pathetic grotesques. They were natural cowards who would accept their losses, lick their wounds, and disappear into the night.

I dug in my heels, spun a few inches to put her in view. "One question's been plaguing me, Lydia. How did my picture get on the art you mailed to the convent?"

She looked at me, brow furrowed. "What?"

"There was a drawing of someone resembling me on it. Erased, but the lab found it. The Eiffel Tower's in the background."

Once again I saw a facial blankness as sudden as lightning, as utter as death. Her eyes glazed over, her mouth drooped. Breathing ceased. Four or five seconds later, the blankness was replaced with an active face. She stared at me.

"I don't know what you're talking about." She turned away and went to the fridge, poured a glass of OJ.

I considered the strange moment; Lydia/Calypso seemed to have processed my question, but, finding the input lacking, dismissed it as irrelevant. Was that how her incredibly focused but damaged psyche dealt with confusion, I wondered; the physical machinery locking up while her mind absorbed and dissected unexpected information – some form of disassociative dysfunction?

"Where *did* the art come from?" I asked. "The art that went to Marie."

She set the juice on the counter, readying for another call. "Even cut into pricey little filets the stuff wouldn't last forever, Ryder, a big reason I started planning my last score. A couple years back I returned to the source for a few final scraps, figured they'd come in handy."

"Forrier."

"Cost me three grand to turn a guard at the crazy house. I told him to grab anything from Forrier that looked like art. My thief slipped out a few snippets from the old days . . . Trey hanging on to the past, I guess. I sent a scrap to Marie, taped a piece above Heidi's rotting body, left one in Rubin's desk. Worth every penny to keep you on task, Ryder."

"Turned out a good thing Forrier survived the beating you people gave him in Paris."

She tapped her temple in the area where Forrier's was indented. "Hard head, I guess. And you're right; I got to use him later, twice, actually."

"You had his masks from the old days. And you kept killing, Lydia. Right? You had to."

She got up from the counter, moved at me like a cat. I took a deep breath, expecting the jump again. Instead, she dropped to her knees and stared into my eyes.

"You ever see the final moment, Ryder?" she whispered, her breath in my face. "Really see it? That split second when you can see what we're made of. The moment spills from the eyes, pours across the floor like mud, all kinds of shit wriggling in it. You can feel heat pouring off. Just amazing. It takes someone special to see it, Ryder."

I turned my head away, frightened of how she was looking at me.

"You left Forrier's masks at your murder scenes," I said calmly, wanting to get her back to braggadocio and away from thoughts of final moments.

Lydia put her hand on my face and pushed herself to standing. She sauntered back to the counter. "Freaky things, those masks. Forrier had been an incredible artist, Ryder. Brilliant, visionary. You've seen snatches of his work, what do you think?"

I could only shake my head. She said, "He lost it; maybe when we busted his head. Those masks were pug-ugly. But they kept me safe."

I stared at the ceiling. Her ability to drain every possible use from another human being – Hexcamp, the girl in the courtroom, Trey Forrier – was supranormal. A prime danger of sociopaths is, unlike the rest of us, they're not burdened by emotion or the myriad tasks of normal life – they focus every cell on their needs and goals.

I watched her dial the phone, slip it calmly to her face. "Hello, Mr Pawalhi? So nice to hear your voice . . ."

Minutes later, she left. I raged against my bonds, shrieked into the tape over my mouth. Kept supine by the broom, I couldn't roll across the floor. I was a mute lump of warm meat, as vulnerable as a naked quadriplegic housed with wolves.

CHAPTER 52

Jacob Willow exited the truck, his shoes sinking into sand. There was no vehicle in Ryder's drive or under the house. Willow climbed the dozen steps to the small porch at the door. He knocked and surveyed Ryder's setting. The street held three houses before abutting a finger of scrubby woods. To the east was a big, fancy structure. Ryder's place and the house to the west were much more modest. It was the beach-front real estate that made them expensive. The truncated street meant almost no traffic. A nice place to live.

Willow knocked again. Nothing. He retreated down the steps, crossed beneath the house, skirting the fish-cleaning table, the kayak, the picnic table. He walked into the sun and looked up at the deck. A light was on in what was probably the kitchen window. He walked back under the house, listened for sounds from above, footsteps, radio. Nothing but silence. Willow went to his truck and grabbed the cellphone to give Ryder a call, but remembered the detective's words: *things are breaking . . . I need the phone.*

He sighed, tossed the phone back in the cab. He was preparing to follow it when he thought, What the hell, maybe Ryder ran to the store for something.

Willow shut the door of the truck, walked to the steps of the stilted house. He slipped on his sunglass, pulled down his hat, and sat in the hot South Alabama sun, wishing he had another cigarette.

I'd heard an engine shut off on the vehicle in my drive, a diesel engine, not Harry or Danbury. Who did I know with such a vehicle?

Willow. His big Dodge truck was diesel. Speaking to him an hour back, I'd mentioned being home waiting for information. Had he gotten the jitters, jumped on the ferry and come to the Island?

It sounded like something the old cop would do.

For a moment, a thrill of hope flashed through me, and just as quickly died. Though Jacob Willow was sixty feet from me, about the length of a tractor-trailer rig, there was no way to let him know I was here. It got worse: Lydia would return in minutes; what would happen if she recognized Willow?

At my knees, the hard-frozen head of Rubin Coyle stared mockingly.

*   *   *

Willow stood from the step, stretched. It was time to do something else; Ryder was probably on the mainland. The breeze nearly snatched his hat before he jammed it down. He shot a look toward the Gulf and paused: churning water fifteen feet out and moving parallel to the shoreline. He crossed quickly beneath the house and out to the strand. He stared past the surf line, the Polarized sunglasses cutting glare.

Willow spotted the dorsal. As he'd thought, shark. Not a big one, thirty inches maybe. It was hunting in the shallow trough between shore and first sandbar, gorging on schooling baitfish. Eat, regurgitate, eat, leaving a trail of red and silver. Sharks never got full: hard-wired to eat from the dawn of life.

Willow watched for a minute until the shark shot seaward over the bar and disappeared into deeper water. Or maybe hovered between the two, hiding in the depths, feeding in the shallows.

He pulled his hat low against the wind and walked back toward his truck. Cresting the dune line and almost beneath the deck of Ryder's house, he heard a vehicle crunching onto the broken shells of the lane. He looked up, hoping to see Ryder. Instead, it was a woman in a blue SUV. She stared as he walked into the shade beneath Ryder's house, then shot a friendly wave. Willow waved back. He watched the woman pull into the drive next door, climbing the steps with feline grace.

Lydia's face was dark when she entered. She glared at me, then strode to the kitchen and rattled through drawers. I heard a drawer flung to the floor, a clattering of silverware. She returned holding a six-inch boning knife and knelt beside me. She ripped the tape from my mouth, and jammed the knife against my neck.

"Someone's at your place. I can't see his face, but he's in a big black pickup. Older guy. Who is it?"

Black truck. Verification of Willow. But she hadn't recognized him.

"I don't know."

She pressed the knife against my jugular. "Don't lie to me. Who the hell is it?"

"Probably . . . a potential client."

"Client? For what?"

"I do a little guide work on my off days, fishing. Vacationers ask around for a guide, sometimes the locals give my name. Check his truck or in the cab, he's maybe got rod holders."

She jumped up and glanced through the window, then turned to me. "I don't know what the fuck a rod holder looks like; tubular things like pipes?" She looked outside again, seemed to relax, the visual input matching what she'd been told. "He looks restless, about to leave. Guess this is one client you'll have to miss, Ryder. The one that got away."

She laughed, walked past me, slashed the knife an inch above my eyes, and went back to the kitchen.

Jacob Willow climbed into his truck, slipped the key into the ignition. He had a while to go before the ferry headed to Fort Morgan, maybe take a tour of the Estuarium at the Sea Lab, it'd been a few years. Make a drive-by after that, see if Ryder was here. Best leave a note. Willow grabbed a pad and pen from the glovebox.

I was here at 3.00. I'm as worked up as you are. Might check out the Sea Lab until the next ferry. Take ten seconds Ryder and CALL AND TELL ME WHAT'S HAPPENING!!!
Sincerely,
J Willow

He tried to jam the note between Ryder's door and frame at eye height. The seal was too tight. Willow grabbed the doorknob and pushed, trying to put a little space between them. To his surprise, the knob turned. Willow gave it another quarter turn. The door opened.

Ryder had left his house unlocked. Willow pressed the door inward six inches, peeked into the cool house, scanned the room. Ryder's white linen jacket was draped over a chair. Something beneath it caught Willow's eye, a webbed strap.

What the hell?

Willow scrambled inside, picked up the jacket. Beneath it was Ryder's shoulder holster and service weapon. *What kind of cop takes off without his piece?* Willow wondered, staring at the blued nine-millimeter tucked into its holster. Willow never went anywhere without at least an ankle gun, like the little .380 AMT he was wearing now; only held five rounds, but at 500 grams, it wasn't a burden. Things were too weird out there not to pack *something*, crazies storming the barricades from all directions.

Willow went to the door, stepped out on the porch. His imagination followed Ryder down the steps, into his vehicle, driving away. Unarmed, probably. Why?

He let his eyes wander to the house to the west, where the woman had gone minutes before. A vacationer, probably; had the look. Willow studied the small sloping dunes between the two houses. There were faint depressions in the sand. By their spacing, they could only have been footprints.

The Gulf breeze blew steadily into his face. Gusting every now and then. Willow wondered how long would it take for prints to fill on a day like today?

What would be a comparative?

Willow thought a second, then walked down to his truck. Beside it were the footprints from his arrival fifteen minutes ago. They were already filling in, smoothing out. He again studied the prints between the houses. Probably not older than ninety minutes, max. Much longer and they'd have disappeared.

Was the woman a vacationer, or did she live there? What if she was a friend of Ryder's? Had he run over to tell her something important?

Questions. Willow had always hated questions.

He tipped back his hat and followed the footprints across the sand.

I heard shoes crunching through the sand and shells outside, someone walking this way. Lydia ran to the window.

"It's that old fuck. Probably wants to ask if I know where you are." She smiled at me and affected a bimbo voice: "'Oh my goodness, I do believe Mr Ryder's gone to Birmingham to visit a sick friend.' What you think, Ryder? Get rid of old Mr Fish and I'll be your guide for a little while? Take you some places you've never been before?"

The feet paused, like Willow was looking up at the house. They continued, louder now, crunching over the shells in the drive.

I played out the upcoming scene in my head. The door opens, Willow's on the stoop. Would she recognize him? When had she last seen him? What would Willow do? Would he know her? Did he ever, or had she simply turned to smoke back in 1972?

Feet ascended the stairs.

Lydia said, "He's coming up, Ryder. Stay put, I'll be right back. Don't despair, we'll get our fun in before I catch my ferry ride out of here." She nodded at the frozen head at my knee, winked lasciviously. "Keep Rubin company 'til I get rid of the geezer."

I nudged the head of Rubin Coyle. Icy. There were drips falling from the softening hair, but the rest of the ghastly thing seemed hard as a bowling ball.

Knocking at the door.

My mind raced, adrenalin blazing through my neural network: the disassociative moments . . . if she wasn't expecting Willow and he suddenly appeared before her, would it stop her engine for a few seconds?

Lydia called out, "Just a second, please. Be right there."

I looked at the head at my knees and studied the shining floor. Lydia took a final glance to make sure I was out of sight of the entry. She tucked the knife into the back of her slacks. Crossed the last few feet.

Opened the door.

I took a deep breath and snapped my legs sideways with everything I had, nudging the head of Rubin Coyle.

Jacob Willow held his hat down against the wind. The door opened. Willow nodded. The woman smiled back, said, "Can I help –"

That was all she said. The moment she looked into his eyes, her face went blank. Absolutely still, like a dead face. She looked like a statue. *Damn* strange, was she all right?

"Ma'am?"

There was something faintly familiar about her face; that was strange, too.

But an even stranger thing happened next. A human head – nothing but the head – skittered slowly across the floor a half-dozen feet behind the woman. It stopped, gently rocking to and fro. The woman didn't seem to notice, her mouth drooping open, her eyes absent.

Willow was reaching for his boot when the woman's eyes returned.

They were on fire.

CHAPTER 53

The head seemed to move in slow motion, almost without sound. I heard Willow say, "Ma'am?"

I held my breath as the head stopped a few feet behind Lydia. All I could see of her was her back. There was absolute silence.

Then Lydia screamed as if she'd exploded into flames. Her hand grabbed the knife from her slacks. She dove out the door, jabbing and slashing. Willow roared with outrage. Someone tumbled down the steps. Then, four gunshots. Fast. They sounded like firecrackers.

Another moment of silence. All I could hear was my heart.

Lydia walked in, knife in hand, the silver blade now crimson. There were two red dots in the center of her blouse. She stopped and studied the room as if it were brand-new to her, or a dream. Then she saw me. There seemed no recognition in her eyes, like she had walked through the last door of madness; I was nothing but easy prey. Lydia lifted the knife and started toward me. She stumbled into the suitcases by the door, kicked them aside. The red dots on her blouse caught her attention. She looked down at them with a kind of wonder, as if mystified at how they'd gotten there.

Her face went slack and she stopped moving.

Two seconds later the machinery clicked on. Her head snapped up and she advanced three steps.

Until her eyes were drawn to her wounds and she again shut down.

Off, then on. She moved to me in a tick-tock motion, closer each time. I shrieked beneath the tape as if my blind terror could ward her off.

Off, on . . . until she stood above me.

Raised the knife high.

And seemed to pause in the middle distance between off and on.

It occurred later I didn't hear the fifth shot. Instead, a small red flower bloomed quietly in Lydia's side. She quivered when it bloomed. Paused to touch it. This time she didn't shut down, but seemed to understand something. The knife dropped from her hand and she fell to the floor with a sound like thunder.

Jacob Willow pulled himself into the house with one hand, the other clutching his side, a wide swash of red following him. He half-crawled, half-swam across the floor, reached out a bloody hand and pulled the tape from my mouth. "She cut me good, Ryder," he mumbled, looking down at his side. "My liver, I think. I got slow over the years."

He stared at Lydia, confusion on his face.

I said, "She's Calypso, Jacob. Call 911, you're bleeding out."

"Calypso? *Calypso?*"

"A switch-off beneath the veil. She's hustled the collectors for years. Get to the phone, Jacob. Now."

The phone was twenty feet away, mounted on the wall. He looked at it and sighed.

"I can't."

"Untie me. My hands."

He struggled to his knees and fumbled at my wrists but the wires were too tight for his wet and failing fingers. His blood-soaked shirt squished as he swayed above me.

"The phone," I said. "You've got to try to –"

He slumped back to the floor, exhausted. "Shhh, Ryder. It ain't gonna happen. Calypso, you're sure?"

I nodded. He thought a moment, then choked out a laugh and tapped my arm, like sharing a joke. "Know what Hexcamp told me in the courtroom, Ryder? Laying there dying. Just before he told me to follow the art?"

"What, Jacob?"

"He said, 'She lied.'"

"She lied?"

"Don't you . . . get it, Ryder?" he said, his voice getting thinner. "She *lied*. Calypso told Hexcamp she was coming to save him. Instead, she sent someone to kill him."

I understood. "That particular game was over. She was ready to move on."

381

Willow nodded, pushed up on his elbow. "Follow the art. Didn't understand . . . until now. Hexcamp was asking me to track down Calypso, his lover, then his murderer." He laughed weakly, his breath almost gone. "I spent . . . thirty-five years . . . avenging Marsden Hexcamp."

"You nailed Calypso, that's what you did. She was a killing machine, a monster. You saved lives, Jacob."

He shifted his eyes to the motionless form at my feet, whispered, "Guess it worked out, then." His head dropped to my chest. His eyes stared fearlessly into mine: we both knew.

A minute later I watched Jacob Willow's final moment. Nothing poured out, no mud, no wriggling horrors, no heat. It was simply as though something else caught his attention, and he wandered that direction.

EPILOGUE

I heard once more from Inspector Bernard Latrelle. He expressed me a large envelope. When I opened it, a color photograph fell out, along with a brief handwritten note:

This photograph documents an object reported missing in April, 1970. If you ever find it, I would swim the Atlantic to see it.
Yours, B. Latrelle

I picked up the photograph and took it outside in the sun. After studying it, I called Dr Prowse at the institute, then Danbury, and finally Harry.

"We're going to the institute, bro."

"Haven't you had a rough enough time, Cars? You don't need to see Jeremy. And I sure don't."

"We're not seeing Jeremy. We're seeing Trey Forrier. You want to be there, Harry, trust me on this one."

I lay in the back seat during the drive up, lost in thought, barely speaking. Harry and Danbury shot each other glances, but asked no questions of me.

Vangie allowed all three of us to meet with Trey Forrier. We went to his room, stark, nothing more than a bed, a chair, a desk, and a battered leather trunk in the corner. The walls were white.

"Harry, this is Trey Forrier."

Harry held out his massive hand. Forrier studied Harry's face for several seconds, then, surprising me, reached over and gently touched his palm. I leaned against the wall and clutched the envelope.

I said, "There are two things I want to talk about, Trey. A piece of your art was outside the walls. It had my face on it, a simple, perfect drawing. Do you know how it happened?"

Forrier cupped his chin in his hand and thought for a long time.

"Je crois qu'il est arrivé il y a déjà des années. J'y suis venu, j'ai rencontré votre frère . . ."

Danbury again translated between us, making conversation as effortlessly as if Forrier and I were speaking directly. "I think it happened years ago. I came here, met your brother. He was sad because he had no photograph of you. You were still angry at his crimes and refused to send him one. Sensing the depth of his pain, I offered to draw you for your brother."

Forrier went to the trunk in the corner, opened it.

"When I arrived, I was allowed a few personal belongings. Among them these small studies . . ." He produced a few pieces of painting on canvas, held them up. The colors were glorious. He turned their reverse sides to us, white canvas.

"He advised me when you were coming for a visit some years back. I peeked out my window as you passed my door and took a mind photograph.

"I practiced sketching you on the back of one of my studies, happy to put it to use. I worked in pencil. Such pointed items are not allowed, but they are here, of course. When your brother was happy with your face I created a lasting drawing for him with pen and paper. He keeps the drawing in his desk and looks at it often. It is his favorite possession. He will never tell you this."

The room began to shimmer. I closed my eyes; swallowed hard. Forrier said, "I always erased the studies. I did not want it known that I draw. The doctors will pick at me if they find out."

I now knew what had happened, thanks to Lydia's boasting. "The art was stolen."

"Thieves are everywhere. Several of my scraps disappeared." He pointed to the trunk. "I now keep it locked."

"The Eiffel Tower was behind me in the drawing, Trey. Why?"

"A view from a little park. It was my favorite place so long ago. Jeremy told me of your difficult childhood, and I decided to place you somewhere happiness could be found."

"Thank you," I said.

"What is your second subject?" Forrier asked.

I pulled the photo out of the envelope, set it on Forrier's desk. Harry and Danbury drew close. "My God," she whispered. Harry just stared, stunned into silence.

In the photo, the color faded somewhat, the paper brittle, a thirtyish Trey Forrier – a decent-looking man with blazing eyes in a normally shaped face – stood in a studio to the side of a large painting. In the bottom quarter, the painting was a nightmare jumble of skulls and blood and excrement and destruction, the section revealed in the mask. Golden worms spun through the carnage.

A quarter of the way up, the painting began to change: horrific blacks and reds and umbers lightened. The chaos was replaced by a sense of calm. The worms began spinning themselves into a shimmering figure both human and ghostlike.

Forrier stepped close. Tapped the photo with a delicate finger.

"Les vers sont la lumière de la creation . . ."

"The worms are the light of creation, the seeds of the soul. They learn to crawl amidst death and filth. It is necessary to the journey, how they learn the direction of heaven."

By mid-point in the painting the figure stretched skyward, ascendant. The central form seemed to glow, the light as pure as the silvery luminescence of Vermeer. In the upper third of the painting, the transformed figure exploded into light and color, the richness of Chagall, the raw power of van Gogh. It was as though Forrier had mixed his paint with photons. Despite the intensity of the expression – or perhaps because of it – the painting emanated a transcendent sense of peace and harmony. It was a journey that ended well.

"Incredible, Mr Forrier," Danbury said.

"It was only a study," he replied.

"A study," Harry whispered, shaking his head.

"There are other paintings?" Danbury asked. "Please say there are."

Forrier walked to his bed, sat. There seemed no more aura of madness in his manner.

"On a préparé mon affaire au procès . . ."

"My case was prepared for trial. There was evidence against me, though I had hurt no one. I could never hurt a soul. It is a transgression."

"But you stopped protesting your innocence," I said. "Admitted everything."

"Me croyant fou, on m'a installé dans une cellule tout seul . . ."

"Believed mad, I was sent here. It was a revelation. Everything was white: the floor, the walls, the ceiling. I began painting on them."

"You said you never did art here," Danbury said, confused.

Forrier walked to the wall and began conducting. No, not conducting. He was wielding a brush, not a baton.

He was painting.

"I realized everything I wanted to do in painting was better without paint. Without canvas. Without brushes. Without people watching, waiting to steal your work."

Danbury stared at the blank wall. "You mean that . . ."

Forrier nodded. "I have covered many of the walls with my art. It is a long process. But I am learning so much." He nodded toward the photograph Latrelle had sent. "I am no longer sad about the painting taken by Marsden. It is crude and ugly compared to my new work."

I opened the door and looked down the white hallway, from it branched other halls. There were resident rooms, meeting rooms, a cafeteria.

All white as snow.

I stepped into the hall and Trey Forrier followed. Harry and Danbury were right behind. I looked into the sea of white. "Tell me about your new work, Mr Forrier."

"Comme toujours, l'art du moment final . . ."

Danbury said, "As it has always been: the art of the final moment. Where everything begins."

I touched the wall, amazed. "And it's all around us?"

Forrier held his arms out to the sides and spun in a circle with childlike delight. *"On passe à travers le cœur de Dieu!"* he laughed.

I turned to Danbury.

"He says we are walking through the heart of God."

Still dumbstruck, we managed to thank Trey Forrier for his time and help. We left him in the charge of a guard and turned toward the door. We were three dozen feet away when Forrier called after us.

"Amis! Friends!"

We turned. From the angle and distance I could not see the damage to his face. He looked as happy as anyone I had ever seen.

"Le monde se sent hors de danger parce que j' y suis enfermé . . ."

Harry and I looked to Danbury.

"Trey says the world thinks it is safe because he's in here. He believes he is safe because the world's out there."

Forrier waved and turned away. He paused, bent to amend an image on the floor, then disappeared into his room.

We walked into the parking lot. The sun was warm on our shoulders, the air sweet as honey. Danbury said, "Do you think – in some way – his painting really exists? On some level the walls of that horrible place are filled with images of indescribable beauty?"

Harry said, "If we believe it does, it does. That's all it really takes, right?"

We got to the car. Harry opened the back door, waved us inside. "Why don't you folks climb in back," Harry said. "I'll drive."

We got in. Harry jammed the car in gear, spun in a circle, clipped a bush, straightened out and we escaped from the gray buildings. We were out on the main highway when Harry slapped the steering wheel and chuckled.

"Hey, Cars, remember when we had the car in the shop for the flat? Rafael was on the case?"

"I'm not senile, Harry, I remember. Why?"

The car veered as Harry bent forward, started patting under the dash, like feeling for something. "Four years back Rafe's kid brother got tight with a gang. Kid had an ugly future if he didn't get wised up fast. I took the kid home for a weekend and laid a little straightening into him; kid's fine now, college. Rafe knows me a bit, knows what I like, figured he owed me a favor."

"What? He put an extra spare in the trunk?"

Harry kept fiddling. I heard a click, like a switch snapped. Just like that, Muddy Waters thundered from speakers tucked somewhere out of sight. "We got tunes, bro," Harry yelled over the music. "Just for every little now and then."

"Ain't we something," Danbury said.

Harry grinned into the rear-view. "Settle in, cousins, we're on the high road to home."

Danbury snuggled against me. Kissed my cheek. Blew one to Harry. He laid the pedal flat and we roared to my place to catch the sunset, about all that's left to do after a long walk through the heart of God.